Like Magic in the Streets

**First published in 2021
by Crackle + Hiss**

Cover design by Jamie Keenan.

All lyrics quoted are for review, study or critical purposes.

A CIP catalogue record for this book is available from the British Library.

ISBN 9798456058010

Like Magic in the Streets

Orange Juice, Aztec Camera, the Go-Betweens, the Smiths, the Blue Nile and the End of Romance

TIM BLANCHARD

CRACKLE
+HISS

Foreword

I've often bumped into Paul Buchanan of the Blue Nile in Glasgow at Christmastime. It seems such a perfect thing, such a perfect fit. A singer emerging alone from the seasonal glitter of Tinseltown, in all likelihood looking for a last-minute present for *the one*, straight out of a Sinatra Capitol LP sleeve from the late Fifties.

On one occasion I was telling him about a new commission I'd got for BBC Radio Scotland.

"Fantastic news," he said.

Yes, I replied, we're going to take a deep dive into classic Scottish albums, one per episode, try and understand the heart and soul of the thing.

"Fantastic."

And, I raved on, we think *A Walk Across the Rooftops* should be in the first series.

"Fantastic!"

So, what do you think, do you want to sit down and do an interview for it?

"Eh…probably not."

Thankfully we did manage to get Paul into the programme we made, but I thought about that story a lot walking down the streets of this lovely book, and what we really mean when we talk about 'indie'.

The 1980s have become a symbol of corporate sparkle: a decade marching to the pulse of a sequencer with each note right on the grid; experimental electronic influences attenuated to three and a half minutes of hooks and a video shot on a boat off the Florida Keys; hairspray and compliance. I once allowed a producer to replace Charlie Charles, genius drummer of The Blockheads, with a beat (I won't say 'groove') programmed at no small expense over several days on a Fairlight CMI™. No such crass missteps for my compatriots. It still thrills me to read about the independence of spirit and thought that drove that 'other' 1980s, where the discovery of new musical possibility sprang from a deep musical capacity — à la Johnny Marr and Roddy Frame — as well as an eccentric humour. A spirit that always built from a punk ethic of DIY do-anything-you-wanna-do fun.

One, sometimes overlooked part of that other 1980s is the 1960s, and particularly the way classic songwriting and arrangements underpinned many key records. Driving into London with my band in early 1985 for a showcase gig, the streets were lined with posters for the Pale Fountains' single 'Jean's Not Happening'. Our tour bus rattled with the majesty of their earlier single 'Thank You', as well as Strawberry Switchblade's 'Since Yesterday' and The Lotus Eaters' 'You Don't Need Someone New'. Recordings dripping with melody, arrangement ideas, pretty orchestration and widescreen reverb. Recordings that understood the heart and soul of the Velvets, the Fabs, and the two Springfields, Buffalo and Dusty. And the Sixties can be heard in the quicksilver José Feliciano licks that found their way into the margins of *High Land, Hard Rain*. The Smiths' 'Hand in Glove' could be a narrative and musical sequel to 'Girl Don't Come', 'Long Live Love' or 'Waterloo Sunset'. But that magical strand back to the source wasn't universally revered at the time.

"I'm not sure this remix guy is really getting this music," I said to my A&R guy later. "I'd like to make a proper record — could we not do something mad and ask George Martin to produce?"

"I think old George is a bit out to lunch to be honest," he replied.
Oh well.

When we record the *Classic Scottish Albums* series we are at heart simply trying to tell great stories about great music, but in doing so also develop a broader story arc about music and its place and impact on our culture. *Like Magic in the Streets* does that beautifully, taking you through moments in time, politics, news stories and all of those things that root music to people and places. But it also understands that the biggest story arc of all is the story of melody, lyric and the lifelong commitment of artists.

Aside from his wonderful music, I'd only known Edwyn Collins from print interviews before he sat down to talk with me about *You Can't Hide Your Love Forever*. As much as I loved the waspish, cheeky, Edwyn-by-numbers from the pages of the *NME* and *Smash Hits*, I was much more taken by the thoughtful artist reflecting on the journey to that album. The eccentricity of the people in the room, the tunes, the sound of the guitars, the colour of the dolphins on the sleeve. Why music matters. Yes, he glee-fully told the story of a certain audience chant that greeted his early gigs (you can read about that here too) but Edwyn was more eloquent on the musical frailties of his group and how those frailties played into something authentic, tender and universal. To put him in a nutshell: Edwyn the artist.

In 1984 I used to scuttle back and forth between Falkirk and Cumbernauld, a 15 minute drive that took me from my home in a traditional Scottish market town to that new-age modernist vista, freshly famous as the setting of *Gregory's Girl*. My manager at the time, a beautiful and under-celebrated music worker called Eddie Trayner, had recently incorporated an independent label, hoping to capitalise on the Sound of Young Scotland energy that pervaded the air. From an office in the town centre — looking out over the clock where Gregory is stood up by Dee Hepburn in the movie — Eddie would plot and plan and almost convince me that we might be able to make a record people would want to listen to. Then I'd head back along the motorway, my belief ebbing with the miles.

One Saturday I heard a song called 'Easter Parade' on the car radio, its vast spaces and stillness seeming to blow the roof off the car. The DJ interviewed the artists, whose accent was my own, who had taken an unbelievable amount of time to make this record, who nobody had really heard of. And the singer, Paul Buchanan, spoke only in terms of artistry, only in terms of the intent and source of the music. The thought that the music might 'sell' or 'make it' seemed not to have occurred to these people, yet the music was transcendent and already somehow connecting with audiences. 'Tinseltown in the Rain' was played next, seeming to rise high and tower over everything across the motorway as I drove.

By the time I reached home I knew it was possible to make music for the right reasons, in the right way, and from a remote part of the globe called Scotland. *Like Magic in the Streets* takes me right back to that day; a listener discovering the heart and soul of the thing. In the right place, at the right time.

David Scott, writer/presenter of BBC Radio Scotland's 'Classic Scottish Albums' and Pearlfishers singer/songwriter.

Contents

Crackle and hiss

*O*rders have been given for some of London's busiest streets to be barricaded, emptied of shoppers and traffic. A city that had been grizzled and age-bent becomes somewhere extraordinary. Horses as black as night are in the Strand; the mounted escort turns dirty shop windows to a streaming ripple of scarlet and gold as it passes; a procession that is being drawn with invisible ropes towards a dove-white Cathedral, where chess pieces have come to life. Kings, Queens, Bishops, Knights of the realm. Fanfares sound, choirs sing, faces tilt upwards towards a reverent sunlight until, at the moment of her choosing, the bride appears in the form of a white bird, her long tail unfolding with the luxury of complete impracticality to run the length of a Cathedral aisle. A son of the House of Windsor — the Earl of Chester, Duke of Cornwall, Duke of Rothesay, Earl of Carrick, Baron of Renfrew, Lord of the Isles, Prince and Great Steward of Scotland — is to be married to the daughter of the 8th Earl of Spencer, the first English royal bride since 1659.

History shows anything's possible with wealth and power, even a fairy tale. The cost of the Royal Wedding in July 1981 was around £100 million in today's money, and remains the most expensive yet staged. Security was the biggest cost, demanding the call-up of 4,000 police and 2,000 military personnel. It was a price accepted as an irrelevance by a country desperate for glamour, dreaming of a shameless prosperity. Because, for once, Britain had more to offer than *Dallas*. In a slick operation, carried out in the teeth of economic despair, miserabilism was banished from the Kingdom. "The Royal Family of England pulls off ceremonies the way an army of Israel pulls off commando raids," observed the *Boston Globe[1]*.

Fairy tales need a frightening otherness to work, a foil for the 'good and glorious', and in 1981 the British hinterlands were nasty with it. The country was in its second year of recession, inflation had reached 20% and unemployment was at a scale not seen since the Depression of the 1930s — meaning new legions of people who were both poor and worryingly unoccupied. A year of riots and fighting with police had begun in April in Brixton before re-igniting in the month of the Wedding and spreading into Southall, then to Handsworth in Birmingham, Chapeltown (Leeds), Toxteth (Liverpool), and Moss Side in Manchester. These were the longest and ugliest of the street battles; other episodes of disorder took place in the Midlands and northern cities, as well as in towns like Gloucester and Cirencester in the west, Bedford, High Wycombe and Reading in the south, Portsmouth and Southampton on the coast, even Keswick in the Lake District. Meanwhile, Trade Unions continued to harry the government, forcing the first U-turn from the Prime Minister on her radical plans to import more coal and close pits. The IRA had twice exploded bombs in crowded city streets.

Her Majesty's Ministers were readying themselves for war. They had a new arsenal of weaponry in the political and media consensus behind the idea of free markets. A government with a conscience didn't do anything for a broken economy. Markets were logical and strict, they would push out institutions — and people — found to be outdated, tired or wasteful. Principles that relied on spending from public coffers only supported weakness and the weak. Opening up the Kingdom to the rule of markets at the same time as limiting the amount of money in the economy to stimulate competition would put needles under the feet of the lazy, and, for the strong and well-adjusted, bring the kinds of riches the Royal Wedding had been a golden advertisement for.

What were once extremist ideas were made to look like common sense and no institution of British life would remain safe from the revolutionary change: not the unions or industry, the professions, universities, the civil service or government itself. No institution except one. The monarchy

---

[1] Sampson, Anthony, *The Changing Anatomy of Britain*, Hodder & Staughton, 1982, p5.

itself was preserved gloriously in amber. As journalist Anthony Sampson pointed out in 1983: "The Queen's own life has remained almost uniquely unchanged. She still pursues her timeless progress between her palaces and country estates, surrounded by the rituals of nineteenth century rural life, concerned with racehorses, forestry or corgis. She is still accompanied by friends from landed or military backgrounds, with a strong hereditary emphasis. The Mistress of the Robes is the Duchess of Grafton; the Ladies of the Bedchamber are the Marchioness of Abergavenny and the Countess of Airlie."[2] Speaking just ahead of the Wedding, the Duke of Edinburgh entered unwisely into the debate on the Kingdom's suffering. "Now that everybody has got so much leisure — it may be involuntary, but they have got it — they are complaining they are unemployed," he said. "People don't seem to be able to make up their minds about what they want do they?"[3]

*

This book is about the mystery of five unexpected LPs that couldn't have been made at any other time than this. Because of this grubby fairy tale world and in spite of it. They were the work of amateurs making use of all they had to hand: the stuff of ordinary lives and what it felt like to live under the rule of Queen Elizabeth II and Mrs Thatcher in the new-build landscape of flyovers and underpasses, concrete shopping centres and civic parks; to be night-walking under the sodium glare of streetlights to empty bus stations, reeking pubs and spangled discos.

The characters come to the door looking nothing special: typically bright-eyed, milk-faced youth. Edwyn Collins, the singer/songwriter of his band Orange Juice is resplendent in quiff and lumberjack shirt combo, wearing a big red-lipped smile. He arrives, still laughing his gurgly laugh, with Roddy Frame, singer/songwriter and guitar virtuoso of Aztec Camera, a boy with a scraggy heavy-metal mop of hair. Robert Forster and Grant McLennan, the Lennon and McCartney of the Go-Betweens, are

---

[2] Ibid., p4.

[3] Ibid., p5.

next. Robert's heavy eyebrows and glare make him look like an escaped strangler, Grant playing the cop sent to track him down. They're young Australians away from home, living in squats and exploring the London life of drugs and haphazard gigs. They seem like polite, enthusiastic Bohemians. At least I really hope they are, because next to turn up is Morrissey (voice and words, of course, of the Smiths) with cocky young friend Johnny Marr (he plays guitar), this time sporting a Fifties look of oil-slick hair and shades. And finally the Blue Nile trio of Paul Buchanan (voice and words), Robert Bell (bass guitar) and PJ Moore (keyboards), the only people who have bothered to dress up smart — if only in a tired polyester kind of way — bringing with them the night air and a gust of guileless integrity.

They're collected in the same small, smoky, thickly-carpeted room. An Eighties party with chicken vol-au-vents, KP nuts and cans of Hofmeister, full of belief in their own songs and nothing much else. But what, if anything, makes it worth getting them together as a bunch? The Smiths are indie royalty, having combined critical credibility with substantial commercial success, while Orange Juice and Aztec Camera messed it up, didn't they? They sold themselves to *Smash Hits* with nothing much to show for it. For all the weak-kneed reviews, the Go-Betweens never managed to break out of obscurity. The Blue Nile look all wrong in this company, having made the kind of mood music you'd expect from the new High Street wine bar.

Then again, there are all kinds of strands of connection between the five: shared band members, producers, managers, tours and sympathies. Edwyn shared a flat with Grant in London for a while, and went on to produce Robert's solo work. Johnny wrote 'This Charming Man' after hearing Roddy's singles 'Oblivious' and 'Walk Out to Winter'. Rough Trade tried to get Roddy to play on some Smiths tracks after Johnny left the band. Morrissey paid attention to Go-Betweens' lyrics, seemingly appropriating some lines[4], and perhaps took a new freedom from hearing Edwyn's wandering vocals. Robert used what he called the 'Roddy Chord' on many of his songs, a major seventh that made for a wistful, Burt

---

[4] Maybe the line "Eskimo blood in their veins" from first single 'Karen' for a Smiths' B-side; and the title and ideas from 'Ask' on *Before Hollywood*.

Bacharach-style lilt. Craig Gannon played guitar with Aztec Camera, the Smiths and Edwyn; Malcolm Ross with Orange Juice and Aztec Camera; Bernie Clarke played keyboards with Aztec Camera, The Go-Betweens and Edwyn; Calum Malcolm contributed enough as sound engineer and on keyboards to be listed as a band member of the Blue Nile, and also worked with Aztec Camera, Orange Juice and the Go-Betweens. And yes, they were young, white and male. Which made them plain and ordinary rather than at an advantage in a business always looking for fruity novelty and the next kind of cool.

There was sniping between them too. "I find most previous Rough Trade groups [like Aztec Camera and the Go-Betweens] nonsensical and unimportant," sighed Morrissey[5]. Orange Juice drummer Steven Daly admitted: "we weren't huge fans of the other Postcard bands [Aztec Camera, the Go-Betweens], although we liked them as individuals."[6] Robert dismissed material for Orange Juice's second LP: "none of it, in the light of their Postcard work, even strong."[7] On tour, a cheeky Edwyn would sometimes dedicate his song 'I Guess I'm Just A Little Too Sensitive' to Morrissey. The owner of Brixton Academy in 1985, Simon Parkes, remembers a tetchy row between Roddy, Edwyn, Everything But the Girl and The Woodentops about who should play the opening slot of their benefit gig for the striking miners: "Well we're no goin' on first," piped up Roddy, "we've organised the whole blinking thing."[8]

All of this is flimsy detail, none of which should brought up at our party. We don't want to stir up bad feelings so early in the night when, anyway, there are far more radical things that join them. Because this was the period when Radio 1 playlists limited the tastes of 20 million daily listeners to its supermarket of ever-changing treats and surprises. In 1982 the most played songs were 'Fame' by Irene Cara, Tight Fit's 'The Lion

---

[5] Trakin, Roy, 'Not the Jones: Morrissey', *Musician*, June 1984.

[6] 'Q&A with Orange Juice', *Anthem Magazine*, 22 November 2010.

[7] Nicholls, David, *The Go-Betweens*, Verse Chorus Press, 2003, p129.

[8] Parkes, Simon, *Live at the Brixton Academy - A Riotous Life in the Music Business*, Serpent's Tail, 2014.

Sleeps Tonight' and 'Eye of the Tiger' (Survivor); 1983 was a year dominated by 'Karma Chameleon' (Culture Club), 'Uptown Girl' (Billy Joel) and 'Total Eclipse of the Heart' (Bonnie Tyler); and in 1984, 'Relax' and 'Two Tribes' (Frankie Goes to Hollywood), 'Ghostbusters' (Ray Parker Jr.), and 'Do They Know It's Christmas' (Band Aid). "The charts at the moment could cause you to question whether there's life before death," said John Peel, Radio 1's constant exception[9].

Inside the machinery of the early Eighties music industry and its cogs and wheels of commercial imperatives and conventions, each of the LPs here was a grind against the gears, a livid spark of freedom. Outsiders were making music that was anti-rock, anti-pop and anti-cool. They were non-professional bands who started out with punk ideals and went their own offbeat and earnest ways; willing to be raffishly literary and poetic — more Romantic than romantic — who looked back to a past age of pop songwriting; who could be excitable and nervy; with an anger that expressed itself in a blithe humour and self-mockery. Because making music could still be a sincere act of expression, not the manufacture of jingles to colour and flavour the silence. And for the outsider bands there was a jag of conflict in everything said and left unsaid by the songs. It was the only way for 'nobodies' to say anything or be heard by anyone.

Listening to music at that time was the kind of thing people listed as their hobby, involving conscious effort, thought and feeling, an encounter with other personalities and experience. And for the potless teenagers spending a whole £5 note on a piece of vinyl or a cassette tape, this wasn't a casual purchase but an investment in identity, the result of careful choices. Record buyers were looking for music that contained echoes of themselves, confirmations and incitement. Is there any other generation that experienced the thrill of carrying home a plastic bag containing a precious piece of vinyl more keenly than this?

The outsiders were making both independent music and an independent attitude. So this is the birth of indie music as we know it. The guitar sound, the look, the scene, all grew out of this early evidence that non-mainstream bands could attract audiences and make money. But none

---

9 Cavanagh, David, *Good Night and Good Riddance - How Thirty-Five Years of John Peel Helped to Shape Modern Life*, Faber & Faber, 2015, p347.

of them had any interest in being part of what became a precious indie culture and pose, there's only mickey-taking at the waves of imitators in duffle coats playing jangle-guitar. "Everyone was getting their name out of [the] Rymans [catalogue]. 30 year-old men with bands called the Pencil Cases or the Pencil Sharpeners," Roddy complained. "All guys ten years older than me with Penguin Classics in their pockets calling themselves the fuckin' School Bags."[10]

The five bands have been classified in all kinds of ways other than 'indie' in the past 40 years: 'new wave', 'new pop', 'new realists', 'new puritans', 'art rock', 'wimp rock', 'alternative rock', even 'new jazz', 'blue-eyed soul' and (cringe) 'sophisti-pop'. Very few bands want to be associated with categories like these, they're only there for the media and marketing blurb. But we're like Saturday part-timers in a record shop. There's a big stack of vinyl to be sorted and we've got to stick them somewhere. 'Post-punk' is big enough and vague enough to do it, but has sometimes been used to include anything that came after punk and wasn't The Nolans. The passing of time hasn't helped. Eighties music has been downgraded to the status of mostly embarrassing. "The early eighties especially are still viewed as a campy comedy zone," wrote music journalist Simon Reynolds[11]. The familiarity of some of the names and songs, the great wash and swill of music in the meantime, means they've lost their look of distinction and difference, become softened and misshapen. What was intended to be contrary, meaningful and vivid, has been erased entirely. The LPs have merged into a morass of soggy pop, safe enough for Radio 2 and use as perky background for retail chains.

I'm going to try to recover these five LPs from the sea, as strangely vivid and intricate artefacts that have been spilt onto the shore from another time, as one-off wonders. The conditions in which they were made in the early Eighties can't come again, can't be manufactured. Those vigorous years of transition, of colliding worlds, were just too violently particular. They began with most people seeing themselves as part of a work-

---

[10] O'Brien, Lucy, 'The Sound of Grown Up Scotland: An Interview With Roddy Frame', *The Quietus*, 9 June, 2014.

[11] Reynolds, Simon, *Rip it up and start again: postpunk 1978-1984*, Faber & Faber, 2005, xv.

ing-class community, short on money and things to do, living in a land-scape of hard times: a wasteland of obsolete industry, scruffy public build-ings, mouldy fly-tip settees, rubble and dog shit. A time and place when there was an acceptance of empty hours and boredom; when love was still a matter of waiting days and days for letters and making calls from a smashed-up phone box; when buying records, let alone paying for instru-ments and studio sessions, was an expensive undertaking. During the same period more families were moving into new towns, middle-class homes and lifestyles. It was the beginning of the Walkman Age when listening to mu-sic was becoming a more private activity; sharp, even unscrupulous busi-ness was suddenly something to be admired; imports of American culture and its consumer porn of TV soaps and blockbuster movies demonstrated how much better life could be, confirming that Britain's tatty streets and frumpy meat-and-two-veg routines were lame. In other words, it was the period of transition into the competitive world of careers and consump-tion that dominates each waking moment of our 21st century world. The conflict between the old Left and the new Right over what Britain should be like, was so all encompassing, so keenly felt and lived, that it was played out in more than just the usual political arenas and the press. It was there in films, TV and music. They were hopelessly ill-matched combatants as it turned out, more a case of the organised forces of 'progress' against a muddle of dreamers, moaners and idealists.

So these five LPs are singularly unrepeatable. Which is why this is the story of vinyl treasure and not bargain rack flotsam. What follows isn't about the rise of indie or how a great musical lineage changed the world; it's about a short-lived and failed romance, a defeat, and why that might be more important and interesting than any Eighties success story. Like first love, this brand of indie music was a bright flicker of possibility that was unlikely to last. The tradition of indie that followed, including what has often been seen as the actual beginning of the indie business — the *NME*'s C86 bands — was already a knowing and cynical affair.

*

There are dangers in taking pop, indie, or whatever you want to call it, too seriously. We're easily distracted by the soundtrack to some heady teenage emotions, ending up confused on the fizz of memory and association and start to see meaning that was never meant to be there. At the same time, let's not be cowed by the dreary norms of modern thinking. We're in a culture where knowledge and ideas of all kinds have been successfully commoditised — they belong to professionals in education, academia, media, politics — so that when 'amateurs' speak out, it constitutes a no-status discourse. It's the guff of the popular mind. True, most pop music is inane. But there are exceptions, signs and signals of truth in unlikely places. And these productions say something fascinating about ordinary people's relationships with the world beyond any 'official' historical documentation, just in their breathing in and out of instincts and feelings free from the crushing weight of the conventional, and, in the end, by declaiming what couldn't be said by any other means. I could use Cultural Studies theory to prop up an argument for pop as a web of social signifiers, but it's an unnecessary rigmarole, and I'd rather keep to a principle of respect for home-made productions as a valid way of understanding a messy complexity and contrariness too often reduced to flat and convenient ideas of what's 'normal', what's obvious.

Taking on individual LPs rather than whole histories of bands makes it possible to look at the intimate story of their making, to pick over how they grew in weathered, contingent, disappointing places, on evenings of tangerine-striped electric fires, *It's a Knockout* and boxes of Twiglets rather than some ethereal cavern of pop inspiration. Getting to the most reliable evidence is the problem. The LPs in themselves provide all kinds of clues that can be interpreted and misinterpreted easily enough. No-one can know what was really being thought and felt when the songs were being written, arguably not even the writers themselves. Different ideas, emotions and perspectives push in and draw out in a relentless tide that leave traces and patterns but no resolution and no permanency of meaning over time. Besides first-hand interviews, biographies and autobiographies I've needed to look to the golden age of the music weeklies for accounts of those days, and those sources can't be trusted either. It was the shooting star of journalism, a success that encouraged a unique mix of Roland Barthes references, cheeky politics and sparkly-pop-love. There were cliques, confrontation and a whole lot of writers competing to surf the wave of the 'next big thing'. The music press were working with inhibited and blurting young people sometimes only playing the system for the sake of gaining extra column inches, other times just groping for what a pop star might be expected to say. A plain honesty was always going to be rare, let alone confessions of a Romantic inspiration. Even among themselves, explanations of real meanings could be a no-go area. "None of us ever talked to James [Kirk] or Edwyn about their lyrics," said Steven Daly[12]. The later interviews are with men of greater confidence and experience and have a more candid look to them, but they can also seem like efforts at detachment from a naive past.

I've not tried to set out a comprehensive record of events. What's documented doesn't tell half of the story, and no amount of detail (of gigs, recording sessions or makes of guitar) is going to be as important as trying to re-capture the landscape and feel of that lost world. So this is a book about the curious stories behind those LPs, trying to better understand what makes them special by conjuring up the ordinary experiences of the early Eighties, the spirit and character of living in what is now a foreign country; not just the recovery of facts, but the recovery of innocence. Which is why the first chapter opens with a scene from early Eighties life, the first in a series of scenes that attempt to infuse these pages with that feel.

It's nostalgia, but meant to be a brisk and questioning nostalgia that always keeps in mind the menace contained within the Eighties fairy-tale, the darkness haunting every step for these bands: melancholy, disillusionment, illness and death.

I think some honesty is the only way I'm going to keep the party going anyway. The conversation's stilted and the supply of booze will never last, not with the Go-Betweens around. Those young faces, at the same time earnest and cynical, are starting to look impatient. I'm going to need to tell them about the future, what's going to happen to them and to the songs. And they're not going to like it.

---

12 Orange Juice, *The Glasgow School* CD sleeve notes, AED, 2005.

1.

Falling and laughing
Orange Juice, You Can't Hide Your Love
Forever (February 1982)

*T*he telly's still on, but the only sign of the existence of human life tonight is the leftover smog of chip pan fat, ketchup and fags. Condensation grows heavy on the windows of number 112 Simpson, turning each pane of glass into an insect's eye. The evening outside, filled with row after row of houses, is a million lights and one single mass of shimmer. Crimson with possibility, yellow with regret.

There's something about Friday night that disturbs the blood. The God of Friday night is everywhere and in every thing, making it feel like something about the day will always be unfinished. It's there in every wink of light on the horizon, the sound of every passing car, in the way the night-time streets burn more brightly.

Nowhere to go, the telly shows Superstars to the settee, an ash tray and a pile of old copies of TV Times and Look-in. A kitchen strip-light buzzes on the right and proper mess of streaky plates and Dream Topping powder. A fresh pack of cigarettes, a lighter, some pound notes and change are waiting, villainously, on the telephone table.

*

> Love is the fart
> Of every heart;
> It pains a man when 'tis kept close
> And others doth offend, when 'tis let loose.

Sir John Suckling, dashing seventeenth century poet and wit, makes an excellent point. Telling someone you love them for the first time is worse than risky, it's leakage from a secret inner life and pathetic. It can be good pathetic or bad pathetic, but still pathetic. No matter how smooth and controlled the persona had seemed, looking solid behind those new Ray-ban shades, there's always the prospect of instant ruin because there's no way back once it's out there. The loved one has all the power. They can make a joke of it if they want to, let their eyes trail away and become distracted. They could think it's a contract with a signature at the bottom. Sometimes they might even just be glad. But this 'love' which is meant to be what makes us human and essential for our fulfilment, still feels like an embarrassing throwback to an age when we weren't so cool or rational or risk-averse. It can't rid itself of the smell of sentiment.

There's nothing natural or immutable about romantic love either, it's had its own inconsistent history. It's meant different things and evoked very different sensations and feelings depending on time and place. In the 15th century, feelings of love were often explained as being part of the religious experience: the brief moment when crude mortals brushed through some threads of the divine. For Sir John, romantic love was contrary to the expediencies of aristocratic life and the need for appropriate marriage; it lacked sense and purpose, a fancy of the imagination. Fey and farty. The eighteenth century's acute sensuality, a hyper-sensitivity to feelings and emotions, meant anxiety over how a flare-up of love could damage your nervous system. The popular book of *Domestic Medicine* (1772) warned that love had the potential to become a "disease" with consequences "so violent, that even the possession of the beloved object will not always remove them." Strong purgatives were recommended as a precaution. In a survey of the inmates of London's Bedlam asylum in 1810, forms of "love" were given as some of the most common reasons for incarceration. 1980s love would be a bad joke to Sir John: a technicolour bubble of pop culture filled with Hollywood ideals and TV soap stories, radio ballads and Mills & Boon; all of which made love more ordinary and imperative, more acceptable and dramatic, more soppy and empty than ever before.

This confusion of love in the Eighties, so unavoidable as an ambition and a panacea, played an important role in the making of each of the five LPs. But if you were going to stand up in public and talk about romantic love, you needed to have some confidence in your audience, that they might at least share some of your views. You wanted to make sure you weren't standing in the outré shoes of Edwyn Collins, wearing a bootlace tie and a Davy Crockett hat, standing on the stage of a sweaty club in Glasgow. Now that would be awkward.

*

Dropping through a mile of cloud, pigeons make an arcing circle away from the hills and head for the river. They fly across a sky that looks troubled by its own changing moods, the changes that come so quick and hard. Below, and stretching to every point of the horizon, is a city made from all the colours of rain: pavement greys, dirty pinks and cold ash blues. The cranes, tower blocks, electricity pylons and works chimneys are like municipal defences, scattering the flocks of birds into motley twos and threes before they can fall and settle. From the rooftops they look down into the streets of a fallen city.

In the 19th century Glasgow was a centre of Victorian wealth and elegance, favoured as the 'Second City of the Empire'. Its location on the River Clyde made it the muscle of Scotland's industrial revolution, ready to take on the manufacture of anything from tobacco to paper and soap before bulking up for the big time of shipbuilding and railways. Money from industry was turned to spectacle: fashionable neo-Gothic and neo-classical architecture, the new churches, mansion houses, grand shopping arcades, museums and galleries. The eventual decline of the city came slowly and painfully as 'foreign' competition and the technologies of a more nimble new age riddled the ground under the feet of what was now a lumbering set of heavy industries. By 1982 Glasgow had become scarred by decades of demolition and clearance, known in the popular press for its violence and low life expectancy. Between 1981 and 1983, the numbers of unemployed in Scotland doubled and, famously, no government support was given to the Clydeside industries to help soften the blow from collapsing markets and the human suffering that resulted.

The fabulous Victoriana of the past was still on show: the palaces of red and blonde sandstone, their towers and spires now fierce with a century of industrial soot; and there was still the grace and mystery of the Greco-Roman pillars, the columns and arches to be discovered looming over wet Scottish streets. But the docks and riverside warehouses grew more remote and meaningless as each year passed. They shared the same miserable story as the other empty and haunted spaces of Glasgow, where the factories, tenements and worker housing had once been, teeming with a bluster of community, and now just part of the spare ground. No-mans-land sectioned off with concrete posts and wire fences. It was a city with nothing much left to do. Modern life — straitened, cold-eyed and on a budget — was characterised by functional high-rise flats and pebble-dashed shopping precincts, ring roads that joined the central sprawl with new-build suburbs and some soggy recreation grounds.

If Glasgow's fall had happened in earlier times, grim-faced barbarians would have poured down from the Clyde Muirshiel and the Trossachs to pillage what remained of its riches, leaving the burning city buried under layers of wreckage for future tourists to re-discover. But modern Scotland had local government instead, the well-meaning officials with small budgets who used compromise and experimental measures to paper over the cracks of social disintegration. From the mid-1950s onwards — and just as happened in many other British cities — the ugly overcrowding of the poorest districts of Glasgow was tidied up. Skilled workers with young families were moved out to the new towns of Cumbernauld, East Kilbride and Irvine. The rest were left to make do (meaning the poorest families, older people, all those least likely to find work) and re-housed in the peripheral estates of Castlemilk, Drumchapel, Easterhouse and Pollok. The intention had been to provide better housing, but it turned out to be better housing in a de-socialised environment. There were no shops, pubs, dancing halls or cinemas in these places (not even any schools), because local authorities wanted to avoid becoming long-term landlords. So if anything provided a sense of social identity and purpose on the estates it was heroin, Buckfast Tonic Wine, sectarian football and gangs — whether you were into them, against them or just trying to keep out of the way.

Cities like Glasgow are made simple for the sake of telling stories. And Glasgow more than any other British city has suffered from myths. In this case myths of slums and drugs and knife gangs, the hot and spicy material needed for photo-features, books and TV documentaries. The city's famous 'neds' might have been the most pungent part of the population, but their influence was diffused by the much larger air of decency surrounding them, by all the ordinary good-hearted families, the bus drivers, shopkeepers, teachers, waiters, housewives, driving instructors and greengrocers, with all their gossip and ordinary longings; the people who went shopping in the same covered markets and department stores, sharing the same on-the-corner pubs and Saturday nights in the social clubs; the same deadpan jokes about the godforsaken place they lived in. Knowing and never saying how sad life can be. There was a medieval university in the city as well as Strathclyde and Glasgow Caledonian and Rennie Mackintosh's Glasgow School of Art; and all of them were part of a rich web of arts and culture. In 1983, when the council launched its 'Glasgow's Miles Better' campaign, badged with a sunburst Mr Happy logo, there was a genuine determination to give the city a more friendly image, to try and attract investors and (at the end of the chain of 'stakeholders') do something to improve the lives of residents.

Glasgow wasn't just Nedville. It wasn't just Edinburgh-civilised either. Not only a place of bohemia or blue-collar grit. Glasgow contained all of this, holding together all the contrasts and tensions that can undermine complacency and conformity, that will intensify a sense of place, of both belonging and not belonging.

*

Some people can't help being misfits. There's something in their background, personality, genes or other circumstances that makes it unavoidable. Edwyn Collins, instead, went to considerable lengths to become one.

He was intent on tearing up the map of where he was expected to be going, just so he might see where a misfit like him might end up. When he bought his first semi-acoustic Burns guitar aged 16, he wasn't dreaming of *Top of the Pops*. "I didn't really want to be a pop star. I was striving for something interesting. I practised daily for months and years, chord shapes and such like. None of that pop star rubbish."[1]

First of all, to be any kind of rebel, there have to be have walls of respectability to climb and leap away from. These existed for Edwyn in the wealthy suburb of Bearsden, a green High Victorian oasis that was close enough to Glasgow's city centre for the young musician to be drawn into the devilish downtown, and far enough away for Bearsden to be viscerally a different land, with its own manner and atmosphere; as civilised and fair-minded as the moods of a Scottish enlightenment philosopher. Home, to Edwyn, meant steep expectations of worldly achievement. His grandfather on his mother's side was Dr Hugh Stewart Mackintosh, the youngest Director of Education in Scotland, renowned for having introduced the comprehensive schools system. A precocious scholar, Mackintosh had begun his degree in maths at the University of Glasgow at the age of 16 before going on to combine a career as an educationalist with playing for the Scotland rugby team. Edwyn had a heritage to live up to, a bedrock of reputation in Glasgow as well as a family 'seat' in the Highland village of Helmsdale with its legacy of generations of builders and stonemasons. "I was a bit of a letdown to the Collins family. I was expected to be a lawyer, a doctor or an academic. My sister Petra became a judge. They found it hard to fathom my love of punk."[2] Edwyn deliberately chose to avoid the university option and went to an unfashionable art school. "But not even that really; it was a design college."[3] Edwyn's wife Grace has observed how: "As he grew up into an awkward and headstrong teenager, who did fine but did not excel academically, relations were not always so easy in this

---

1 McKay, Alastair, 'Orange Juice: "If anything became too smooth, Edwyn Collins liked to fuck it up"', *Uncut*, June 20 2014.

2 'This much I know: Edwyn Collins', *The Guardian*, 27 April 2008.

3 Reynolds, Simon, interview notes for *Rip it up and start again: postpunk 1978-1984*, Faber & Faber, 2005.

tight-knit family, but affection and loyalty remained firm."[4] There wasn't any dramatic split, but clouds of incomprehension gathered. These lines in a letter from Dr Mackintosh hint at the pleasant quality of doubt and disapproval: "I do hope that this sudden and most welcome publicity that he and 'Orange Juice' has got is not something that has happened more or less accidentally."[5] Collins' family life was civilised, high-minded and bookish. Edwyn's father was an artist and art lecturer, his mother also studied art, and the most likely soundtrack to evenings at home was classical music. It was a setting that encouraged introspection, creativity and some quaint bedroom-based pursuits like collecting stamps (it was this collection, including a much-prized Penny Black, that was sold at a Glasgow pawnshop to pay for the Burns guitar). Young Edwyn had also been an expert in spotting different types of warplanes just from their silhouettes in the sky, a hobby that evolved into a fascination with native British birds and his beautifully observed and felt drawings. He collected stuffed birds as well as having chance to get to know their wild, palpitating existence more intimately.

> I think I was eight or nine when I found a fledgling greenfinch in the garden…My neighbour called it Tweety Pie. A female. I kept it in a shoebox in my bedroom. It would tweet from 5am onwards, but I was too lazy to get up until about six or seven…I fed it from my finger and she gobbled it up…When she flew off she would sometimes come back in to visit if I left the window open.[6]

It's easy to see how wild birds could take a hold inside the imagination of a misfit in the making. Their self-sufficiency, their fugitive haunts, their frailty and innocence. In birdwatching there is an appeal to the sensibility of an artist in the need, first of all, for seeing, for patience and for discrimination. Those summer holidays in Helmsdale, the excursions to the re-

---

[4] Maxwell, Grace, *Falling & Laughing: The Restoration of Edwyn Collins*, Ebury Press, 2009, p256.

[5] Ibid., p256

[6] Ibid., p268.

mote cliffs and headlands to watch for birds, exploring a magical shoreline and its secrets, would always stay with him as luminous memories of freedom and adventure away from home.

The family circle was broken by his parents' separation when Edwyn was 15. Edwyn and Petra went to live with an aunt and uncle and he only returned to Bearsden later to live with his mother. A home with his curious-looking bedroom, filled not only with beady-eyed taxidermy and the clutter of an artist's bric-a-brac, a debris of paper and pencils and paints, but also his books and stacks of vinyl in slides and spills over the floor. By then it was time for the misfit to take his contrary spirit out into the work-a-day world and its staring, assessing pairs of eyes.

> A salmon flapping in the dunes of the Sahara was less of a fish out of water than Edwyn at [the Glasgow College of Building and Printing] …his lankiness, his fringe, his sensible patent shoes, his drainpipe jeans, and the tangible aura of blazing strangeness.[7]

Edwyn would often take the bus into town to Paddy's Market in the railway arches in Shipbank Lane and hang out in the frowzy jungle of cheapo clothes and piled up boxes of subsoil from Glaswegian days of old. What had been cellophane-wrapped and hopeful in the Sixties, now left sun-faded and dejected. Paddy's was filled with old-timers, oddballs and students along with the chuntering wail of cassette tape decks playing the usual Country and Western favourites. It was a place of rank city smells, the musk of fags, traffic, rotting food and piss-stained corners. It was somewhere else for Edwyn to explore away from the mainstream, a local habitat of musty leftovers that might turn up an unexpected find, maybe a discarded cowboy jacket with a funky fringe, some Rupert Bear trousers or even a Velvet Underground LP. After he'd left the market for main city centre streets, Edwyn gave the pubs a wide berth and met his art school friends in the more reasonable habitat of the local cafés and their scuffed, sugar-sprinkled formica. When he got a job, the one and only job he ever had, it was uncannily suitable. Edwyn was employed by the Glasgow Parks

---

[7] Goddard, Simon, *Simply Thrilled: The Preposterous Story of Postcard Records*, Ebury Press, 2014, p48.

Department to produce illustrations used in its nature trail leaflets, given the freedom of the city's biggest green and leafy spaces to draw its wildlife, the mallards, chaffinches, moorhens and squirrels. A job that was more like a hobby. The harder work for Edwyn was finding an identity, how all his need for being different, his mix of talents and sensitivities, could be resolved into something tangible. Saying no was the easy bit; no to a middle-class education and career, no to trendy fashion, no to chart pop, even no to the wrong kind of punk. Edwyn eventually stood up to proclaim a kind of yes with the band he formed with friends and fellow Bearsden suburbanites, James, Steven and David, if only in a tentative and erratic kind of way. "We were never the kids at school that people wanted to hang out with," said Edwyn. "When we met each other, we were all coming from an outsider perspective, it informed the way we were with each other."[8] They were a geeky little band who came together first of all to make an outsider's fanzine, *No Variety*, mixing esoteric Velvet Underground reviews with political comment, before committing themselves to their own songs and evenings of rehearsing.

Meanwhile, waiting to abuse them, was a gig scene that was still stuck in the Seventies. The roster was filled with blues guitar and rock music for the geezers in denim and lads in sports casual, doing their thing in pubs and clubs made fetid by second-hand Kestrel Super and Snakebite. Local journalist Allan Brown has grimaced at the memory.

In environments so avowedly masculine the music prevailing was growly and two-fisted, a hirsute heavy rock that took its cues from Free, Deep Purple, Uriah Heep. At this time, the mid-to-late 1970s, Glasgow was effectively a Saxon city, permanently on a war footing. The messiahs were The Sensational Alex Harvey Band, native boys gone national, and Nazareth, yet another outfit with a vocalist, Dan McCafferty, who gave the impression he was in the midst of passing a particularly sizeable kidney stone...Each and all were truly, shudderingly horrible.

---

[8] King, Richard, *How Soon is Now — The Madmen and Mavericks who made Independent Music 1975-2005*, Faber & Faber, 2012.

Although in their twenties, the musicians seemed wreathed with the seedy fatigue of drunken uncles.[9]

So Orange Juice didn't just stand out because of the musical style they'd created. "They thought we were effete nancy boys," said Edwyn[10]. Members of another local band liked to stand next to the stage and get a chant going of "poofs! poofs! poofs!" in time with the beat of Northern Soul thumper 'Lovesick'. One night, when the usual chants had started up among the Saxon army, Edwyn got right to the heart of the issue of what it means to be unconventional versus thinking and doing the same as everyone else. Looking back into the eyes of a red-faced heckler: "I'm no' a poof!" he roared, "you're a poof!"

*

Boys start bands to get girls, or so it was said at the time. Being in the limelight of a band at least meant the backdoor to acceptability for a misfit. "On a personal level, I went from having very few friends to suddenly knowing 100 people," recalled Robert Forster of the Go-Betweens. "It was incredible, it was like a coming-out, like some sort of old-fashioned Victorian belle or something...Life suddenly had a purpose."[11] Everything But The Girl's Tracey Thorn made the same discovery. "Like many other fundamentally shy and awkward teenagers both before and since, I'd realised that joining a band could be a shortcut to the kind of local status and prestige I'd dreamed of."[12] But as another cliché of the time goes, after punk anyone could make music. True stardom was in short supply. New bands were sprouting up everywhere, and so many of them had a comic-

---

9 Brown, Allan, *Nileism: The Strange Course of The Blue Nile*, Polygon, 2010, p24.

10 Scott, David, *Classic Scottish Albums: You Can't Hide Your Love Forever*, BBC Radio Scotland, 2006.

11 Stafford, Andrew, *Pig City: From the Saints to Savage Garden*, University of Queensland Press, 2004, p83.

12 Thorn, Tracey, *Bedsit Disco Queen: How I Grew Up and Tried to Be a Pop Star*, Virago Press, 2013, p30.

ally inflated sense of their profile. The Blue Nile's PJ Moore was working behind the bar at the Rock Garden in Glasgow when he fell into conversation with one of the customers: "I'm in a band," they confided, impressively, "as you probably know." It was a line PJ, Paul and Robert never got tired of repeating. At least being in a band felt like you were doing something. Aztec Camera's bass player Campbell Owens remembers there being a new sense of the possible. "There was that post-punk moment, all bright and hopeful, the excitement of stirring things up, unleashing creative energies. We thought everything was going to be new, it was all going to change. It wasn't about being pop stars, it was about just being in a band and going on tour."[13]

In its guide to the youth culture of 1980, *The Sun* listed the tribes of the time as punks, rockabillies, new psychedelics, heavy metallers, New Romantics, skins and mods. Each of these subcultures was an outlier, a small minority, as much about fashion as the music. "There was no confidence on display here," Eighties commentator Alwyn Turner has argued of these musical tribes, "no obvious unifying thread. And the decade went on to witness the sightings of a wide variety of the alleged sociological groups — Yuppies, Sloane Rangers, Young Fogeys — as though the cultural confusion were not merely related to music but to the future of the nation itself."[14] In his book on teenage culture, Peter Everett described how a "psychologist [in April 1983] told delegates at a London advertising conference that teenagers 'had been left in a backwater'. Musical tastes were 'diverse' and 'anarchic'. There was 'a trend to individual listening boosted by Walkman-type stereo headsets, on which teenagers can listen to their favourite songs, safe in their private world.'" There was so much attention given to subcultures because of the overwhelming ordinariness of the majority, said Everett: "If 90% of youth...drifts back to dressing from Debenhams and listening to the Top Twenty, the 10% that holds out for an alternative, *any* alternative, is the bit that gets noticed."[15] None of our

---

[13] Owens, Campbell, telephone interview, 9th November 2018.

[14] Turner, Alwyn W., *Rejoice! Rejoice! Britain in the 1980s*, Aurum Press, 2010, p61.

[15] Everett, Peter, *You'll never be 16 again*, BBC Publications, 1986, p147.

five were part of a definably flamboyant, visually style-bound sub-culture. They were defined more by what they weren't.

The biggest enemy was mainstream rock. Rock had grown to a dominant cultural position since the Fifties as the music of an upwardly-mobile baby boomer generation. It had been funded by the first flush of youth consumer culture and gone on to proliferate its own universe of symbols for what was meant by 'cool': fast cars on the open road, living hard and loose, a burning cigarette in the corner of the driver's mouth. It was a posturing and extroverted (white) male world in its celebration of noise, machines and physical strength, a universe where women were scenery and entertainment. As the baby boomers got older and their ambitions evolved, the music stayed with them, becoming a soundtrack to some fogeyish consumerism. Rock and roll meant having a big house (Tudorbethan, decked out in Laura Ashley), fast cars (classic) and expensive holidays (Caribbean cruise). The squares weren't the boring middle-aged suits anymore because the rock fans were themselves the suit-wearing management. The squares were now the small and weedy, the 'unsuccessful', the sensitive. Rock had become part of the capitalist system, offering a release valve for frustration at the paltry, muted reality of things, an escape into fantasy for the careerists (who'd just better be tidy and sober and back at their desks on Monday). And when the rock revival came in the Nineties with Britpop, the new rock n' roll lads and ladettes were less likely to be freewheeling on the road than slumped on a Habitat sofa, can of Stella in hand, worrying about the negative equity on their new Barratt Homes flat.

It was cowardly to have let rock music become so pre-eminent, argued Subway Sect's Vic Godard. Courage was needed to stand up to the oafish conventions of rock as the sound of cool and find something new, an ethos that was more real and relevant — and a lot more likeable. "We oppose all rock and roll," sang Vic on 'Rock and Roll Even (Different Story'. Edwyn followed in Godard's footsteps on the early Postcard single 'Poor Old Soul' with its protest chant of "No more rock and roll for you!". Steven Daly has suggested the only real common ground, "something in the air", between the Postcard Records bands was their anti-rock feeling, "rock seemed like an exhausted form and we couldn't imagine that anyone would still want to play it for much longer."[16] "Many people who go into this business think that they have to have a very aggressive machismo or a very aggressive stage image," said Morrissey in 1984. "It's time for a different version: not everybody is like Ozzy Osbourne. The normal rock 'n' roll terminology sounds like a chant of agony."[17] Later he added that: "the traditional, incurable rock and roller never interested me remotely. He was simply a rather foolish, empty-headed figure who was peddling his brand of self-projection and very arch machismo that I could never relate to."[18] Instead the Smiths had Johnny Marr, "perhaps the first non-macho guitar hero"[19]. Morrissey handpicked all of their gigs in the early years in order to avoid the rock "treadmill", hoping to secure attention with vinyl rather than gigging. The Blue Nile went further and spent almost all of their time on private rehearsals and songwriting. After the success of *High Land, Hard Rain*, Roddy Frame went straight into the heart of Rockville, living and recording in the USA. Everywhere he went, radios and MTV were playing Van Halen's mega-hit 'Jump', an archetypal anthem of rock triumphalism. In response Roddy recorded his own downbeat version, turning the song into an ironic comment on the boneheadedness of the rock industry, expressing a feeling that was more suicidal than elated. The line "can't you see me standin' here, I got my back against the record machine" becomes something else, "like I've got my back against the record industry" explained Roddy[20]. If the emptiness of rock was bad, when it tried to make itself seem meaningful it was even worse. "It was just something I couldn't have articulated at the time, but it was an innate suspicion that a lot of rock was stupid and silly," Edwyn said. "Particularly the rock that people

---

[16] Orange Juice, *The Glasgow School* CD sleeve notes, AED, 2005.

[17] Savage, Jon, 'The Smiths: Deliberately', *The Sunday Times*, 8 January 1984.

[18] Kent, Nick, 'The Smiths: Dreamer In The Real World', *The Face*, May 1985.

[19] Maconie, Stuart, 'Johnny Marr: Set The Boy Free', *Daily Mail*, 26 November 2016.

[20] *Rockin' On* magazine, Japan, 1985.

found most profound — that was the *most* absurd. Siouxsie and the Banshees. Or Ian Curtis, who by all accounts was a little uptight nutty Tory."[21]

Punk, on the other hand, still mattered. It mattered even if the original daemon of what was meant to be a temporary and self-destructive phenomenon - a detonation that left everyone looking at a smoking hole - was long gone by 1980. Just the hangers-on and their 'oi oi music' were left. "I think right from the start we could see that being in leather and chains was exactly what punk was not about," said Robert. "Punk was more the New York thing, where you could have hair down to here, like Joey Ramone. It's variety; it's individual expression; it's diversity."[22] An attitude that helps to explains why all of these bands, so adamant with delicacy and elegance, could still have been made from their emotional response to punk. It was where the courage to be genuinely different came from. "I don't think The Sex Pistols were silly — that kind of manic intensity, that kind of anger you see in Rotten, it seems real to me. the things he's saying are very clever…and he's the reason why I'm talking to you [the music press] now." (Edwyn)[23] The Blue Nile were first of all fans of the Clash, Television, the Sex Pistols, and their model of angry possibility: "The first time we heard Talking Heads, we were thinking, 'I could do that'…We went into it knowing we weren't musicians."[24] Being amateur and artless was part of the deal. "Even our friends thought we were crap," said Orange Juice's David McClymont[25]. When the hits started coming, that's when Edwyn reverted to type, as drummer Zeke Manyika remembered: "we had a lot of singles that went to the edge of the Top 40.

[21] Reynolds, Simon, ibid.

[22] Stafford, Andrew, ibid., p83.

[23] Reynolds, Simon, ibid.

[24] Kelly, Jennifer, 'At the Source of the Blue Nile: an interview with Paul Buchanan', *Pop Matters*, 30 January 2013.

[25] Stenders, Kriv, *Right Here: the story of the Go-Betweens* film, 2017.

But [Edwyn] had a strong punk ethic, where if everything became too smooth, he liked to fuck it up."[26]

So not punk and not pop, but instead an attempt to bridge the market-generated chasm widening under their feet. On one side there was radio-friendly commercial music, where the sun was shining and the sea was blue, and on the other, alternative music: cold and lonely in its bedsit with a pile of unpaid bills. There was a danger that all the most interesting and sincere, 'real' music, was going to stay sidelined by the magnetic appeal of chart pop. Something had to be done. Alan Horne, impresario behind Postcard Records, sounded off to the *NME* in 1980:

> "Music should always aim for the widest possible market. The charts are there. That's where you need to be. Postcard was not really that well organised, it was just at the back of my mind that the punk ideals had failed, all dropped away. Groups like Buzzcocks, who knew the importance of getting into the charts, could have been so powerful, so strong, and they could have led the ways for other groups. They didn't."[27]

An early mover into smart indie pop was Green Gartside's Scritti Politti on Rough Trade.

> "We realised that a lot of independent music had become ghetto-ised and trivialised. Despite all Rough Trade's good works, lots of other independent labels didn't spring up and together invade the high streets. Our music and that of a lot of other independents became merely marginal. Marginal music has never transcended its own history or invaded the mainstream. As a consequence it ends up asserting little other than its own marginality, its difference from the majority. But

---

[26] McKay, Alastair, ibid.

[27] Morley, Paul, Alan Horne interview, *New Musical Express*, 4 October 1980.

mere difference is not enough, especially when it soon created a tradition as stale as that of the mainstream, as stale and as self-enclosed."[28]

Changing the nature of 'pop' was never going to be easy. The new mainstream bands, more dazzlingly promoted than ever before, had already delivered a revolution. ABC, Culture Club, Duran Duran, Human League, Kajagoogoo, Spandau Ballet, Wham! weren't just radio-friendly but TV-friendly and press-friendly, setting themselves apart from those who couldn't pay for wall-to-wall PR and advertising, or the high production values needed for watchable video. They had media platforms designed to tap the commercial potential of the new product line to the full: *Smash Hits, i-D, The Face, The Sun*'s 'Bizarre' column, diverting readers from the muso old school of the *NME, Melody Maker* and *Sounds*. The new pop stars offered a feelgood ethos with mass appeal to early Eighties Britain. Nothing complicated — they were just young, rich and famous. Music was suddenly a profession that required an assertive business plan and the ability to make rather than follow fashion. For this reason, a place like Soho's Blitz Club became a seat of power, visited by industry royalty like David Bowie and Mick Jagger. Bright young things with connections across the music industry as well as the London media and club scene would gather to applaud the business success of the New Romantics, competitively dressed in monocles and velvet capes, frilly pirate shirts, satin knickerbockers and silky batwing dresses. "Hair-styles here command airspace of their own," observed the *New Standard* in 1983. "It's pointless wondering why that girl has coloured her breasts green or why that young man sports fishnets beneath shredded jeans."[29] But Adam Ant knew exactly what it all signified, what it all really meant. "To be a new romantic you had to be working and you had to have a lot of money to spend on very, very expensive clothes."[30] British culture was going through another Restoration, the return of pop royalty, meaningless extravagance and careless celebration of wealth after the years of grey social awareness and soul-searching.

---

[28] Cooper, Mark, Green Gartside interview, *Record Mirror*, 5 December 1981.

[29] Everett, Peter, ibid., p144.

[30] Ibid.

The new pop wasn't thinking in terms of playing gigs or writing new songs, it was a bunch of activities designed to maximise profit. As Martin Fry explained, with 'ABC' they were looking to create a "new brand name"[31]. "With the punk thing everyone was making impractical attacks on being rich," said Boy George, "But they all wanted to be rich. You have to be. I've got plenty of money…And I worked for it, really hard."[32] Adam Ant, in his instant 1981 biography, said: "Cult is just a safe word meaning 'loser'"[33].

For our five bands, then, pop appeal was a tightrope. A post-punk group like Scritti Politti decided to leave the squats and the nights of serious political discussion behind them and go for ultra-pop. "What has meaning is what sells," confirmed Green[34]. But while he wanted mainstream success, Edwyn was determined not to be lumped with the pap, especially when there were suggestions that Orange Juice might be successors to *Smash Hits'* favourites Haircut 100. "I don't envy them, these groups who've put the 'a' back into pop music. Ha ha. I really don't. I know there are certain factions who insist that Orange Juice propagated this *wonderful*, golden age of pop, but quite frankly if I thought we'd been in any way responsible, I'd feel we'd have a hell of a lot to answer for. Because I think most of it is shit…I hate them the same way I hated progressive groups in '77; hate was the good thing about punk."[35] There had to be a way to stay on the tightrope of sincerity and shift attitudes, and Morrissey believed he was ahead of everyone in doing this, striding forward at the highest of heights with eye-catching poise. "I think what The Smiths are is something quite beyond popular music, which could almost sound like an absurdly brash comment but it really is the truth. I think

---

[31] Beckett, Andy, *Promised You a Miracle — Why 1980-82 Made Modern Britain*, Penguin, 2015, p186.

[32] Ibid., p191-2.

[33] Ibid., p191.

[34] Ibid., p xix.

[35] Bohn, Chris, 'Orange Juice: From A Postcard To A Postage Stamp', *New Musical Express*, 2 October 1982.

that's why I'm asked very serious questions. If we were simply blending in with modern popular music...we wouldn't be having this conversation [he told the *NME*]."[36] Johnny Marr shared his confidence. "We really should be up there on all these television programmes giving them some sort of credibility."[37] The *NME* saw exactly the same quality in the Go-Betweens: "The common goal [between them and The Smiths] is the reclamation of pop as a vehicle for esoteric wit and everyday insight, the trashing of Pop as a constricting collection of platitudes."[38] "We're doing something new and something very emotional, and we're experimenting," said Grant McLennan. "It's just a matter of the focus. I do think we're right at the centre, and eventually all the other dreck that's around will be just washed away."[39]

New and experimental though? Not really. Post-punk has been defined as being the period from the late Seventies to the mid-Eighties when everything in music had to be new, "yesterday's innovation was today's kitsch"[40], and the reason why the essential book on the period by Simon Reynolds was called *Rip it up and start again*. But our five weren't just re-inventing the old, they were embracing it with affection. Being self-consciously unfashionable meant nothing from the past was off limits. They could raid the shelves and cabinets at home for old LPs, and all those earnest smiles, rolltop jumpers and cardigans they found there were just fine. It's this combination of punk with an enthusiasm for Sixties crooners and janglers that makes each of these LPs sound so strangely out of time — classic because they don't seem to belong to the early Eighties, or maybe to any age at all. When Steven first met Edwyn he was wearing a Buddy Holly badge. "I could possibly make the music sound more con-

---

[36] Hoskyns, Barney, 'These Disarming Men: The Smiths', *New Musical Express*, 4 February 1984.

[37] Shaw, William, 'The Smiths: Glad All Over', *ZigZag*, February 1984.

[38] Watson Don, 'The Go-Betweens: Up From Down Under', *New Musical Express*, 26 November 1983.

[39] Barber, Lynden, 'The Go-Betweens: Mysteries of Exile', *Melody Maker*, 1 October 1983.

[40] Fisher, Mark, quoted in *Post-punk, now and then*, ed. Gavin Butt, Kodwo Eshun and Mark Fisher, Repeater Books, 2016.

temporary; even with Orange Juice the music was either anachronistic or ahead of its time. Never in tune with the times. But then, I often haven't liked the times, so why be in tune with them?" said Edwyn[41]. "People stopped using the word 'hipster' after the 60's. I still liked it, Daddio. Although some words were forbidden in punk times. For instance, 'cool' or 'yeah' or 'man.' Verboten, totally verboten."[42] There was an older vibe with a quality and distinction that had become lost to modern pop. "We're not a trendy band, we're a groovy band, and I like that," offered Grant. Lindy Morrison was more assertive. "I never gave a shit. We did not look the part, we did not sound the part, we were not the part. We were too intelligent."[43] There was a ten year gap between Roddy and some of his older brothers and sisters which meant exposure to record collections full of sun-spangled Americana, Bob Dylan, Burt Bacharach, Neil Young, Simon & Garfunkel, Ike & Tina Turner. The Blue Nile, just like the Go-Betweens, started out by playing their own version of American West Coast guitar pop. Morrissey's first vinyl loves were the working-class female singers of the Sixties, Marianne Faithful, Cilla Black, Sandie Shaw. Faraway voices emanating from a velvet darkness. Their innate taste for storytelling drama would stay with him (along with some of the lyrics — like Sandie Shaw singing 'Heaven Knows I'm Missing Him Now'). The new indie guitar sound came from a fascination with acoustic and vintage guitars, Gretsch and 12-string Rickenbackers, and all the brittle musical edges and crisp corners they could produce. "I feel very traditional about what we do," admitted Johnny. "Which is why I can always relate to people like Muddy Waters and not feel bad about it. I could never deny listening to Duane Allman, or whoever it is that's got long hair and is uncool."[44] Paul Buchanan looked back further, to his father's Frank Sinatra LPs, and, most

---

[41] Brown, Len, 'Hope Springs Eternal: Edwyn Collins', *The Cut*, Fall 1989.

[42] Collins, Edwyn, *Tim Burgess's Twitter Listening Party*, 6 April 2020.

[43] Stenders, Kriv, ibid.

[44] Garvin, Rex, 'Johnny Marr: The Man Who Caught The Common Cold', *ZigZag*, August 1984.

unfashionable of all, to what was most quiet and introspective about Sinatra, rueful and self-abnegating.

There was nothing consciously retro going on, the more diverse and perverse the influences the better. Part of what makes the later indie imitators look unimpressive is their seeming belief in a formula that really had no authenticity: there was no original, cohesive source. Clashes in taste were part of what made the outsider magic work. "The idea of doing two songs in the same 'genre' seemed lazy to us — an absolutely disgrace, in fact. We went for something different every time — usually more than once in a song," according to Steven Daly[45]. Edwyn listed the ingredients to the mess that was Orange Juice to Paul Morley in 1980:

"I'm interested in all kinds of music, '50s, '60s, '70s, disco — I think the O'Jays' 'Love Train' is great. David is into Eno and Kraftwerk, who personally I can't stand. James likes jazz and C&W, his licks are really C&W. When it comes to a group like Creedence [Clearwater Revival], I can just tell intuitively that they were honest and passionate. I think that's a really good influence, as well as the Velvets…No one uses C&W at all. It's ethnic, it's good. It's really accessible. And we're combining it with a lot of other musical styles. What people don't seem to realise is that if they take one group as a blueprint and try to emulate that, it won't work. There are so many influences. How many years of popular music have there been…50? You start listening to everything and that's how you're going to start new music coming through."[46]

Edwyn talked about Nile Rodgers being his first choice for producing *You Can't Hide Your Love Forever,* and early gigs would begin with the chant from Chic's 'Dance Dance Dance (Yowsah Yowsah Yowsah)'. At the same time he cited the influence of Noel Coward (whose lyrics crept into the early single 'Poor Old Soul') and the 'Tin Pan Alley' generation of American songwriters: "real pop started in the 1890s with vaudeville. It's people like Gershwin (brother Ira is even better!) and Cole Porter, these are the boys

---

45 Daly, Steven, *Tim Burgess's Twitter Listening Party,* 6 April 2020.

46 Morley, Paul, ibid.

that go right through to Bacharach and Lennon-McCartney"[47]. The distinctive sound of the Smiths depended on the marriage of spiky blues guitars with Morrissey's operatic lament. Around the time of the recording of their early LPs, both Aztec Camera and the Go-Betweens were listening to a lot of jazz. Aztec Camera's bossa nova rhythms and acoustic Spanish guitars were a vigorous two fingers to moody synth pop. Touring in the USA for the 'Love' album in 1987, Roddy was suddenly playing white boy soul — more Anita Baker than Bob Dylan — when he bumped into members of the Ramones backstage. With a nice delicacy of perception, the band saw through to the particular essence of Roddy's attitude to indie when they suggested: "you really don't give a fuck do you?"[48]. And yet, of all five, perhaps the most shockingly different were the Blue Nile and their minimalism, the way frail and piquant emotions were made taut and intense by electronica, spilt into warm waves of disco.

*

My sister's going out. "Stay out of my room." Why would I go in a girl's room? "Because, Adrian, you're sad." She says I'll be dead if she catches me in there again. And she goes out. Stairs, slam. Cartoon stinklines of hairspray and perfume in the air.

So I go and look in her room, click on the anglepoise and lie on her bed. I play her cassettes for a while and then read her boring diary. D did this and D said that. V is after D. She thinks she's pretty but she's fat. I know D is for Danny, who drives around in his Dad's Escort. Don't know how he even sees through his flick hairdo to drive. I feel sorry for Danny though. He's told Sarah he's going to be called up for the Falklands. But there's no way he's going to get any sympathy from her. He'd just be messing with her plans by going to war and being dead.

I'm looking for secrets in the shadows left by the lamplight. Red zigzag curtains, polka-dot wallpaper, matching red-handled furniture. Her red lips poster from Athena she's put into a proper frame with glass. Her rack of tapes. Dollar, Shakatak, ABBA, Kool and the Gang, Julio Iglesias. It's all about one big secret. About going out rather than staying in. A secret that smells like hairspray and cherry lip gloss. Something about

---

[47] McCullough, Dave, 'OJ are OK', Sounds, 24 October 1981.

[48] Craig Gannon interview, *earcandy*, February 2012.

love, that's black and silver and glows all around the edges like the door to the nightclub in town. I don't want it anyway. What's it got to do with me? It's all fake, all that make-up, those goofy faces, sweaty bodies and heavy breathing.

I play another tape and start to doze. There's something pure about the night-time.

Sarah comes back, crashes in. She doesn't shout this time, she tells me quietly to go fuck myself. I must be looking surprised as I leave. "Isn't that your favourite hobby?" she says.

*

Being different wasn't a musical pose for our outsider bands, it was a matter of everyday life and the living of it. No rock sneers or thrusting groins because these were self-consciously polite, articulate and well-mannered types, harbouring youthful ideals. "We can't relate to drugginess," said Edwyn. "I hate dopiness, hallucigenicness, amphetiminess...I'd like to see a return to high romance rather than all this emphasis on sex."[49] Cheap thrills were out. Edwyn's wife Grace remembers Orange Juice gigs when girls would crowd the front and scream his name. "Now, where every other bugger can cope with that, Edwyn comes out, and he goes, 'Well, you can cut that out right away.'"[50] Early Postcard single, 'Simply Thrilled Honey' is the tale of how a demure Edwyn turns down the offer of no-strings sex: "I think it's really important to only go to bed with someone if you love them," he explained[51].

17 year-old Roddy talked about being "into this 'new Puritan' thing where you don't touch girls... I like those lyrics of Mark Smith's a lot. I used to be against drugs and drink, that sort of thing."[52] Instead, Roddy had a one-track mind: "It's just something that occupies my mind a lot. I dunno, I think I wanna get married some day. That's really important. It

---

[49] Pye, Ian, 'Juicy, fruity, cheap 'n cheerful', *Melody Maker*, 17 January 1981.

[50] McKay, Alastair, ibid.

[51] McCullough, Dave, ibid.

[52] McCullough, Dave, 'After the Fall...Aztec Camera', *Sounds*, 3 January 1981.

always has been and always will be."[53] Music journalists could be taken aback by the gentility they encountered in interview situations. "These charming men? Morrissey and Marr share a polite yet earnest nature," said *Sounds*[54]; "Roddy Frame's favourite expression is 'It's just great', and when he says it, his eyes light up. He has a wonderful smile and a slightly mistrusting expression on his face most times."[55] Grace remembered first meeting Roddy and being struck by his "beautiful manners", "in true Post-card visitor style"[56]. She also suggested, in hindsight, that there was nothing consciously moral about any of this, the Postcarders were rejecting rock clichés. But there looks to be a spine of idealism there, people finding a pleasurable frisson in having principles, from being different to a brash industry and some braggart rituals. Hard drinking was one of them. The name Orange Juice itself comes from the band's favourite rehearsal drink (as well as being an intentionally strident response to po-faced post-punk band names and the trend for the brutish: the Slits, the Ruts, the Clash, Wire, Crass, Buzzcocks, New Order). None of the band drank alcohol or smoked in those early days. Sent to review an early Aztec Camera gig at the London Lyceum, an *NME* writer couldn't resist a dig, revealing that: "somebody actually smuggled in a bottle of...chocolate milk."[57] The Blue Nile's collaborator Calum Malcolm had previously lived with the excesses of Nazareth and their "crates of booze and masses of cocaine", and appreciated breathing fresh air again with "three, quiet, equable graduates": "We thought, well, maybe we can be a bit, not clean, but a bit more respectful, of situations and people...there was lots of humour throughout, that was the principal part of it. But we also had a moral stance and it was

---

[53] Gumprecht, Blake, 'Aztec Camera', *Matter*, September 1983.

[54] Black, Bill, 'The Smiths: Keep Young and Beautiful', *Sounds*, 19 November 1983.

[55] Hewitt, Paolo, 'Aztec Camera: I'm Gonna Live Forever', *New Musical Express*, 7 January 1984.

[56] Maxwell, Grace, ibid., p6.

[57] North, Richard, Aztec Camera gig review, *New Musical Express*, 2 April 1983.

a nice feeling."[58] The gentlemanly demeanour was one emanation of a particular state of mind, a self-aware sensibility. "To me, that is the beauty of our music," Grant said. "Those are two nouns I'm quite interested in — subtlety and sensitivity. We don't go in for the demon look, so people just think we're sort of simple and naive. Most people just aren't prepared to look at music any more closely. It's cosmetic and taken on initial appearance."[59] By 1986, Simon Reynolds in *Melody Maker* was able to wonder whether there might be something bigger happening, particularly around the Smiths. Was "[a] new kind of youth culture taking shape, based in romanticism and ascetism? Make no mistake, 'How Soon Is Now', 'Still Ill', 'You've Got Everything Now', these were the lost 'Satisfaction' and 'My Generation' of our time. Lost because the independent scene is just an island, an asylum, that no-one wants to know."[60]

In 'Walking Around', poet Pablo Neruda wrote how: "It happens that I am tired of being a man", "I go into the tailor's shops and the movies/ all shrivelled up", "the smell of barber shops makes me sob out loud"[61]. Walking the Eighties streets offered plenty of reasons for men to feel weary in the same kind of way. The girlie calendars and Page 3 cutouts on workplace walls; the public bars, working men's clubs, bookies and sports matches occupied by gruff circles of masculinity; the breasts revealed by buying bags of pub peanuts; the casual, easygoing chauvinism and racism; the assertive stink of Brut, sweat, cigarettes and stale beer. Average masculinity was inattentive, shabby and contented, and it was plain from any demonstration of empathy or idealism that you didn't belong. This Eighties masculinity, strongly rooted in the habits of previous decades, was becoming jostled from all sides. The certainties of the role of 'bloke' were being made unsteady: sensible, water-sipping Steve Davis was picking up more fans than wild man Alex Higgins. The collapse of heavy industries and manufacturing in particular meant traditional assumptions

---

[58] Brown, Allan, ibid., p78.

[59] Gumprecht, Blake, 'The Go-Betweens: Past Hope, Past Care, Past Help?', *Matter*, April 1984.

[60] Reynolds, Simon, 'Younger Than Yesterday', *Melody Maker*, 28 June 1986.

[61] Neruda, Pablo, 'Walking Around', *Pablo Neruda: Selected Poems*, Penguin, 1975, p67.

about work and men as the sole earners in a family unit were breaking down. Fatherhood in itself was becoming uncomfortable. It was still only the few who would ever be seen out with a pram or taking the kids to the park, even fewer cooking food and doing housework. Arguably, the threat was felt more keenly by young whites, without the same kind of sociable networks and support from black and Asian families. Girls were getting better results than boys in school exams, and more were going on to Higher Education. Margaret Thatcher's premiership was a beacon of unflinching — and, for some, even strangely sexy — femininity for the Eighties. In 1983, three-fifths of married women were now working[62], meaning a greater degree of independence and a refusal to just accept the deal they'd been given: just 27,000 divorces were granted in the UK in 1961. By 1985 the figure had risen to 191,000[63].

"Ever since I was a boy I absolutely detested 99% of male society because they stick to the masculine role model," said Grant. "You talk of one-parent versus two-parent families; if you just have a mother you tend to have a completely different perspective and approach, and I think I've benefited a great deal from that. I don't think anyone could argue against the determining thing in the relationship between most men and women is the power wielded by men."[64] "I think we're tough romantics," claimed Paul Buchanan. "You have to be strong and firm to be able to hold out and express the tender moment, accept each other's strengths and vulnerabilities in equal measure, and I think that's the way, for instance, to be manly rather than to be always coming on macho."[65]

Others went further, seeing strength in those prepared to be openly camp. For Edwyn, the real rebellion of punk wasn't nihilism or aggression but Pete Shelley's limp delivery and stage foppery with Buzzcocks. In his lyrics for 'Consolation Prize', Edwyn set out the problems faced by a sens-

---

[62] Jones, Margaret, *Thatcher's Kingdom: A View of Britain in the Eighties*, Collins, 1984, p76.

[63] Abercrombie, Nicholas; Warde, Alan, *Contemporary British Society*, Polity Press, 1994, p294.

[64] Snow, Mat, 'The Go-Betweens: Money Can't Buy You Love', *New Musical Express*, 13 October 1984.

[65] Interview with Rickie Lee Jones, 1989.

itive youth trying to take on the challenge from virile masculinity: "I wore my fringe like Roger McGuinn's...So frightfully camp, it made you laugh/ Tomorrow I'll buy myself a dress...I'll never be man enough for you." The desire to wear dresses wasn't a comedy one-off. In promotional pics around the time of *Before Hollywood*, Robert and Grant sported make-up and dresses while doing the household chores. But Robert would also occasionally wear a dress for live encores, aiming to look something like Emmylou Harris in "an ankle-length hippie dress". "Why? I don't really know. They felt comfortable and lithe, for a start, and like the red flares and capes I favoured, were part of a set of feelings I had concerning the group's image — never be bland."[66] According to Lindy, Robert would sometimes wear dresses about the house at home. When a reviewer for *Sounds* first heard Aztec Camera he thought Roddy wrote songs "like a girl"[67], and for the follow-up LP to *High Land*, Roddy is represented on the front cover with flowing locks, wearing a dress. At his local working man's club, Roddy's nickname as a teenager was 'Little Nell' (the sentimental female heroine of Dickens' *The Old Curiosity Shop*) because he'd wear his Dad's big work coat with the letters NEL (for National Engineering Laboratory) stencilled in white on the back. And then there's Morrissey. A dress would surely have been too vulgar and blatant a statement for his taste, he kept his femininity more immanent and part of the mystique. "No major pop male sings in female persona as often as Steven Morrissey," suggested the *NME*[68].

Sometimes more overtly than music, fashion could be the language of expression. Record sales in Britain peaked in 1978 at 89 million singles and a similar number of LPs; by 1983 the figures were down by 17% for singles and 39% for LPs[69]. Meanwhile, clothes shopping (and the art of shoplifting) was booming. Farrah, Pringle, Lacoste, Tacchini, Fiorucci and Adidas were the labels of distinction for the mainstream of soul boys, cas-

---

66 Forster, Robert, *Grant & I: Inside and Outside The Go-Betweens*, Omnibus Press, 2017, p203.

67 Aztec Camera review, *Sounds*, January 1984.

68 Sinker, Mark, 'England: Look Back In Anguish', *New Musical Express*, 2 January 1988.

69 Everett, Peter, ibid., p150.

uals, trendies and mall girls. They were the kinds of clothes that provided status and protection from abuse on the streets. Nothing our five wanted to be seen out in (except for an unmissable appearance by Aztec Camera on TV show *The Switch* in 1983, when the whole band was decked out — surely ironically? — in red-collared Sergio Tacchini tracksuits). They swam against the tide. "Edwyn looked like a fish out of water," said David McClymont. "He was wearing straight grey flannel trousers, black Oxford shoes, a tartan shirt and an anorak with a hood. He was tall and lanky, and he really stood out. When you'd walk down the street with Edwyn in Glasgow, people would stare. It was like they were looking at someone from Mars."[70] Where was this new indie fashion coming from? Was it, as argued retrospectively by *MOJO*, a kind of Walter the Softy from the *Beano* thing?[71] Part-Bohemian, part middle-aged square from the Sixties, and anything but sports casual. However it's described, it was dangerous. Wearing unconventional clothes marked you out in the pebble-dashed town centre squares, shopping arcades and covered walkways as pretentious, someone who thought 'normal' clothes and the agreed kind of 'trendy' wasn't good enough for them, and it wasn't safe. DJ and pop historian Stuart Maconie has talked about his obsession with Postcard Records and his dream of moving to East Kilbride to be part of the fresh new scene: "I was obsessed to the extent I would wander the streets of Wigan in a bootlace tie and a big check shirt. I would routinely get beaten up but I didn't care. I would have worn a racoon hat if I could have got hold of one."[72] The Postcard 'look' got bands noticed from the start. "[Aztec Camera] wear Jim-Bob shirts! And Sensible Shoes! And it is unaffected, natural. Aztec Camera deserve, in fact need to be separate from the whirly world of mainstream r'n'r, the world of fat men and big signings, of ill-conceivedness and arbitrariness."[73]

---

[70] McKay, Alastair, ibid.

[71] Eccleston, Danny, 'Aztec Camera Vs Sergio Tacchini', *MOJO*, 9 September 2013.

[72] Stuart Maconie interview with David Scott, *Classic Scottish Albums: High Land, Hard Rain*, BBC Radio Scotland, 2006.

[73] Aztec Camera review, *Sounds*, January 1981.

Rather than being effortless, getting the look involved time and planning. For Edwyn, it was afternoons in Paddy's Market picking out Tweed suits, trilby hats and Boy Scout shorts, as well as the hours at home spent on his hair. "He had a high-maintenance quiff, which took a very long time to assemble…" said Grace. "The main component of the operation was Extra Hard Hold Elnett Hairspray. Choking clouds of the stuff. We were late for everything because of the quiff."[74] What wasn't necessary was lots of money. Roddy worked at imitating Mark E Smith's "indoor look". "Here was a guy singing about the computer centre over the road or eating a packet of crisps and you felt it was coming directly from his life… Before the Fall I liked the Sex Pistols, but they had that New York Dolls glamour to them. You just ended up thinking: 'Where am I going to buy clothes like that? It's not going to happen.' Mark E Smith, meanwhile, would be wearing a tank top from Marks & Spencer. From then on, I started buying my clothes from the Co-Op."[75] Cowboys were a thing for Roddy: fringed jackets, plaid shirts and high boots. He only stopped short at being seen out in a star-spangled sailor suit. Robert had a "Sherlock Holmes-inspired wardrobe" while living in London, taking influences from James Joyce and Samuel Beckett[76]. Morrissey was the least demonstrative, attempting the impossible of having no image at all. Contrary to intentions he became the one to spawn legions of imitators with his slouchy old cardigans and horn-rimmed specs — while also being the most androgynous and the most insinuatingly sexual. Looking like the typical eternal student, ready for another day at the library with a tartan flask and homemade sandwiches, he balanced butch with effeminacy.

*

Postcard Records lasted only a couple of years, released just 12 singles and one LP, little of which output was given any radio airplay. None made the mainstream top 75. And yet Postcard — a label set up by Edwyn with

---

[74] Maxwell, Grace, ibid., p107.

[75] Hodgkinson, Will, 'Home Entertainment', *The Guardian*, 16 August 2002.

[76] Forster, Robert, ibid., p184.

friend Alan Horne, and run from Alan's tenement flat at 185 West Princes Street — continues to have the reputation as being the fount of indie music. Why? Most of the giant corporate record labels started out with a single fan sitting in their bedroom (like Atlantic, Virgin, Island). The Postcard story mutated into legend because it was short-lived (the James Dean effect); because the music was a pick-me-up tonic for grey years; because everything about Postcard was fun, from Edwyn's homemade cut-and-paste artwork to the piss-take press releases. And because there was Alan Horne. "There's someone knocking on my door. A loud rap. I'm woken up with a start. I open the door. Standing there is little Alan Horne, a morose kid in transparent-framed spectacles. He runs Scotland's Postcard Records, a label he's convinced will surpass any of the achievements of Factory or Zoo. This lad is angry all his waking life. He's standing there with Edwyn Collins, well fringed fidgety singer and rhythm guitarist with Glasgow's Orange Juice," wrote Paul Morley in the *NME* in 1980.

> Horne wipes away all obstacles, ducks under impracticalities, thinks little of reputations. The week he'd been in London he'd been to see John Peel, who explained he would like to do sessions with the Postcard groups but there were 60 groups on the waiting list. Horne was not happy. He wanted to know how his groups could jump the list, because they were 'better than all that shit.' Horne almost goes out of his way to retain punk's original arrogance. These days his attitude is refreshingly spiteful and unimpressed. He's been let down a lot.[77]

With his insinuatingly camp manner and acidic humour, Horne was the punk Alan Bennett. Depending on your point of view, he was also either Glasgow's answer to Andy Warhol, a smart Svengali with the energy, intelligence and big ideas to create a Scottish Motown — as per his epic promotional strapline of 'The Sound of Young Scotland' — or just had a big mouth. Either way there wasn't much Scottish nationalism involved, the real focus of the mantra was "pop music for the young made and con-

---

[77] Morley, Paul, ibid.

trolled by the young"[78]. "I consider that we're the only punk independent because we're the only ones doing it who are young. Everybody else has come from the back of a record shop or are business men [criticisms aimed at Rough Trade and Factory]. We started with no money and just built it up from Orange Juice's first single…We want to get our records out as we want them, cut out the majors, all the old middle men, and get into the charts. There'll be no money going to old men, it will be totally independent," he said[79]. Postcard advertised itself as "the only true punk label, we don't do new wave". The label also revelled in not being especially grown up. Edwyn tells the story of Postcard's 'House Designer', a Polish girl who would make herself foam at the mouth with Alka Seltzer tablets, pretend to have an epileptic fit, and then chase Alan around the tenement flat HQ with a bread knife. She'd be "running about like a squealing stuffed pig. She was completely off her head." When the Inland Revenue enquired into the new enterprise, Alan would advise them they needed to speak to the Postcard accountant, Mr Higgy. Mr Higgy, of course, was always out, but, as the head of Postcard Records further explained, when he was around he could usually be found under the kitchen sink. Visitors to West Princes Street would be expected to make themselves useful by colouring in some Postcard sleeves with felt tips. Roddy remembered how CBS had once called from the US to make Alan an offer for Aztec Camera but were told to "fuck off and call back" because he was having his dinner. Alan and Edwyn shook each other up like bottles of Irn-Bru: "we were just merry pranksters, mischief makers"[80]. This included a hobby of winding up the music press, convincing *Sounds* that Postcard had signed David Bowie's 10 year-old son Zowie; and that Barry White was going to produce an Aztec Camera album at Sigma Studios in Philadelphia[81].

---

[78] Bohn, Chris, ibid.

[79] Morley, Paul, ibid.

[80] Sloan, Billy, Interview with Edwyn Collins, Radio Clyde, 1987.

[81] Goddard, Simon, ibid., p172.

"[Alan] would go around with huge cat's whiskers painted on his face saying, 'I'm catman and I make purrrfect records'."[82]

Everything about Postcard was designed to jiggle the executive leather chairs of the major labels in London and mock the pretensions of the in-crowd. The Postcard logo summed it up: a kitten banging on a drum taken from a series of pictures about making enough noise to annoy the parents: "WHEN ONE WEE KITTEN'S IN THE HOUSE IT'S ALL QUIET AS A MOUSE; WHEN TWO ARE THERE IT'S NOT SO QUIET, BUT ENOUGH TO CALL A RIOT!" says the print pulled from a 1913 storybook, *Happy Rhymes And Funny Times*. Edwyn used other cut-outs from a 1960s book of traditional Scottish pursuits — country dancing, Highland games, hill walking, shooting and fishing — a lot of tartan-clad, shortbread-biscuit-tin tease, making fun of Scottish stereotypes.

Postcard materials have sometimes been seized on as an early manifestation of 'twee', but wrongly. There was nothing soft-eyed about it, it shared very little with the school of Twee and its affection for owls and narwhals, it was bracingly sharp. As Stuart Maconie has written, Postcard was rough and tumble, "tousled mischievous fun"[83]. "People always thought of Postcard as a home for wayward wimps but it was actually nothing like that," Edwyn told the *NME*. "The characters around the label were just nutty characters. It consisted of social misfits from all kinds of backgrounds, just like the original London punk scene. Alan seemed to have a penchant for collecting weird people."[84]

Interviews with Alan demonstrate how calculated his ambitions were. For Alan the success of the business was very important, more so than the success of the musicians themselves according to some members of the Postcard roster. "He was a control freak...Alan used to say that the great thing about punk is that it's brought in an era where the manager is as important as the group — 'cos in early punk interviews, the manager

[82] Henry, Julian, 'Orange Juice', *Underground*, 20 March 1987.

[83] Maconie, Stuart, *Cider with Roadies*, Ebury Press, 2004, p156.

[84] Edwyn Collins, *New Musical Express*, 23 April 1983.

[like Malcolm MacLaren] often assumed the same importance as the singer," said Edwyn[85]. For Postcard to reach the next level in terms of chart positions and radio-play, it needed backing from a bigger operation. Rough Trade was a serious indie label, with its physical premises and smart distribution network overseen by a gentlemanly Cambridge graduate — as well as being the kind of "brown rice independent" staffed by "old hippies", that Alan was determined to overthrow. A 'no' from Geoff (who didn't like the combative nature of the Horne hustle and felt "the songs fell in between punk and professional pop") sent Alan into despair according to Edwyn: "We left the offices very downhearted and Alan seemed to go into a crazed depression and started wandering about in the middle of the road saying, 'Let them run me over, let them kill me'."[86] When Geoff later changed his mind and gave Postcard a standard distribution deal, Alan crowed that he'd landed an arrangement that would "bankrupt" Rough Trade. "I think that not having embraced Alan's genius immediately counted as a big blow against me," said Geoff[87]. Things would get worse.

Orange Juice made Postcard Records and Postcard, in turn, made Orange Juice. They grew up together like a pair of squabbling brothers, and the time together sharing the same home, like sharing the same bedroom, needed to come to an end. Edwyn's lyrics to 'Poor Old Soul' are like a diagnosis of some of the problems and how the sniggering-behind-our-hands fun could turn into irritation: "My friend, The Harlequin, The Rogue/ Befriending the meek/ His tongue tucked firmly in his cheek/ You better come clean/ How could anybody be so mean/ You better come clean/ I will not be a party to your scheme…The things you do just make me want to scream." Postcard Records was unique. The label set off fireworks into cold post-industrial skies that would influence bands and musicians for decades. Radio 1's John Peel, for one, would never forgive Orange Juice for the impact they had on his beloved Undertones. The two

[85] Reynolds, Simon, ibid., p347/8.

[86] Henry, Julian, ibid.

[87] Taylor, Neil, *Document and Eyewitness: An Intimate History of Rough Trade*, Orion Books, 2010, p191.

bands had got to know each other while touring in 1981 (Edwyn knew them as "The Underpants") when the Northern Irelanders had fallen for the possibilities of mixing punk guitars with soul tunes, causing them to dump the raw grunge of songs like 'Teenage Kicks'.

"Almost single-handedly [Postcard] had made melody, fun and love songs cool again," wrote Simon Reynolds. "But it was 'Love Action', The Human League's romance manifesto that got into the Top 5, not Orange Juice's 'Simply Thrilled Honey'."[88] Over the passing years the power of Postcard has often been overstated. "Without Postcard Records there would have been no Prince, possibly no Bruce Springsteen, and certainly no U2," said Edwyn later, with tongue tucked firmly in his cheek[89].

*

The original Orange Juice line-up lasted barely long enough for *You Can't Hide Your Love Forever* to stagger onto vinyl. They had never seemed like a group with a career ahead of them. Not from either the look of their fraught local gigs that exposed a lack of confidence in their playing, or gawky Postcard singles that only attracted the usual indie delight at the plucky and eccentric. The first, strangled-sounding recording of 'Falling and Laughing' was Record of the Week in *Sounds,* but only 1,000 copies were ever pressed. It was no surprise when the Postcard recordings for a planned LP, *Ostrich Churchyard,* were scrapped. Alan didn't think they were impressive enough in the context of the label's ambitions, the tapes needed cleaning and tidying up. Some added bounce, crackle and sheen. In other words, they needed more money spending on them. Alan managed to convince Geoff at Rough Trade to fund new recording sessions to re-do some of the standards like 'Falling and Laughing' and 'Felicity' and add new material like 'Untitled Melody', 'L.O.V.E. Love' and 'Upwards and Onwards'. Once the LP was all paid for and in the bag, Alan agreed for the tapes to be sold to major label Polydor. "I don't know if Geoff Travis still hasn't forgiven me because we kind of stabbed him in the back really,"

[88] Reynolds, Simon, ibid., p360.

[89] Sloan, Billy, ibid.

fretted Edwyn[90]. "I just thought it was Alan Horne acting ridiculous," said Geoff, always sanguine about the affair. "I moved on and we got the money back. I suspect that at the back of my mind was a suspicion that though the album was good, it wasn't that good, and certainly not worth arguing over."[91]

The band had spent the summer of 1981 in London. There was news of outbreaks of rioting and confrontations with police on the telly every evening. Deaths of IRA prisoners on hunger strike. On the streets they saw the latter-day punks on parade; Modern Romantics doing their best to suck in their cheeks and angle their fringe as they passed by. They were warm hazy days with a Motown soundtrack, the Sound of Young America was everywhere: 'Being With You' by Smokey Robinson and Michael Jackson's 'One Day in Your Life' filled stuffy bedrooms and back-garden BBQs with the possibility of evanescent summer romance. Back to reality, it was The Specials' 'Ghost Town' that told it like it was, with its scenes of urban breakdown and a woozy unsettling fear of what the future might hold. Even for Orange Juice it wasn't much of a party. They should have been living the dream in London: Glasgow boys on tour with major label backing, suddenly with a modern sales and promotion machine behind them. But apart from the recording sessions at Regent's Park Studios, band members mostly spent the time doing their own thing, going out to gigs when they could. Edwyn and drummer Steven were staying with producer Adam Kidron at his smart place in Hampstead while fellow songwriter and guitarist James Kirk and bass player David got digs with a fan of the band based in Finchley.

In spite of their naturally spiky cynicism, Orange Juice still managed to become infected by Wedding Fever. "The wedding of Prince Charles and Lady Diana Spencer occurred during these recording sessions. Even though the studio was costing us hundreds of guineas an hour, we all agreed that we should down tools for the day & celebrate," Steven has remembered. "The engineer thought we were mental, putting up all

---

[90] Goddard, Simon, ibid., p232.

[91] Taylor, Neil, ibid., p191.

that bunting!"[92] But tensions in the band were building, divisions taking their natural course. They'd been abrasive school friends. Digs, sarcasm and put-downs were the norm (like the song title 'Tender Object', which came from James's nickname for Edwyn), but the banter degenerated into something less comfortable and workable at Postcard. Relations were embittered by Alan and his love of provocation, what Edwyn called his "insidious quick-wittedness". "I used to be very close to Edwyn, but once Alan came in I didn't speak to Edwyn again for about six months," said David. "I thought Alan was taking over the group, and rather than making some rash statement like, Alan! You're taking over the group, I crawled back to the flat and just whimpered." James and Steven were sacked before the record was released in the winter of the following year. "I wouldn't talk to [Steven] at all, we didn't get on, so the rhythm section was rubbish," explained Edwyn later. "And we would just laugh at James..." David joined in: "James was always dizzy-eyed, playing novel things on guitar and wanting to write stupid twee comedy songs, like those you get in musicals. A lot of people came to see us especially for James, because he would always do something wacky, like fall over."[93] Meant to be providing the structure and cohesion, the rhythm section of David and Steven was always arguing. When guitarist Malcolm Ross was brought in by Edwyn from fellow Postcarders Josef K (without consulting anyone else in the band) he was shocked by what he found: "All this backstabbing...It was a horrible atmosphere. I just wanted to leave..."[94] "Strange mix of personalities in the group, to be fair," wrote Steven. "We actually invented 'social distancing'."[95]

When the LP arrived there was a general feeling it was too late, Postcard had gone flat. *You Can't Hide Your Love Forever* was made to look like a naive mistake, a blurting of some gauche romantic ideas to be laughed at

---

[92] Daly, Steven, *Tim Burgess's Twitter Listening Party*, 9 April 2020.

[93] Bohn, Chris, ibid.

[94] Ibid.

[95] Daly, Steven, ibid.

by those who knew better. *Sounds* magazine — maybe with the Zowie Bowie incident still fresh in their minds — put the boot in.

> Ahh, St Valentine's Day! Dingle-dongle Meepy Goblin loves Fluffy Bunny Wunny, Rickiepoos wants Leggy Plumplet-Puds to be his Potato Dumpling and Owange Juiciepies expect their debut albumypoos to be taken seriously. Just fancy that! Yeuch. A rapid downhill slide to 'Untitled Melody', E's warble wobbling wildly and amateurish offkey guitar and organ plodding away in the middle. A ham-handed tape-recorder-in-the-front-room job. Office opinion at this stage: a resounding, nay, explosive thumbs down and cries of 'Pipsqueaks!' rent the fetid air. Icky man, icky. Are these OJs honestly s'posed to evoke visions of Byrds and Velvs? *"I'll never be man enough for you,"* they chorus. Too true, puppypopsters.[96]

Sounds had found a band ripe for exposure as a fraud:

> remember when Edwyn used to joke about onstage delays and mechanical incompetence, the lack of technical ecstasy somehow serving as a symbol of Orange Juice's refusal to play the big league rock'n'roll numbers game? It was uncomplicated, nothing too tense, a happy shrug of the eyebrows and one in the eye for the highbrows. Just the sort of thing critics loved, and they made the band because of it (and the fizz in the music). Now Edwyn only alludes to all that broken-stringed smiling and limping in order to get the audience on his side by stating that if there are any critics in the audience he'd be happy to see them in the bar afterwards 'for a good kicking'. I hope someone obliged him. Smirking up there in The Venue lights he looked like he deserved one. Rock star? Simply ill, sonny.[97]

Here was the crux of the problem. Press attitudes to Orange Juice changed immediately after they went to Polydor, because they weren't part of the

---

[96] Page, Betty, Review of *You Can't Hide Your Love Forever*, *Sounds*, 20 February 1982.

[97] Robertson, Sandy, Orange Juice gig review, *Sounds*, 30 January 1982.

indie club anymore. "But although Orange Juice's main danger has always been overstepping the boundaries of unflustered fluidity, and staggering bashfully through exaggerated surges of nearly-right chords, a polished and slick Orange Juice would be as worthless as a pleasantly euphonic Fire engines, a dour and professional Haircut, or a non-panicked, harnessed Rip Rig," said the *NME*[98]. "Orange Juice are a minor group trying hard to be bigger and more significant than they really ought to be. Their wan series of Postcard singles served them better than any fetchingly polished album ever will: their real dimension is best considered through the blurred viewfinder of those scratchy, bashful records."[99] There was more sympathy from the pop press, where *You Can't Hide* scored an eight out of 10 from *Smash Hits*, and the follow-up single 'Rip it up' was being toasted as the band's breakthrough. "[I]f you'd spoken to Edwyn a few months back you'd have been lucky to have squeezed out (sorry) a solitary mono-syllable. The album had come out and he was cast in a pit of gloom. Black clouds weighed down his usual effervescence to the extent where he nearly bottled Orange Juice altogether," reported *Flexipop!* in its interview with Edwyn. "'If you'd have spoken to me then I would have been totally unresponsive and fed up...I didn't retreat or anything like that. I just didn't project and I was pretty introverted. It did seem a really depressing time.'"[100] He could afford to be dismissive of past events because, finally, Orange Juice had made it on to *Top of the Pops* in March 1983. It was what he always had (and always hadn't) wanted. History would go on to show that the real success was behind them, in the troubling memory and magic of the one that had been cast aside.

*

You Can't Hide Your Love Forever turned out to be wonderland, a rackety journey by Willy Wonka train where the treats and surprises come thick and

---

[98] Sanai, Leyla, Review of *You Can't Hide Your Love Forever*, *New Musical Express*, 20 February 1982.

[99] Cook, Richard, Orange Juice: 'Rip It Up' review, *New Musical Express*, 13 November 1982.

[100] Needs, Kris, 'Orange Juice: Fruit Of The Loon', *Flexipop!*, April 1983.

fast. One moment you're bumping along to a Chic disco shuffle, the next winding a way through singed and frazzled Country and Western. A left turn into a beatnik basement and some plangent Velvets, then a sudden reverse into dainty 1920s musical comedy. Contrary to received wisdom, the guitars don't jangle, they buzz, spike and prickle, they ring like bells and make a dirty roar. Edwyn and James are the lovably unreliable train drivers in uniforms that don't fit, sometimes shown up up by their smooth and professional support from keyboards and backing singers who add sugar and ice to the passing soundscape. In the Postcard singles, the band seemed to be pushing the Orange Juice jalopy up a hill, but here they're freewheeling back down again. It's erratic, but it's going places fast. Examining that reckless progress, critics have heard overly elaborate bass lines, out of tune singing and some white boy drumming that lacks the necessary groove. "In a sense it's a failure...but a glorious failure, and that's what's interesting, it's ramshackle," said Belle and Sebastian's Stuart Murdoch[101]. "They had the courage to fail," argued Stuart Maconie. "They wanted to be The Velvet Underground, they wanted to be The Delfonics, they wanted to be Sly Stone and the Buzzcocks all at the same time, and they were prepared to make fools of themselves in the attempt"[102], later adding the LP was "wonky and beautiful", "it sounds like it's going to go wrong at any moment, it's not too polished, it clangs and clatters a bit, and that's part of the charm of it."

This isn't genius by accident. David Scott summed up the LP neatly as "the sound of soul music played awkwardly and artfully"[103]. There's an engineering to the LP that keeps the train on the tracks, and working with producer Adam Kidron helped with that. Never short on ambition, Alan Horne had wanted Creedence's John Fogerty or alt-rock god Alex Chilton to be in charge. It was only through Geoff Travis that they secured 21 year-old Kidron, fresh from working on *Songs to Remember* for Scritti Politti, where he'd demonstrated an ability to juggle styles into an oddly thrilling

---

[101] Interview with David Scott, *Classic Scottish Albums: You Can't Hide Your Love Forever*, BBC Radio Scotland, 2006.

[102] Maconie, Stuart, 'Best of the Zest', *New Musical Express*, 27 June 1992.

[103] Scott, David, ibid.

concoction. He'd also worked with Roddy, maybe less successfully, on the 'Mattress of Wire' single for Postcard[104]. Adam was a soul/funk/reggae fan and a musical *wunderkind* of the time (Julie Burchill reportedly once blurted he was like a young Phil Spector), who has since gone on to work as a digital music entrepreneur. His father was a celebrated Marxist economist; his sister is film director Beeban, now Baroness Kidron (best known for her BBC TV adaptation of *Oranges are Not the Only Fruit* (1990)). Steven Daly has accused Adam of using their LP as a shop window, showboating with brass; but with *You Can't Hide* Adam managed, most importantly of all, to avoid the processed Eighties studio sound, the keyboard and drum effects that have mouldered over time. There's air and space around the playing. "After dealing with Green and his insecurity for six months I was looking for something to do that might be braver melodically," said Adam. "Less theoretical and more performance based. I saw that in Edwyn and I heard the blues."[105] All the layers of 12-string guitars, some fighting against each other, have been skilfully entwined to make just enough chaos. Adam brought in the slick talents of keyboard player Mike McEvoy, who arranged the horns and backing vocals. An American who'd moved to Britain and later wrote music for Soul II Soul, Mike plugs away with funky abandon on tracks like 'Tender Object'. "More than me, Mike was responsible for the album's unique sound," Adam admits[106]. And there was a guest star appearance from Green Gartside for some characteristic 'ooh-oohs' on 'Upwards and Onwards'. "When he showed up at the studio it was absolute scenes," says Steven. "The staff thought they were getting a visit from Princess Di!"[107]

Listening to the LP for the first time in more than 30 years in 2019 brought back some foggy snapshots from Adam's memory:

---

[104] Asked if any of his songs had ever made him cry, Roddy said only when he heard the mix job on 'Mattress of Wire' by "Adam 'More Snare' Kidron" (Mathur, Paul, 'A Fine Romance', *Melody Maker*, 13 February 1988).

[105] Kidron, Adam, Email exchange, 29 September 2019.

[106] Ibid.

[107] Daly, Steven, ibid.

Recording the slowed down horns on 'Wan Light'; the hours getting the snare to sound like a US funk record; the Elvis piano on 'Felicity'; the backing vocals Mike McEvoy multi-tracked into a gospel choir on 'L.O.V.E' — which was dipping into the 'Faithless' well perhaps [from *Songs to Remember*] — but over a track that was funky and now, on reflection, wasn't quite good enough for prime time. We struggled to get that long pressed snare on 'Tender Object', but it works to build suspense. Edwyn singing 'Dying Day' was as close as I got to his heart; the guitars took us close to U2 but not so close as to be stealing. I over-gated the snare and the drums needed a bit more space! I also now remember the struggles I had with 'Intuition Told Me' because rock and roll wasn't my bag, and thinking when we were done that the Postcard version was better (ugggh). I was so excited by the doodling piano at the end of 'Upward and Onwards' because I was a huge fan of Al Jarreau. 'Satellite City' was the most fun to record — which is a little lame, as it's probably the most derivative track on the record. Unlike much of the post-punk-funk at the time though, it was actually funky and recorded to a click-track, so unlike 'L.O.V.E' we all kept time, and the guitars — all of them — worked. I had quite a lot to do with the rather strange but cool backing vocals on 'Three Cheers for our Side', and they sounded as unlikely then as they do today. 'In a Nutshell' was my favourite song on the album because the tempo let the harmonics jangle and Edwyn sounds like Frank Sinatra.[108]

What raises the LP above the mass of pop and post-punk is that it never falls into the clichés of either. With all the different ideas going on, the unlikely chord changes and shifts of gear, the use of diminished sevenths and ninths, Orange Juice are just about hanging on with their fingertips as they go round corners, and that only makes the experience more exhilarating. Edwyn's vocals are a big part of the risk: "the glottal bleat of an aged Scottish bishop" offered the *NME*[109]; or "not unlike a tipsy man

---

[108] Kidron, Adam, ibid.

[109] Snow, Mat, *New Musical Express*, 9 April 1983.

launching into an after-dinner speech with his mouth still full of port and walnuts." (*The Guardian*)[110]. His voice is a naturally rich, wounded, sometimes quavery thing, on the verge of not quite finding its way to the tune. A poisoned punk wail was available when needed. The band took chances with the material in general so that a song like 'Felicity' was recorded as a live take with vocals added on top. Adam talked Edwyn into covering Al Green's 'L.O.V.E. Love' on a "whim". "Although 'cultural appropriation' wasn't a thing at the time, I have always felt that we should acknowledge our references, and I heard a bit of Al, Marvin and Stevie in Edwyn. I also thought that he might do for 'L.O.V.E' what Sid Vicious did for 'My Way'. But perhaps I was an obstruction by making it too faithful to the original."[111] The band learnt the music by playing along to the vinyl single, Edwyn providing what he always knew was tuneless accompaniment, but with "a poignancy [he] kind of liked"[112]. Reverend Green has since said he enjoyed the wobbly version that resulted.

Most important of all to the *You Can't Hide* engine was the dynamic between Edwyn and James, band members who, manpower-wise, offered the same contribution as singer, songwriter and lead guitar player. The future of indie guitar was made from their sparring — the introduction of Country and Western sounds from James in particular. Edwyn picked up the rhythm from the *Bonanza* theme tune, as well as the Memphis Scales used by Sam & Dave on 'Soul Man' and Mark Knopfler on 'Sultans of Swing'. Meanwhile James competed for space on the LP with his own songs, 'Wan Light', 'Three Cheers for Our Side' and 'Felicity', and there was no doubt he added a special something to the band, a thoughtful eccentricity that was met with both scorn and admiration. "James Kirk often sounded like a teenager in his bedroom fumbling a Byrds riff whilst knocking over furniture with his guitar," said one gig reviewer[113]. But "James had no notion of how brilliant he was, or how strong a character he was in

[110] Petridis, Alexis, *The Guardian*, 4 November 2010.

[111] Kidron, Adam, ibid.

[112] Scott, David, ibid.

[113] Kinney, Fergal, *Louder than War* website, 13 February 2014.

the group," according to Grace. "If people cite him as the one that made Orange Juice particularly interesting, I would agree with them every time."[114] Unlike Robert and Grant, who competed in the same way for space on Go-Betweens' albums, Collins and Kirk never managed to work out a partnership. After being dumped from the band James went on to a long career as a chiropodist back in Glasgow, continuing to be an obscure musical hero — the source of the name of Tim Booth and co's band (as well as Strawberry Switchblade, named after one of Kirk's songs). For some, James Kirk's long delayed solo appearance with *You Can Make It If You Boogie* (2005) — including two songs co-written with Alan Horne and the bass playing of Campbell Owens — was more of a follow-up in spirit to *You Can't Hide* than what the remainder of Orange Juice actually delivered.

The LP cover has added to the album's lasting appeal because of its visual sympathy with the music's optimism and sense of restless adventure: a leaping pair of dolphins in sparkled, nostalgic sunlight. Mammal-fish out of water, still having fun no matter what. The cover was designed by Steve Bush, who later went to become editor of *Smash Hits*. Stuart Murdoch first came across the *You Can't Hide* album in a bargain bin going for a pound. Its status as an indie icon meant he wanted to use the dolphin cover on the back of Belle & Sebastian's *Fans Only* DVD, a model holding the LP over her naked torso. Polydor wanted an eye-watering £10,000 for the privilege, but Edwyn stepped in to make sure the model's modesty could be dolphin-covered for free.

"I knew, even at the time, that it needed a little bit more polish to be a U2-sized record, and I didn't make it happen." In retrospect, Adam Kidron was disappointed that he hadn't delivered an LP with the dazzling pop perfection later rendered by Scritti Politti on *Cupid & Psyche*. And worse still, the business side had the money all zipped up. "I have never seen a penny in royalties from that record or any others I made at the time — and I mean, not a penny."[115]

---

114 McKay, Alastair, ibid.

115 Kidron, Adam, ibid.

*

The house has stopped now that mum and dad are back from the social. They've been going out a lot more since he became one of the Unemployed. Until last month I used to think UB40 was just a band.

You can only hear the street. There are no footsteps or voices or car doors anymore, but that doesn't mean there's silence. There's fidgets and ticks from the car metal. Streetlights drone. Along with all the sounds that spaces make.

The moon fills my room with silver and makes me see everything I don't want to see. It doesn't look like it should do, not smart and new like Dean's. All of it old. There's too many things I can't just throw away, a Flying Fortress hanging from the ceiling, all the other Airfix kits that were bought for me, half-made and broken, the jigsaw puzzles, the gyroscope, the shelf of Enid Blyton books. The label maker I had for Christmas and the labels that won't come off. DOOR. CHAIR. SHELF. CARPET. Mum says it looks like I'm holding a dirty protest. Which I think is in really bad taste.

Even Radio 1 isn't free from the past. It's Nan's old radio, a wooden box with a dial, a red needle and faded station stickers, still gummed up with all those years of Jimmy Young and David Jacobs, cups of sugary tea and plates of Rich Tea biscuits; dull from sitting in the soft light from net curtains. Though it doesn't want to, it plays music from the future, a croaky crackly Mike Read, Tony Blackburn, Peter Powell, Tommy Vance and the Top 40. I just need a tape recorder to record things, and that means I'm going to have to steal my sister's.

Lights are still on in windows all across the estate, in sad squares of orange and brown.

*

We're back with Edwyn on a Glasgow stage in his Davy Crockett hat, singing a bunch of love songs. White-faced and sweating, his Munchkins beaming. "The early Juice stuff was all love," said the be-quiffed one. "I was writing from…an adolescent angst-riddled perspective hyukhyuk [that gurgle laugh]."[116] One reviewer suggested that *You Can't Hide* was just "the

---

[116] Brown, Len, ibid.

sound of lovesick schoolboys"[117], another that the lyrics to songs like 'Falling and Laughing' were basically only "sixth-form poetry". (As Edwyn pointed out, that wasn't so surprising as he'd been in the sixth-form when he wrote them[118]). "This record deals with human relationships and the games lovers play better than any other album ever made," claimed Steve Sutherland in his *NME* review, "it can be more cynical than Kraftwerk, more sexy than Oakey, more cuddly than the Mode and more crucial than Joy Division, purely and simply because it all comes so naturally...So each and every song on this album is a brave potpourri of puns and romance, the busting giggle of a bunch of bright lads who are happy and healthy and absolutely convinced that there's more to a girl than a three-minute grope and then off down the pub...makes you feel like flinging your hat high in the air, like skipping down the street when you think no one's looking, like you did when the postman delivered that Valentine...They understand entirely that having to catch the last bus home or the untimely arrival of a pre-date spot can be the greatest disasters in the world. And that tragedies go just like they come. Daily."[119]

Except the LP isn't really about love at all. 'Love' is too easy a catch-all to describe the mess of emotions and responses experienced while the world is opening up, opening in ways that are both daunting and thrilling. There's no simple story going on in the songs, no trajectory towards resolution or rejection. Love is out of reach, just there as a preoccupation, the animus to an oblique and reticent conversation. The biggest part of late teenage and early twenties years for most of us is spent in emotional limbo, outside of commitment, caught up in all the shambles of daydream, possibilities and impossibilities, disillusionment and despair. And the LP is more an expression of that giddy in-between life, exploring an imagined realm of romance in Glasgow and its suburbs: walking in and out of town; hanging out on park benches, sliding down railings, gurning in shop windows, getting lifts on the back of scooters. Sitting around with

[117] Reynolds, Simon, ibid., p343.

[118] Scott, David, ibid.

[119] Sutherland, Steve, *You Can't Hide Your Love Forever* review, *New Musical Express*, 20 February 1982.

long-empty cups of coffee. Making the most of those occasional nights out at crap gigs and the cheapo sparkle of Shuffles and Satellite City. Most of all, night after night, sitting in a bedroom with only a record player for company, swallowed by the seductively remote landscapes of dreams and fictions conjured by the music. It's a life filled with fleeting romantic sensations that work on their own, and outside of what might be seen as a meaningful (or even meaningless) relationship. Al Green's 'L.O.V.E' was a fortuitous choice. It does the workmanlike job of spelling out what's going on — when the other songs have been too busy leaping about with an awkward glee — because as Al says, rather than being only a contest, love instead is about a walk down main street, an apple that is so sweet, making for a heightened experience of life just in itself. "Is this what life is all about?" sings Edwyn in the twirling party-time ending to 'Wan Light', James Kirk's exposition of medieval romanticism, where Eighties-erection-section-love is subverted by something more rarefied: "An unchartered world which will be unfurled/ Wander constantly by glistening streams".

Modern romance was always going to be a challenge for a wannabe misfit. There had been a tightening of the standards of what made someone an acceptable proposition, who was 'fanciable' as prescribed by film and TV and in the ideals of magazines and chart hits. Grace has explained how she'd never seen Edwyn as a natural romantic ("Edwyn is touchy-feely phobic"[120]) and *You Can't Hide* is loaded with tensions, cynicism and ambivalence. The title of the LP comes from 'Hi, Dear', the Jonathan Richman and the Modern Lovers song, "I know you still care about me / Even when you don't let it show…You can't hide that love forever/ But take your time, dear". Lyrics that lend their tone to the whole Orange Juice LP: a funny, ironic way of coping with likely rejection and the knowledge that romantic relationships aren't everything anyway. Because love gets painful, especially when it comes to the hotspots for seeing and being seen, like the 'Satellite City' nightclub and the rough emotional waters of its dance floor, ("You smash your heart against the rocks"). So we get 'Falling and Laughing': "What can I do but laugh at myself?", "I want to take the pleasure with the pain pain pain" (delivered punk pogo-style); a

---

[120] Maxwell, Grace, ibid., p82.

determination to be phlegmatic: "Your knife edge caress/ Cuts me so deeply/ There's no bitterness/ Cause you did it so sweetly". There's nothing ever straightforward for these Modern Lovers, carrying their burden of awareness of the posing and pretence around them, the doubts over who's feeling what and who's in charge, summed up by 'Untitled Melody' and its flipping of roles. One moment Edwyn is the confident loved one and the next saying: "You need me more or less, I need you more and more." Despite knowing all about the typical male playboy ("I don't mean to pry but didn't that guy/Crumple up your face a thousand times?") there's no steadfast romantic hero who's going to save the day, just the loser/joker: "I'll be your consolation prize". And then the impossibility of turning feelings into words that make sense (articulated by the "shoo-shoo-shoo shoo-doo" refrain of closing track 'In a Nutshell'), and instead an insistence on using the kind of language that would have marked someone out as truly Undateable: "Goodness gracious, you're so audacious"; "Ain't you guessed by now? I dote on you." Dreams weren't any easier to realise back in the real world. There'd been hopes that a pin-up of Edwyn's — the Velvet Underground's ice maiden of choice, Nico — would record her own version of 'In a Nutshell'. After an uncomfortable meeting between the young fan and the ageing siren in her London flat, she turned the offer down[121].

Each new generation re-makes the idea of 'love' in ways that are both in line with, and reacting against, their immediate culture. The Fifties and Sixties were a golden age for giving love a rosy-cheeked makeover. Teenagers were suddenly fully-fledged consumers, equipped with the motive and opportunity to explore romantic possibilities, with their own music, fashions and places to go like the coffee bars and dances. While the squares and parents were at home with the wireless, love scenes were being played out as a delightfully perilous kind of leisure activity. There was still a balance between commerce and innocence in this period, a respect for the value of genuine emotions. Parents, in general, were strict in upholding family values and there were restrictions and prohibitions that only added to the felt degrees of sensitivity, excitement and heartbreak. With experience came sophistication, a more confident assertion of freedom over responsibilities, and the golden balance between the two was tipped

---

121 Goddard, Simon, ibid., p180.

over onto the side of cynicism. By the Eighties there was a fully commercialised environment for romance. A popular attitude that love was a means, like the clothes you wore and the car you drove, to establish status, it was a domain of winners and losers. Sexual liberation was a tired kind of freedom and it's been noted that, if anything, Eighties' teenagers were less promiscuous — even before they'd heard anything about the nightmare of AIDS — because their permissive parents offered nothing to rebel against. "The Sexual Hangover, No Sex, Defunkt Sex, Post-Sexual Sex, call it what you will, but sex just isn't sexy anymore," wrote the *Melody Maker* in a feature on The Smiths[122]. "In America, No Sex has reached epidemic proportions and it's not just the fear of AIDS and herpes. For 30 years we've had sex saturation in the guise of a sexual revolution and candid sex has now become candied sex — sex as the boundless sweetshop of sexual identity and consumption."

The difference between the Eighties and 21st century varieties of love is mostly just the mode of delivery for making arrangements. Digital technology means a great deal of the intimacy, the physical and formal elements of starting relationships has evaporated. Upfront negotiations in person had been needed, whether through the language of glances across a room, some painfully obvious conversation starters, the intervention of a mate with their eyebrows raised, or an animal gravitation towards slow dancing in a club. It was high drama. It needed courage or carelessness or both. Hearts and minds would be strung out over the days and nights, waiting for a call, a letter, another chance meeting - because there was often the need for luck, to be out and in exactly the right place at the right time. As well as the felicity of feeling a swell of confidence at the particular moment when it was most needed. A break-up was more final. There were no simple, private ways to smooth over the cracks. No social media pop-ups to remind anyone of what they were missing. So the parting could be more haunting, a disappearance and an emptiness with no digital streams of social life to fall back upon, only the awkwardness of having to explain why. Who dumped who. And it meant the smallest of reminders would resonate painfully: any schmaltzy playlist love song could have its claws in

---

[122] Owen, Frank, 'The Smiths: Home Thoughts From Abroad', *Melody Maker*, 27 September 1986.

the psyche, playing again and again on a radio somewhere at home, on *Top of the Pops*, in the shops in town. Since then some socially embarrassing and unhygienic rituals have been made safe, replaced by online processes for remote interaction. There are giant databases of opportunity and algorithms to ensure some suitability, social media tools to make the introductions easy and to act as a prop for making conversation something automatic.

The five LPs capture a reflected glimmering from the re-making of love for the early Eighties. They were all writing love songs of one kind or another, none of them conventional, because there was a need to bust out of the neatly packaged, cynical, commercialised version of romance. "Morrissey and Marr could just be penning the best love songs since The Buzzcocks," wrote the *NME* after an early gig in 1983 — meaning love seen through NHS spectacles, looking at the ugliness of life and accepting that "'love' is a miserable lie"[123]. There was a longing for something real, to return to a time when 'love' meant something honest, direct, and not strewn with the rubbish of ego, image and manipulation. "The actual experience of being-in-love is presented differently, not as wracked passion, but as an almost out-of-body experience, a dreaminess or entrancement, a rapture not of the senses but of perception and intellect," wrote Simon Reynolds. "Which is why indie groups tend to choose a vocal style that denotes 'purity'... the folk idiom used by Morrissey or James or other voices of male vulnerability (Pete Shelley's campness, Edwyn Collins' preciousness...)."[124]

Women could seem to be from another planet. "As for myself," confessed Robert of the Go-Betweens, "having grown up without a sister, gone to a boys' school and arrived at university without ever speaking to a girl for longer than twenty minutes, there must have been waves of uncertainty and strangeness coming off me that were detectable to the few young women I did meet."[125] Being in a band wasn't a ticket to sexual adventure:

---

123 Hoskyns, Barney, 'Ridiculous and Wonderful: The Smiths/The Go-Betweens at the Venue, London', *New Musical Express*, 15 February 1983.

124 Reynolds, Simon, 'Younger Than Yesterday', ibid.

125 Forster, Robert, ibid. p43.

"Grant and I, by swerving away from university and full-time employment, had been taken out of the currents where young men and women mingled. Plus we weren't hunters, high-charged heterosexuals confident about coming on to women, and in this regard we'd perhaps gone too far the other way, being regarded as too odd or eccentric to be reliable partners for sensible girls."[126] The Blue Nile's *A Walk Across the Rooftops* is a series of ordinary moments in love, built around admissions of vulnerability. "A phrase as trite as 'I'm in love' finds its way into at least three of the record's seven pieces and comes off gloriously heartfelt every time. Buchanan has a way with a line like 'Stay/ And I will understand [you]' that draws one in, trusting every syllable," said *Rolling Stone*[127]. Paul Buchanan talked about the importance of love to the integrity of a personality, how broken relationships lead to a loss of dignity, bad decisions and a loss of faith in who we want to be[128].

Johnny Marr explained Morrissey's aversion to relationships as the natural result of shyness and hyper-sensitivity: "Morrissey is really capable of a truly loving relationship. Every day he's so open, so romantic and sensitive to other people's emotions...Personally speaking – I don't *know* this but yeah I think – I don't think he'd turn away from the perfect opportunity. But try and imagine the hang-ups most people have in bed. All that *'Is she enjoying it? Is there something more than this?'* Confusion. Now magnify that a hundred times and you've got the beginnings of Morrissey's dilemma..."[129] Morrissey knew sex could be an obstacle standing in the way of sincerity and trust. "I know that wind-swept mystical air/ It means I'd like to see your underwear" ('Miserable Lie'), "Let me get my hands/ On your mammary glands" ('Handsome Devil'). Transparently animal; just another dollop into the piggybank; giving into a social convention that didn't seem to have anything to do with the all-important business of having and keeping hold of a soul. So Morrissey becomes the most celebrated

---

[126] Ibid., p58.

[127] Interview in film by Rudden, Bernard, *Flags and Fences*, BBC Scotland, 1991.

[128] Holmes, Tim, Review of *A Walk Across the Rooftops*, *Rolling Stone*, 1984.

[129] 129. Kent, Nick, ibid.

and despised celibate on the planet. In the *Virgin Yearbook* of 1984, Barney Hoskyns, like many others, assumed Morrissey was just homosexual, plain and simple: "Gay men paved pop's way this year...The subtlest victory was Morrissey's – his the least fairy-tale, the least gaudily exhibitionist."[130] Morrissey liked to claim it was "involuntary" celibacy, but as with many of his interviews, it's hard to unpick the truth from what's being used to build a suitably rich and mysterious legend.

High Land, Hard Rain might sound on first listening like the LP most likely to have fallen victim to slush, but not at all. "Aztec Camera's songs destroy, as [Vic] Godard tried perhaps to destroy, the trash pop view of love as a simple thing," noted *Sounds* in 1981. "Love or hate, good or bad, win or lose, happy or sad, love shall or shan't!: they are all unceremonially kicked out the door marked 'Easy Cliché' by Frame. His attitude in all the songs is that love is complicated, confused, difficult to comprehend but the important thing."[131] The gushing, heart-stopping romance of 'We Could Send Letters' is cold and worldly stuff. "It's not a nice song, it's just sarcastic. 'We could send letters', it's just about having no contact with someone even if you think they're not far away," explained 19 year old Roddy[132].

The Go-Between's *Before Hollywood* is the anti-Hollywood when it comes to love, with a sense of there being no pattern of beginning, middle and end but a lack of control, a twist to relationships that's only ever random and hopeless: "I haven't heard a voice that I can trust/And all this sweetness turns a throat to rust" ('Two Steps Step Out'); "Who broke who/ Who screamed who/ There's no two things/ Lovers can do" ('By Chance').

A common thread between the bands is how they succumb to the more fragile and unworldly essences of love, to the bigger relationships of people to the outside world (that walk down main street), without giving in to the dictates of popular culture, not being kidded, sidelined, humiliated or exploited. "I remember for a long time feeling totally charmless and unhandsome and I know there are so many others who still feel the same

---

130 Hoskyns, Barney, 'The Year Of The Smiths', *The Virgin Yearbook*, 1984.

131 McCullough, Dave, ibid.

132 Roddy Frame interview, *Alternatives to Valium*, May 1983.

way. It's time that all those people moved in on this whole shebang and if necessary pretend to have charm. For too long this sphere of entertainment has been dominated by the big mouths and the small minds," warned Morrissey[133]. Maybe there could be a new kind of love, suggested Barney Hoskyns: "[Morrissey] does not say *'You are mine'* or *'It feels so good when we touch'*, he says you are charming and handsome and he is not precisely certain of your sex, or where or what your sex is. He observes the routes desire takes. He sees it flow between you. He catches it on the breeze."[134] As per the line in 'You've Got Everything', there could be a strange rush of liberation from taking a backseat and being the love-less outsider: "But I don't want a lover/ I just want to be tied to the back of your car."

*

Love was just a question, not an answer. So what else was there to fill the void?

---

[133] Black, Bill, ibid.

[134] Hoskyns, Barney, 'These Disarming Men: The Smiths', *New Musical Express*, 4 February 1984.

2.

The Boy Wonders
Aztec Camera, *High Land, Hard Rain* (April 1983)

A blue-eyed schoolboy walks home from school. Head up, fringe down, he's walking with a self-conscious head-bobbing swagger. His feet make their own meandering route from one underpass to another, avoiding the green ice of broken bottles, the skids of dog turds. He's reached a network of estate footpaths, more concrete steps, moving from one block of grey utility housing to another, between the geometric patches of landscaping, squares and triangles of fledgling shrubs and trees. Greens are greener, clouds are whiter, now he's able to wander in backways like these, where people and places are just themselves, with the kind of indecipherable truth that never makes it into the textbooks. It's not so deep, he's not so slow.

Another seven months and three weeks of sitting at a desk facing a blackboard. If he got a job as a postman he wouldn't need to do anything else except this, just walking around, watching the Scottish springtime in motion: the unrolling sky; treetops razzling in a breeze; the curious shades of light on moss-grown rooftops and TV aerials, purplish and grey one moment, orange-pink the next; the sun staining the face of the Westwood flats.

He changes mechanically in his bedroom and puts on a pair of cowboy boots, making sure to tuck in the bottoms of his jeans. He picks up his guitar and heads across town. The Westwood shops are empty, metal shutters pulled down. Just a kid on a bike making loop after loop round the precinct, she's still waiting for tea and hoping someone comes along and buys her chips. Through Murray and its flats and tower blocks, over the ring road, into the Town Centre Park, up the hill to the concrete mothership of The Key. The sun's going down. The wind's picking up again over the fields and hills, a mass of hair covering his face from the sights of downtown East Kilbride.

Inside is thick with youth centre fug, the sourness of bodies made sweet by Wrigley's Juicy Fruit breath. He can feel the eyes on him as soon as he arrives in the main hall, like they've been waiting for him. The black stage blocks are being dragged into place in front of a set of ceiling-to-floor orange and brown curtains. The older lads have lined up against a wall before the bands start, the closest thing to punk the town can manage. Cocky in their hodge-podge of C&A and market stall outfits, grinning, they nod one after the other. "Ey lads. Look at this guy," says the head punk, lifting Groucho Marx eyebrows. "It's mini Ziggy Stardust."

*

So Roddy Frame meets Campbell Owens in a scene that sounds like something out of *Gregory's Girl* (1981). And that's because it kind of is. The band's early music was made from experience of similar places and the feelings they evoked; they were both reacting to the same mainstream culture, and had found the same kind of unassuming lyricism to express themselves. A first awareness of love, and at the same time, awareness of what it means to be alone. There's a shared melancholy.

Bill Forsyth had grown up in sight of the Clyde shipyards with a dream of doing something quite different, of becoming a writer. The closest that reality could offer him in the early days was a position as an odd-job man for a small firm making public information films and travelogues. It wasn't until his mid-thirties that Bill wrote his first feature film script and started to find the ordinary and unaffected actors he was looking for at the Glasgow Youth Theatre. *Gregory's Girl* was turned down for funding by the British Film Institute (an organisation conscious of its bigger purpose of supporting high-minded art projects rather than minor-key comedy). Instead, Bill made the cheapest ever full-length feature film,

That Sinking Feeling (1979), with a budget of around £5,000. It's a marvel of modest means, made with the leftover lengths of celluloid from his documentary work, some willing amateur performers, and the skills of a filmmaker used to capturing different moods and sensations evoked by the Glasgow cityscape. Its unlikely success meant Bill could finally go back to his gang of actors with a budget of £200,000 from the BFI. Now in their late teens, *Gregory's Girl* was a script the Youth Theatre players had become very familiar with from the drama workshops of their school days. They'd also gotten to know Bill — the writer who in the old days had just sat quietly at the back of the theatre — as a director. These weren't middle-class wannabes mimicking regional accents. John Gordon Sinclair (Gregory) has since explained he'd had no acting ambitions. As a 15 year-old it had been a straight choice between Friday afternoons spent in double English or the relative freedom of joining the Youth Theatre (sometimes the group would even be taken to the pub for pints of beer); he had to take holiday from his job as an apprentice electrician to take part in the filming. Clare Grogan (Susan) wasn't in the theatre group at all, but a waitress at the city's Spaghetti Factory restaurant where Orange Juice would play gigs. Each one of the young actors relied heavily on Bill's gentle guidance. As John admitted, he didn't understand the film script at the time, he was just saying the lines and making faces — he only looked up words like 'mater' and 'pater' much later.

 Gregory's Girl is another one-off from that moment in time, a cinematic outsider running contrary to prevailing trends: the Glasgow TV programmes drenched with crime and violence; the hooliganism on football terraces; Hollywood's High Schools ruled by jocks and bitchy cliques. Along comes *Gregory's Girl*, where a girl is best at football and the socially awkward boys are busy making buns. A film offering a simple-hearted but realistic vision of what being young in a Glasgow new town might really be like. It was a disingenuous alternative to the noisy propulsion of American film romances, and its innocence is relentlessly disarming. It's a film that doesn't feel so much made as found, free from the distracting sense of being crowbarred into a shape that would guarantee a box office hit. "The trick is to learn to speak your own emotional language clearly, and then stick in a couple of jokes," Bill explained[1]. The small budget and simplicity of the film's making was essential to its special look and feel. Very few films before (and not many since) have included scenes filmed at twilight without using artificial effects: the fragility and transience of the light was too risky for large production crews working on complex shoots, too reliant on extended windows of time for re-takes. Having a single cameraman with a handheld camera made it possible to capture the last greenish light of an early Eighties summer day on celluloid.

Aztec Camera's first Postcard single 'Just Like Gold' was released a month before *Gregory's Girl* in March 1981. The *NME* called it a "love-drunk wonder", that was "as sparkling, as profound and essentially as Scottish as Bill Forsyth's cinema"[2]. Roddy Frame would often be asked what it was like to grow up in East Kilbride, and each time he'd give the same answer: it was like *Gregory's Girl*. "That's Cumbernauld, but it looks exactly the same."[3] Campbell shared that sense of recognition and affinity. "When I first saw *Gregory's Girl* I thought it was East Kilbride, it's so similar. It was like many of the British new towns of that time, like Milton Keynes — lots of trees, lots of green space. It was a brave new world for overspill families, for our parents y'know. We felt lucky."[4] Roddy also talked about an intangible something that linked *High Land, Hard Rain* with *Gregory's Girl* when the LP was released[5], how they shared a poetry that was all the more affecting for its backdrop of asphalt and concrete ordinariness, a wide-eyed new town optimism. "Back in 1981 I would happily have moved to Cumbernauld or East Kilbride," wrote Stuart Maconie. "That must seem truly bizarre if you actually lived there. I just wanted to hang out in that park where John Gordon Sinclair and Claire Grogan lie down and dance on that endless, luminous summer evening at the film's close. Maybe Roddy

---

[1] *Sight & Sound*, Autumn 1981, p243.

[2] Weston, Don, Review of *High Land Hard Rain*, 16 April 1983.

[3] McKay, Alastair, 'The Boy Wonder Matures', *The Scotsman*, 2 August 2002.

[4] Owens, Campbell, telephone interview, 9th November 2018.

[5] McNeill, Kirsty, 'Tartan Tearaway', *New Musical Express*, 11 June 1983.

Frame and Edwyn Collins would come by on their way to the 'Dip' [a local pub, The Diplomat]."[6] While it was a nasty surprise for the indie music press, there was something fitting about Roddy's decision to work with Mark Knopfler on the album after *High Land*. More than an MOR guitar legend, Knopfler had been responsible for the pitch-perfect sound-track to Bill Forsyth's own follow-up, *Local Hero* (1983). Roddy wasn't chasing the sound (or necessarily even the sales) of Dire Straits, but that wistful spirit of Highland melancholy.

At least one member of the *Gregory's Girl* cast was in tune with the Postcard vibe (not Gregory, whose bedroom in one scene includes a Rush poster, rock favourites of John Gordon Sinclair). Clare Grogan was one of what Edwyn called the "Munchkins", the smiley young girls who lined the front row at Orange Juice gigs. Alan Horne had played around with the notion of bringing her band Altered Images to Postcard, but was never going to be in the running against Epic Records who'd signed her up during the film shoot. It guaranteed her *Top of the Pops* appearances a good year before her hero Edwyn (who had written off Altered Images as "kindergarten Banshees")[7].

*

Gregory's Girl wouldn't have worked if it had been set in and around the Glasgow tenements. The sparse new town, its country park and recently-opened Abronhill High School, are aglow with just the right quality of fragile, kindling possibility. A world that, bit by bit, is becoming open for discovery. And this time not for the fast metropolitans or other stereotypical cinema heroes but the ordinary and ingenuous. An incipient awakening. "I thought to myself, why don't we set the film in an adolescent town?" said Bill. "I remember saying to someone, 'Even the trees in Cumbernauld are teenagers so everything fits.'"[8]

---

6 Maconie, Stuart, *Cider with Roadies*, Ebury Press, 2004, p156.

7 Goddard, Simon, *Simply Thrilled: The Preposterous Story of Postcard Records*, Ebury Press, 2014, p147.

8 Rees, Jasper, '10 Questions: Film-maker Bill Forsyth', The Arts Desk, 28 April 2014.

It was a brittle newness that was in keeping with the cultural turn of the early Eighties. There had been a growing fear in the previous decade that Britain was living on past glories, wars and Empire, aristocracy and pluck. The nation was always looking back for things to be proud of, and it couldn't go on that way, the cosying back into chintz sofas while the rest of the world was busy making the future. Auberon Waugh called it the "British sickness". Here was a society stultified by its class system, a stuffiness created by closed doors: "the public schools, a tradition of non-communication between the classes, simple, old-fashioned snobbery and the resentment it generates", and on the other side: "primitive tax-structure, powerful unions and indulgent welfare system leading to a collapse of discipline in family, schools and factories". In short, the problem was "a paralysing wetness"[9]. Like a gaggle of spoilt, lazy, disorderly schoolchildren, Britons needed to be taken in hand. That stern shake-up was coming, but there were insidious motivations and agendas. Nothing could have been as innocent or earnest as the 'newness' expressed by those Cumbernauld estates and their freshly-mown little lawns.

The great disruptive force for change in the Eighties was new money and the bustle and jostling to be on the receiving end of it. Rupert Murdoch had originally complained that in Britain "gentlemanly professionals, Oxbridge and the whole establishment...don't like commerce." But that tradition was being tumbled over in quick order. Peregrine Worsthorne of the *Sunday Telegraph* talked about the emergence of a new "bourgeois triumphalism"[10]. The Field Marshals and Eton Old Boys who'd filled wood-panelled boardrooms were being replaced by zealous middle-classes with the brilliant smiles and energy to trample over anything standing between them and bigger profits. Because that was the great advantage of re-building enterprise in a moribund economy, there wasn't much that couldn't be improved almost instantly with a new business plan and investment. Everything was up for grabs. Banking, insurance and tourism were the biggest successes of the new economy, alongside home electronics and media, while traditional industries like manufactur-

---

[9] Waugh, Auberon, *Another voice: an alternative anatomy of Britain*, Fontana/Collins, 1986, p260.

[10] Turner, Alwyn W., *Rejoice! Rejoice! Britain in the 1980s*, Aurum Press, 2010, p321.

ing had too much of the smell of death about them. New money wasn't vulgar anymore (whoever could have said it was? asked the newly monied élites) and old money could sit back safe in the knowledge that their returns on land and property would only grow larger.

At the same time as the upper classes were being eased from the top of institutions, their culture — if only in ersatz forms — was being appropriated for the wider British public. Post-War egalitarianism had made ridiculing the accents and manners of posh types a mainstay of popular radio and TV. Now the aspirant masses liked nothing better than to wallow in the upmarket worlds of *Brideshead Revisited* (1981), *To The Manor Born* (1979-81), *Chariots of Fire* (1981), *The Jewel in the Crown* (1984) and the first Merchant/Ivory heritage films. The fairy-tale made palatable on screen, bringing with them a re-affirmation of the myth of class — that the privileged possessed a natural superiority and grace. National Trust membership rocketed. A failing remnant of aristocratic Britain, *Tatler* magazine suddenly found new life among readers who felt they were made for higher circles of society, far from the coarseness of everyday streets and behaviours. The committed student look was out, along with beards and being serious. A froth of cocktails, masked balls and dandyism were in[11].

For the majority of the population, being employed (and living in the south of England) made your family far more likely to be part of the new toffery. Between 1982 and 1983 average earnings rose twice as fast as inflation, but levels of unemployment were high (around 9% in the south east compared with 17% in the north and 15% in Scotland)[12]. The 'haves' were setting themselves apart. Share ownership became popular as a demonstration of affluence — as much about self-image as actual dividends — and by the end of the Eighties there were more shareholders than trade union members[13]. For the first time, a home was seen primarily as an investment, leading to the idea of there being a 'property ladder'. Earners were beginning to feel they had spare cash again. Shopping

---

11 Beckett, Andy, *Promised You a Miracle — Why 1980-82 Made Modern Britain*, Penguin, 2015, p198-201.

12 Jones, Margaret, *Thatcher's Kingdom: A View of Britain in the Eighties*, Collins, 1984, p304.

13 Turner, Alwyn W., ibid., p227.

morphed from being a simple necessity into a mass leisure activity, leading in turn to an ascending spiral of smarter outlets, more affordable luxuries, higher expectations, more spending and more borrowing on credit. If everybody you knew was buying a new house, getting new kitchen appliances, new curtains and soft furnishings, then it was difficult not to do the same without looking and feeling left behind in the grisly Seventies. Having new things was exciting. Still unexpected. A happy splash of wealth. In 1980 a video player cost around £178, more than half the average monthly salary; another must-have, an early home computer like the Sinclair ZX80, was £100[14]. When Dad (as it was then still more likely to be), came home with the latest TV with Ceefax and a remote control, a video cassette recorder or new hi-fi, he would be a hero. There would be some ceremony, an excited unveiling of the box and its polystyrene-jammed contents; whole weekends spent reading instruction manuals from cover to cover, exploring every single plastic switch, button and feature.

The thrills of the home consumer age came with more than just financial costs. Old bonds and values, especially those of local communities and the routines of places to be, the pubs, social clubs, church groups and whist drives, were seen to have no place (or just a depressing one) in the aspirational, individualistic New Britain, and were dwindling away. Historian Alwyn Turner has summed up this period as involving "a radical transformation of society, away from the solid, if imperfect, certainties of the post-war era to something akin to a state of permanent revolution, in which traditional values of respect, loyalty and consideration for others appeared to hold little sway."[15] In the 21st century we've grown immune to the alarms of constant change. Change is a cliché; but in the early part of the Eighties the sudden rush of change was both refreshing and a nerve-jangling helter-skelter. The insecurity and competition for careers, the need to be a conspicuous consumer, to have a modern lifestyle, were all part of the tightening grip of a new 'normal'.

Commerce had encouraged a brighter, greedier, more cohesive mainstream culture, what Mark Simpson has called the "shiny High Street

---

[14] McSmith, Andy, *No Such Thing as Society*, Constable, 2011, p8.

[15] Turner, Alwyn W., ibid., p273.

version", the bunching of a pop consciousness into: "the wake-me-up-be-fore-you-go-go-kajagoogoo-morning-in-America-do-they-know-it's-Christmas-the-price-is-right-for-I-am-your-laydee-and-you-are-my-maan-this-lady's-not-for-turning...isn't-Princess-Di-pretty-Eighties."[16] In this there was, to an extent, the guiding hand of Tory party think-tanks and policy advisers. After the 1981 riots, the Prime Minister had pointed irrit-ably to a lack of social constraint. People didn't feel enough pressure to behave. Where had the sense of right and wrong, the aspiration for 'better' gone to? And so there was a co-ordinated campaign to spread middle-class imperatives of career, wealth and status as a common and binding ideal in political language as well as through popular media and advertising. Everyone should be looking over their shoulders and feeling the same anxiety about money, work and possessions. Margaret Thatcher once re-portedly said that anyone still travelling by bus at the age of 26 should consider themselves a failure. Suddenly the popular press had found a new breed of villain: the work-shy, the scroungers, the loony Lefties, all the losers who were still taking the bus. Britain was entering a cycle of stand-ardisation, the world was getting smaller and more uniform as the popula-tion compared itself with models of successful lives propagated by news-papers, advertising, TV and pop music.

For people moving into new homes, the shrinking was found to be literally the case. One of the biggest reforms of the age, with long-term effects on the whole physical landscape of a nation, was when the Gov-ernment — quietly and discreetly — scrapped the Parker Morris standard for the minimum acceptable size for housing in 1980. Much to the delight of landowners, developers and house builders, the minimum space re-quirement for a two-storey terraced house, 84.5 square metres, could be ignored. The average size of a new build home in our century, even when figures include the largest, five-bed 'executive' homes, is now 76 square metres[17].

*

[16] Simpson, Mark, *Saint Morrissey*, SAF Publishing, 2004, p23.

[17] Morgan, Malcolm; Cruickshank, Heather, 'Quantifying the extent of space shortages: English dwellings', *Building Research and Information*, June 2014.

With a car full of children, the Frames packed up their family home in Faifley, Clydebank, and moved to another planet. One year-old baby Roddy was among them. It was 1965 and East Kilbride's futuristic architecture was still bright and unsullied by age and the weather; pavements were uncracked, flyover bridges were free from graffiti, the roads were quiet; the maisonette railings and house fronts were smartly painted in moss greens, greys and purples. But like an unpopulated city on a lunar surface, there was something mildly sinister about the new town. "My parents didn't like it because they came from Glasgow and they missed the sense of community, the warmth of the tenements," Roddy said. "But then my Dad would remind my Mum, 'Remember when you were pacing the block waiting for me to come home because there was a rat in the room.'"[18] Set up in their smart modern home, Dad went to work each day at the National Engineering Laboratory, the state funded workshops for testing the potential of new materials for manufacturers. The kids would eventually end up at Duncanrig High School, a huge glass-fronted aircraft hangar of a place. In modern Sixties' fashion, the entire length of the main foyer was filled with artwork; in this case a giant mural setting out the history of the Clyde river, its farming and industry. This was nothing like the traditional Scotland of "tartan and shortbread tins". "My world in East Kilbride wasn't about any of that," said Roddy. "My Scotland was T. Rex, double nougats and *Starsky & Hutch*."[19] The Frames shared a homely, Protestant, council house life, with older brothers who introduced him to the wider possibilities of pubs, sex and getting into fights; and older sisters to their going-out routines, applying make-up to a soundtrack of The Beatles, The Move and Hermann and the Hermits. But home was also a town that the East Kilbride Development Corporation wanted to sell to industry as a model of good urban planning, open spaces and functional-

---

[18] O'Brien, Lucy, 'The Sound of Grown Up Scotland: An Interview With Roddy Frame', *The Quietus*, June 2014.

[19] Thomson, Graeme, 'Candid Camera: Roddy Frame opens up on new album *Seven Dials*', *The Herald*, 9 May 2014.

ity. Well-organised but boring. "I used to read Enid Blyton just to get a sense of adventure!" Roddy once said[20].

This East Kilbride experience was transmuted into the lush indie-flamenco romance of Aztec Camera. It began with the 1940s classics sung by his Dad in the social clubs, the kind of ballads made famous by Mario Lanza and Josef Locke like 'Galway Bay', 'Dark Lochnagar' and 'Cara Mia'. "He had a perfect voice. A very beautiful voice, strong high notes," remembers his son[21]. Roddy's introduction to music and performance was in those hot and smoky, have-another-round places, where families would get together for a mix of old-fashioned sociability, and later in the night, some shiny-eyed sentiment. Plastic chairs and sticky lino. Darts, snooker and card games. There were jazz standards, popular arias and folk songs: a music and a mood that worked better when it was shared in unfussy, unpretentious places like these. Roddy was only 12 years-old when he picked up his first guitar job at East Kilbride's social club playing alongside Billy Bain, once Lonnie Donegan's double-bass player, getting paid a tenner a gig. And it wasn't as if Billy was just doing Roddy a favour. Roddy had first asked for an electric guitar and an amp from a Father Christmas in a department store when he was four, and had already become a very capable, self-taught guitarist. What else was there to do on those drizzly East Kilbride evenings? He was already a long-time Bowie fan, spending Saturday mornings in the town's Impulse Records store flicking through the boxes of singles. He'd started to read the music press and was getting into punk via the Sex Pistols and the Clash, as well as New Wave: the Fall, Alternative TV and Roxy Music. But it was those Friday and Saturday nights at the social club that hardwired the musical language of Roddy Frame's songwriting and guitar-playing.

"My whole interest was the ballads — people miss out on the beauty of those, things like 'The Bewlay Brothers' and 'Quicksand'. I'd lie on my mum's bed when I was nine with the lights out, listening to *Hunky Dory*. It was another world."[22] There was a secret in there somewhere. "I'm always

---

[20] McCullough, Dave, 'After the Fall…Aztec Camera', *Sounds*, 3 January 1981.

[21] McKay, Alistair, ibid.

[22] Brown, Glyn, 'Frame by Frame', *The Independent*, 30 July 1999.

trying to find that special thing in pop music. For me, it started with 'Space Oddity' by David Bowie — it has that semi-tone shift which fascinated me. I played it endlessly to my mum and it made me feel this yearning. It's a kind of sweetness, and it can turn up in the strangest places."[23] At any hour of the night, in the crush of the Frame household, Roddy would be found huddled over his guitar, occupying his own starlit corner: "I like gentle music. And there's the fact that I do most of my writing at about four in the morning, so I can only use an acoustic guitar in case I annoy people."[24] He'd picked up Wes Montgomery's trick of playing with a thumb rather than a plectrum to keep the noise down, and used the opportunity it gave him to try and catch the essence of those otherly moments, and find ways to make listeners feel the same. The semi-tone shifts were like a miniature window on something important, a quality to life that went missing or forgotten most of the time. But what? It wasn't as if Roddy had been given the formal musical training to intellectualise his feelings and turn them into crafted plans for notes and chords. "Because I don't read music, I don't even know what half the chords are called so then when you hear proper musicians talking about music, it sounds like mathematics."[25] He was instinctive and exploratory, unburdened by expertise, and with that came the felicity of the beginner's mind: a combination that meant jazz guitar really could be blended with a slug of Clash. "He would sit opposite you and dazzle," said Robert Forster. "Fingers swooping up and down the guitar neck picking out single notes, to freeze in a tangle-fingered chord that I would squint to decode. The tonal tinge that made his song-writing so distinctive came from these jazz-like chords that he would strum with a wrist-snapping flourish."[26]

Roddy couldn't get away from Duncanrig High soon enough. "School on the whole was horrible. I always wanted to leave. I only went to sec-

---

[23] Hodgkinson, Will, Roddy Frame interview, *The Guardian*, August 16 2002.

[24] Hill, Dave, 'Aztecs Inca Contract At Last', New Musical Express, 4 September 1982.

[25] Shepherd, Fiona, 'Roddy Frame releasing first solo album in 8 years', *The Scotsman*, 29 November 2014.

[26] Forster, Robert, *Grant & I: Inside and Outside The Go-Betweens*, Omnibus Press, 2017, p143.

ondary school with the intention of leaving as soon as possible; I knew the day I *could* leave years before I did. The exact date…The teachers were really *stupid*. I always thought I hope I never have to do anything as pathetic as being a teacher."[27] His teachers didn't see much of the misunderstood poet in him, just working-class truculence. Young Frame would "[parade] around my class like a recalcitrant navvy" one has since complained[28]. All the formal rules of learning and knowledge, the nagging sense of their irrelevance, turned him into a brooding outsider. "I didn't have many friends at school, I was probably a bit much of the loner, typical intellectual artistic type. I kept well away from team games."[29] Roddy wasn't a pariah — just different enough to have to learn to be able to smile at himself, and lie low when necessary. "It's a running joke between me and my friends… all those beer swilling guys in East Kilbride! I hate sport! I hate football! And I'm not gay! I'm more romantic, I suppose," he told *Sounds* magazine[30] when he was 17. "I was quite sort of bitter about a lot of things – in a quiet, stupid, romantic way – a lot of the time. I wasn't the best person to have at your party. But now I can cope with those things much better. I was a real moaner. I dunno, I used to just read books."[31]

Roddy left school as soon as he turned 16 in January 1980, pretending to his teachers that he'd got a job with Tesco. He walked out into a Scottish winter with just the thin hope of turning his newly-formed band into a career. A year later, Postcard had released the frighteningly precocious 7" single 'Just Like Gold' (an inimitable marriage of teen New Wave and jazz guitar); and, by the time he died in 1989, Roddy's Dad had seen the lad who'd been with him on so many rainy club nights and playing at local

---

27 Paphides, Pete, "I was arrogant enough to think that my stuff was too good to be buried." Roddy Frame, *Medium*, April 2014.

28 Hewitt, Paolo, 'Aztec Camera: I'm Gonna Live Forever', *New Musical Express*, 7 January 1984.

29 Dessau, Bruce, 'Roddy Frame', *Jamming!*, October 1984.

30 McCullough, Dave, ibid.

31 Gumprecht, Blake, 'Aztec Camera', *Matter*, September 1983.

hotels, swamped by that old NEL work jacket, become a *bona fide* international pop star. If only for a while.

*

The high point of that pop career came in 1988 and wall-to-wall radio play for 'Somewhere in my Heart'. It was an unremarkable track in the context of the Roddy Frame songbook, originally intended as a B-side, but it was also very much a song rooted in the East Kilbride he'd come from. A teenager walking those ordinary streets, the places of home that could be comforting and familiar but always kept something empty and hopeless about them: "A star above the city in the northern chill/ A baby being born to the overkill/ No say no place to go/ A TV and a radio." It's one example of a bigger tangle of feelings that was common to the lyrics and attitude of all five bands: how they shared difficult feelings about home. A sense of boredom and the need to escape colourless, inhibited lives. But deeply muddled with affection and regret, because there was still reliance on those little worlds of home; memories of the years of balancing tea on laps together in front of the telly. Banal and unnecessary, cherished memories. From this ambivalence came a sympathy with the ordinary, the grounded and unpretentious, an unwillingness to be part of the social climbing that was so much a part of an Eighties' life.

The bands were all made up of outsiders from unfashionable cities and their even less glamorous suburbs and satellites. Glasgow, Brisbane and Manchester were all side roads off the slick, bolting new highway of politics, finance, business and media. There was no easy route into the music business via a conservatoire or family connections for them. Hindsight means we don't have to worry about the prospects for our bunch of drop-out students, the shy and unworldly, unemployed and mostly unemployable teenagers who thought they were going to save themselves from poverty and the grind of normal careers by writing songs. We know it worked out to one degree or another (The Go-Betweens didn't bother to tussle over royalty payments when the band split, The Smiths did). At the beginning of our story, however, they were all leading unpromising lives, often isolated, dreaming and detached. Roddy relied on dole money and luncheon vouchers provided by his sister to get by. He'd meet with Alan Horne in the Equi Cafe in Sauchiehall Street when he went into Glasgow, but wouldn't even be able to afford to have a cup of tea with him. Playful as ever, Alan would make Roddy sit and watch as he consumed one tall glassful of Knickerbocker Glory after another[32]. A conventional job wasn't a serious option. "I've only ever had one job which lasted for one day. I had to clean floors in a Glasgow council building," said Roddy. "I decided that I didn't really like the view on my knees."[33] The Blue Nile were sleeping on the floor of friends' flats when their first LP was being recorded. The reason it took nine months to respond to early interest from a record company was that they didn't have a phone and were embarrassed at having to call from a phone box. Despite the band having part-time jobs (sound engineer, freelance journalist, press officer), Paul Buchanan remembers a boho lifestyle. "You'd sit and and play guitar all day and then at eight o'clock somebody would say, Have we got any money? Yeah, we've got enough for two portions of boiled rice and a naan bread. Fantastic, there's a tin of pineapple in the cupboard, we can mix that in."[34] The Go-Betweens were serial squatters without the money to go out in the evenings. Since he'd seen his father's overalls on the washing line as a boy, "still dirty after having been washed", Robert Forster never wanted to join the ranks of the slavishly employed[35]. "I knew the suburbs were a trap. The image I had in my head was *living with vampires*: one bite of the neck and I'd have a local girlfriend, be going to teenage parties, and it would all be over by the time I was twenty."[36] To survive in the music capital of London, Robert worked at St Mary's Hospital in Paddington as an X-ray clerk (where he once purloined the X-ray of Nicholas Roeg — director of David Bowie in *The Man Who Fell to Earth* — as a keepsake). Lindy took jobs

---

[32] Turner, Luke, 'Independent Label Market: Edwyn Collins & Friends Talk AED', *The Quietus*, 30 November 2012.

[33] 'Aztec Camera', *Chartbeat*, 1984.

[34] Brown, Allan, *Nileism: The Strange Course of The Blue Nile*, Polygon, 2010, p48.

[35] Forster, Robert, ibid., p4.

[36] Ibid., p33.

cleaning the big homes of wealthy Londoners while Grant McLennan was mostly only busy while horizontal, reading novels and film magazines. After leaving school at 16, both of Morrissey's short-lived jobs sent him underground, into the cellar of Yanks record store and then the basement of the Inland Revenue as a filing clerk.

They all had time on their hands. Time that was invaluable for waiting for their muse to descend from its cloud, for making instruments feel a natural extension of hands and fingers, for wearing grooves and scratches, for exploring chords and sounds, patterns and rhythms. Time for creating an unorthodoxy, what could be made from reading too many books, from just walking and talking. Sitting around with mugs of sugary Mellow Bird's. Free to roam with jokes and ideas. But time could also be a dangerous thing, eventually revealing itself as more void than opportunity. They were nobodies who could just as easily have been seen — by themselves as well as by others — as ridiculous rather than exciting hopefuls.

Mass unemployment fell hardest on older jobseekers and school-leavers. The baby boom of the mid-Sixties had meant an extra 100,000 extra teenagers each year were competing for jobs[37]. It led to an entire culture of doing nothing. Traditions and habits for how to fill days and nights of nothing. So there were routines of staying in bed, *Pebble Mill at One* on TV, dossing around parks and shopping precincts, learning to live out each day with no money and no way to get around, no easy way to communicate, and no end to the tedium in sight. A survey in 1982 claimed 10% of all British teenagers were regular glue-sniffers, and deaths from glue rose from thirteen in 1980 to 61 in 1982. Political instability in Iran had led to an increase in opium farming, making heroin relatively cheap and easier to find[38]. Between 1974 and 1989, the number of younger men (15-35) taking their own lives rose by around 70% (Office of National Statistics). The worst of this blank existence came out in newspaper stories of youth suicides. One story reported how a 19 year-old had taken to staying at home all day. "Well, there's nowhere to go Mum. There's no jobs, no money, there's nothing to do," he had explained. "You just walk up and

---

[37] Beckett, Andy, ibid., p57.

[38] Turner, Alwyn W., ibid., p88-89.

down the street. It's the same every day." A few weeks later he was dead. He'd stolen a car with a friend so they could kill themselves with exhaust fumes[39]. It's with this picture of early Eighties life in mind that Morrissey's years as a teenage recluse, rarely leaving his bedroom — the posters of James Dean on the walls, obsessed with *Coronation Street* and the New York Dolls — look filled with peril.

It's a paradox of the time. The wasteland of lives also meant there was the space to create, and there wasn't today's stigma around unemployment because it could be unavoidable. Teenagers had to look at what they could do for themselves, what was inside themselves and what they could make happen. There were student grants that made Higher and Further Education a possible way out for some. With their low entry requirements and loose schedules, art schools in particular could provide purpose and a ready-made community of likeminded souls without too heavy a drag on time. Art schools were the making of Orange Juice and other post-punk radicals like Green Gartside.

This relaxed scene of creative idling has since been tidied up. Trying out music — doing mostly nothing — now looks like the ultimate of luxuries, because stepping off the accepted ladders of education and careers creates ugly gaps in a CV that can have implications. Aspiring musicians now need at least a grounding of security to work from. One signal of what that actually means for the musical landscape was spotted by the Sutton Trust in its report on *Elitist Britain*[40]. Just 6.5% of children go to public schools, but even in a field like rock and pop music, 30% of current 'pop stars' have been privately educated. That includes the lead singers of two of the most successful 'indie' bands of the new millennium, Coldplay's Chris Martin (Sherborne School) and Thom Yorke of Radiohead (Abingdon). Many of the musical forms that originated with the working classes, as a way to share stories and ideas, to share feelings of protest, have been appropriated in the interests of commerce and celebrity.

None of the five bands were looking to forget where they came from or to transform themselves into pop exotica. "I'd never rewrite

---

[39] Ibid., p87.

[40] *Elitist Britain*, The Sutton Trust, June 2019.

'Starman' or 'A Hard Rain's A-Gonna Fall'," wrote Robert Forster in his autobiography, "but then Bowie and Dylan hadn't grown up in The Gap [a Brisbane suburb], looked for golf balls in the tall grass behind the fifth hole at Ashgrove Golf club, or driven the rollercoaster hills in a beat-up Ford aching for a girlfriend."[41] There's no fantasy in the lyrics: a kitchen sink, back alley and bedsit ordinariness rules; because, anyway, having money didn't necessarily mean living on a higher plane of existence. "So who is rich and who is poor? I cannot say," sang Morrissey on 'You've Got Everything'; and Paul Buchanan, equally uncertain on 'Heatwave': "Are we rich or are we poor? Does it matter anymore?". Very un-Eighties.

Instead the lyrics of all five LPs are threaded with associations with the kind of working-class culture that had asserted itself and created its own mystique in the Sixties. "It was seen as an antidote to the stuffed-shirt, stiff-lipped (Southern) British bourgeoisdom," Mark Simpson has argued. "Culturally, big-heartedness was gaining the upper hand over small-mindedness, and the common people were now hip and in the charts."[42] There was a freeing spirit and character to ordinary lives that the bourgeois struggled to appreciate, their vision too often clogged by niggly standards of proper behaviour and competitive consumption. The appeal of Sandie Shaw, said Morrissey, was the way it felt like "she'd just walked in off the street and begun to sing, and strolled back home and bought some chips."[43] There was an iron streak of stoic humour there, exemplified for Morrissey by George Formby: "His more obscure songs are so hilarious, the language was so flat and Lancastrian and always focused on domestic things. Not academically funny, not witty, just morosely humorous and that really appeals to me."[44] This web of strength to working class culture, its ingenuous quality, was what led to Morrissey's choice of name

[41] Forster, Robert, ibid., p37.

[42] Simpson, Mark, ibid., p51.

[43] Fletcher, Tony, *A Light that Never Goes Out: The Enduring Saga of The Smiths*, Windmill Books, 2012, p58.

[44] Kopf, Biba, 'The Smiths: Morrissey A Suitable Case For Treatment', *New Musical Express*, 22 December 1984.

for the band, as the most ordinary and unsensational name he could think of. "When we began, nothing could have been more deflationary than 'The Smiths'"[45]. It was also intended as a form of defiance. "I sometimes wonder whether we're the last dying breath of that '60s grim working class thing!" said Johnny Marr. "I often feel like we're that one solitary clog left in the middle of the Arndale Centre!"; "To me popular music is still the voice of the working class, collective rage in a way, though seldom angst ridden," added Morrissey. "But it does really seem like the one sole opportunity for someone from a working class background to step forward and have their say. It's really the last refuge for articulate but penniless humans."[46] Once the assertive burble of modern life — work! consume! achieve! — was shut out, there was a simpler, unadulterated plane of experience to be found. There might sometimes be a difficult stillness to it, suggesting melancholy and boredom, but also a more honest and unifying reality. The Blue Nile's poetic evocation of the ordinary has been compared with Edward Hopper's paintings of the lonely light and mood in American lodging rooms, early morning streets and remote lighthouses. Paul recognised the connection: "[Hopper] seemed to live a very private life, staying in one apartment for years, going to the movies a lot. To me that's the way it should be [for an artist]. You should just be drifting about. You should be the guy at the next table. You drive past a terraced house with the curtains drawn, and wonder: what's really going on in there? It should be about your senses. Music releases them. I'm trying to address what we have in common. Smell the petrol, the tarmac, the heat, the coffee, the soap."[47]

The question is, were the five bands really interested in their own contemporary ordinariness, full of the scratchy demands of the present, or an easier nostalgic ideal? That rose-lit Edward Hopper, haunting Sixties pop, Ealing comedy version of ordinary that was closer to their parents' world than their own. It looks as if they shared a sense of longing for the

---

[45] Cooper, Mark, 'The Smiths and Echo & The Bunnymen: The Smith and the Bunnyman', *New Musical Express*, 28 April 1984.

[46] Kopf, Biba, ibid.

[47] Roberts, Chris, 'The Blue Nile', *Uncut*, August 2004.

kind of dimly nostalgic half-history found in old home movies. They shared the feeling of the loss of a childhood that had slipped away with the flickering of time. "How I wish I was young again," sang 21 year-old Edwyn on an early song 'Breakfast Time'; "Worldliness must keep apart from me" ('Simply Thrilled, Honey'); "I can remember the halcyon days/ We leapt on stage/ Though we couldn't play" ('Satellite City'). *Melody Maker's* Simon Reynolds spied an emotion common to indie music: "grief for a lost spontaneity, impulsiveness and unselfconsciousness; desire to recover the ability to dream, to have a magical, wide-eyed relation to the world; a hope of remaining unsullied"[48]. "It's time the tale were told/ of how you took a child/ and you made him old," lobbied Morrissey (on 'Reel Around the Fountain'), just the start of a batch of lyrics on *The Smiths* LP that are troubled by schoolyard worries and regrets, and filled with the hinterland places that children hang around in. A Peter Pan refusal to grow up? To an extent, but it's also nostalgia for the cocoon of home, however imperfect. "Family life is chaotic and full of primitive drama as everything is felt intensely [wrote Morrissey]…The switching on of street lights each evening tells us all that we ought to be at home, or heading there, for where else? There is nowhere else to be…Cross-legged, I sit on the floor and lean into the screen for *Champion the Wonder Horse*."[49] *Before Hollywood* is dedicated to The Go-Betweens' parents, and it's most celebrated track, 'Cattle and Cane', is about Grant McLennan's boyhood memories. "I wrote [it] to please my mother. She hasn't heard it yet because my mother and stepfather live (on a cattle station) and they can't get 240 volts electricity there, so I have to sing it over the phone to her…I come from [a background of] just songs, singalong songs, Scottish folk songs, old war songs, going out to all the properties and the picnic races… hearing all the country songs."[50] For the band's final album Robert wrote 'Born to a Family': "It was my story and Grant's too: wayward eldest sons

[48] Reynolds, Simon, 'Younger Than Yesterday', *Melody Maker*, 28 June 1986.

[49] Morrissey, *Autobiography*, Penguin Classics, 2013, p17/18.

[50] Nicholls, David, *The Go-Betweens*, Verse Chorus Press, 1997, p126.

who 'belonged', yet had to go their own way."[51] Paul sang about the confusion of feelings involved with his own walk out to winter on the Blue Nile's 'Rags to Riches': "I leave the home of a lifetime/ Like any son/ I have hope and good intentions/ And wandering into the daybreak/ I learn as I go/ To fall laughing into the water."

*

Muddy-coloured like a polaroid picture, but it happened alright. Mum got out of the car, kissed the man in the driving seat on the mouth and then walked away. All like it was normal. Doing that flick-thing she does with her perm when she's pleased with herself. The tippy-tappy heels coming up the street, too full of her own thoughts — of him — to even see me watching. Telling Danny will be something, thinks Sarah. Even if he's got nothing to say about it, the picture won't only be stuck in my head and nowhere else.

Outside the shopping centre waiting for a phone box to be free. There's always a queue at this time on a Saturday afternoon, when shops are closing and people are calling to say they're ready for a lift. It's kids. Four kids crammed inside and mucking about until the glass turns cloudy with the smell of them. Sarah tries to catch the eye of the woman in the other phone box, but she's not taking the hint. She just turns away to face in the other direction.

Left standing around with the fag butts, bus ticket stubs and ring pulls. Shoppers are picking up treats, bag fulls of them, hurrying home out of the cold. Technicolour shopfronts, electric dazzle. A trick row of funfair rides. It's only Rumbelows and Radio Rentals. The shop staff look bored, hovering by the windows again. What could it be like to be there all day, treading round and round on the same carpet, under the hot lights, smelling that same electronic ozone smell of warm plastic and wires? At least it was still Saturday, when things were happening, the very last signs of life before Sunday when everything would be shut and empty, when the rows of TV screens in the windows would all be dead.

The woman gives Sarah a look, checks her handbag, tightens her coat and head-scarf and emerges slowly from the phone box.

Sarah takes the few pieces of change from her purse, just enough for a short call. The air in the phone box is sour with old cigarette smoke and something like meat pies.

51 Forster, Robert, ibid., p337.

She feels the hardness of the coin's edge, the stiff resistance of the metal slot. Cold metal of the dial. Danny probably wasn't even in. Sure enough.

Strangled distorted beeping, like an old machine left forgotten somewhere, breaking down.

*

Being signed to a record label at 16 wasn't enough for Roddy. There was a lot more going on behind his sometimes winsome pop image. "Alan Horne said he was a wolf in sheep's clothing," explained Campbell. "Not in a bad way, he was very pleasant and mild-mannered — but he was a strong character and knew what he wanted."[52] This was the upstart who phoned up Siouxsie and the Banshees to offer his services. "The girl said, 'Oh, I think at 15 you might be a bit young'."[53] "When I was sixteen and I was judged a 'child prodigy' — the new Neil Reid of the indie scene [Neil was a Scottish child star who won *Opportunity Knocks* in 1971 and had five minutes of fame before his voice broke] — I was pissed off," Roddy said. "I wanted to be judged alongside the great songwriters, your Lou Reeds and your Leonard Cohens, not judged because of my age. But looking back I can see what they were on about. Compared to what I see now, it's extraordinary that someone of sixteen — fifteen in some cases — was writing those songs."[54] When Adam Kidron first met Roddy he thought he was "Bob Dylan redux in a more listenable Frame"[55]. Roddy had learnt about the power of being cocksure from one of the very best. "I owe Alan Horne a huge debt. He imbued me with confidence and a healthy cynicism. I picked up some of his contrariness...Alan was like my Andy Warhol and Julie Burchill rolled into one. He was very cynical, very stylish. Postcard was the perfect apprenticeship. So years later when a manager was on the phone saying, 'Where's the record? The record company want

---

[52] Owens, Campbell, ibid.

[53] McKay, Alistair, ibid.

[54] Aiken, Kit, 'Roddy Frame', *Uncut*, September 1999.

[55] Kidron, Adam, Email exchange, 29 September 2019.

a new record, a new cover, a blurb…' I'd say, 'Fuck off.'"[56] Alan was also the first label boss to get a taste of Roddy's determination to secure the attention he felt he deserved ("we didn't always get on too well with Alan…a lot of the time."[57]) Roddy wasn't prepared to put up with Postcard's half-baked schemes, and it was Alan who blinked first in letting Aztec Camera go to Rough Trade.

Soon after *High Land, Hard Rain* was released, Roddy was coming across in press interviews as an *enfant terrible*, a talented gobshite with the world at his feet: he didn't want anything to do with the indie movement, he wanted hits; but he also wanted to be on *Top of the Pops*, as a subversive, a guerrilla in enemy territory[58]. And there was never any question that Aztec Camera was his band to mould however he liked. "Then as now, I was a little control freak. I wanted the drums to be like this and the bass to be like this. It was very much my thing."[59]

Underneath the bluster, the young Roddy was a mix of natural ability, grace and an awkward kind of confidence. DJ Billy Sloan has talked about the early appearances at the Bungalow Bar in Paisley, when the fresh-faced guitarist had to be smuggled in round the back because he was too young to be there. Bashful under the lights, seeming to want to hide behind a flop of greasy fringe[60]. "[Roddy and Campbell] were lovely, very shy and very young," said Dave Ruffy, recalling the time he joined the band as drummer from The Ruts[61]. There was no masterplan, Roddy was muddling through. Rumours suggest the first ideas for a band name were Aztec Triangle and Pink Camera. "We were seen as a bit gauche because we were very working class. I was still learning. I wore my influences on my sleeve.

56 O'Brien, Lucy, ibid.

57 Hill, Dave, ibid.

58 McNeill, Kirsty, ibid.

59 Davis, Hays, 'Aztec Camera - Roddy Frame on 1983's "High Land, Hard Rain": A Shootout on Mainstream', *Under the Radar*, 9 April 2014.

60 Sloan, Billy, interviewed for *Classic Scottish Albums: High Land, Hard Rain*, BBC Radio Scotland, 2006.

61 McKay, Simon, 'Dave Ruffy (Ruts)', *Eccentric Sleeve Notes* website, 2008.

If I heard something like Wes Montgomery that would be on the record. Or The Clash. I was finding my way on the guitar. That's why so many chords and lyrics are flowery and abstract. I wanted to write like [Magazine's] Howard DeVoto," said Roddy[62]. "We were following bands like Magazine, who were popular with us, getting away from the punk three chords, ram-a-lam-a-lam," remembered Campbell. "Then Roddy was such a phenomenal talent he did his own thing. We weren't born punk rockers, we both liked jazz. Django Reinhardt was a big influence on both of us. I used to have 78s of Django. Black music and Spanish flamenco come from things like Arthur Lee's Love, all the acoustic guitar music, Bowie and his 12-string acoustic guitar. Roddy once went to see Don McLean play. It was all about the melodic, a connection with plaintive melodies."[63] He might have still been learning, a blank sheet of paper coloured by every kind of influence, but his technical ability, along with a fatal way with a chord change, made something new possible. "Some of the chords Roddy was using were quite advanced and sophisticated for that time," said fellow band guitarist Craig Gannon, "mostly used in jazz or songs by people like Burt Bacharach or Jimmy Webb — you'd rarely hear them in new wave or pop music at that time."[64] Early reviewers of the band were enthusiastic, but taken aback by Roddy's youth and unsure what category to put him into. He was "perhaps the missing link between Joy Division and the Eagles," suggested *Sounds*[65]. "[Aztec Camera] were as strikingly unexpected as frail Vinny Reilly after railing Blurt [a noisy, *avant garde* jazz group] on a hot, het-up Factory night, their haunting melodies alternately chilling and warming," said *NME* in a review of a 1981 gig in

---

[62] O'Brien, Lucy, ibid.

[63] Owens, Campbell, ibid.

[64] Gannon, Craig, Email exchange, 4 June, 11 July 2019.

[65] McCullough, Dave, ibid.

London[66]. Meanwhile, Alan Horne was still touting him as a young Bob Dylan.

*

Roddy and Campbell set off from East Kilbride in May 1982 to travel down to London. They took the bus from Glasgow's Buchanan bus station in Killermont Street, a hive of dust and carbon monoxide, equipped with their guitars, a few clothes, toothbrushes and a packed lunch. They were setting off for halcyon days, pulling away from the concourse and the all-too-familiar skyline of the city's grey tower blocks, making for the M74. They passed the M8 flyover hiding the art school buildings where they'd spent so many hours rehearsing, leaving it all behind for the open road and the vistas of Strathclyde.

Everything in those days seemed easy. As if it was all meant to be. "There was a magic about that time. The stars had aligned," said Campbell. "We met recently [in 2018], Roddy and I, in Glasgow, and we were talking about the old days and getting excited about it. We were so on fire and it all went so quickly."[67] Like Orange Juice before them, signing to Rough Trade meant they could make an LP. There was only a smallish budget, but it was an LP made with the professional networks and backing of Geoff Travis.

There were gaps in the band roster. There was no drummer. "Dave Mulholland was the original, but Roddy didn't see eye to eye with him. When we moved to London to do some more demos we were using Patrick Hart, who'd played drums for Haircut 100, but that didn't work out either."[68] The memories of Craig Gannon, who went along as a 16 year-old to audition as second guitarist for the upcoming tours, give an insight into what Roddy was really looking for.

66 Sanai, Leyla, 'Josef K, Aztec Camera: The Venue, London', *New Musical Express*, 15 August 1981.

67 Owens, Campbell, ibid.

68 Ibid.

As Aztec Camera were one of my favourite bands it was an opportunity I couldn't pass up. I don't know how many guitarists were there to audition that day but there was a lot. I was the last one in as I'd been caught up in traffic on the way down to London and the band were all dejected and a bit depressed they hadn't been able to find anyone 'just right'. Some were great players but maybe didn't have the right look, others looked right but didn't have the right attitude. Roddy always said I was the only one they thought had everything. *High Land, Hard Rain* hadn't been released when I joined the band but I knew some of the songs from hearing a few live sessions on the radio, songs like 'Back On Board', 'Walk Out To Winter', 'Release', 'Down The Dip', and also the songs they'd released so far like 'Oblivious', 'Just Like Gold' and 'Pillar To Post'. I'd also seen them live in Manchester in 1982 and I remember watching and memorising a lot of Roddy's finger positions for the chords, when I could see clear enough.[69]

They also needed a producer. Roddy asked Geoff if he'd approach John Brand because of his work with Magazine. John had served his time as a sound engineer, rubbing shoulders with George Martin and Tony Visconti, and had worked on material by artists like George Harrison, Elton John and Kiss before bagging his first solo production job with the Ruts. In later years he went on to produce the Waterboys' *This is the Sea*, develop the Highland guitar sound of Big Country, and manage Stereophonics. John first met Aztec Camera at a studio in Shepherd's Bush: "They were both very young and quiet but Roddy was obviously smart, a super talented guitarist and a songwriter with a unique voice. They were just pretty wide eyed about the whole music business and Roddy in particular was keen to learn everything about the recording process. I spent a lot of time talking to him during the time we worked together, telling him about the many pitfalls of the industry, and how to deal with success — which at the time seemed inevitable."[70] John brought in Dave Ruffy from the Ruts on drums; as well as Bernie Clarke to play keyboards and help out with production

---

[69] Gannon, Craig, ibid.

[70] Brand, John, Email exchange, 11 June 2019.

duties. After the reggae punk of the Ruts, Dave had begun to get a feel for different rhythmical possibilities by working with a songwriter like Prefab Sprout's Paddy McAloon. He found he was playing with more "gentleness and depth"; around the singer rather than just laying down a linear rhythm. Aztec Camera was a natural enough step. "They had some great songs — although they weren't very tight," he said of that early meeting[71]. Dave and Bernie added rigour to the mix and the new foursome used the London studio for rehearsals, and to record the single 'Pillar to Post', before heading for the seaside in September to record *High Land, Hard Rain*.

*

ICC was a small studio with 24 track recording on a two-inch tape, costing around £2,000 a week to hire. ICC stood for International Christian Communications and had strong links with Cliff Richard and many of his famous recordings. It was chosen as a cheap studio, not too far away from London and one that John had already used with the Ruts. A four-storey Georgian residence in a quiet residential street, just around the corner from the seafront at Eastbourne; close enough to hear a faint rush and sigh from the tide moving over shingle, the far-off cry of gulls. Along the promenade and its gardens of weather-beaten palm trees, the band would have recognised the strains of big band music, Glen Miller and Count Basie, coming from the doorways of imposing Georgian hotels, grey-white like imperial ivory. For the four weeks of the Eastbourne trip they lived together in the studio's own residential accommodation ("quite small and intimate" said John[72]) and adjusted to the sedate, out-of-season, seaside vibe.

Maybe it's no coincidence that the video for 'Walk Out to Winter' was filmed in another, even more desolate seaside resort, in Hythe, a Kent seaside town that's featured regularly in lists of Britain's "crappiest" places to live. The camera follows young Roddy as he walks the lonely streets in his tasselled jacket. He leaps onto the shingle and spreads himself among the

---

[71] McKay, Simon, ibid.

[72] Brand, John, ibid.

stones like a sea-worshipping satyr. Clips are interspersed with footage of an elderly lady, buttoned into her Sunday best dark coat and matching hat, the epitome of old English conservatism.

The band enjoyed the irony of their Eastbourne location. The Christian studio set-up around them, life in a Golden Years resort made for afternoon tea dances and gentle evenings watching the movements of the tide from the promenade. And here they were, a band with a smouldering determination to have a good time. "It was pure debauchery," admits Campbell. "Me and Roddy were the young ones and we learnt a lot from Dave and Bernie, not just about music. They were our mentors. We were in the pubs all the time, and managed to get barred from one of them because of all the shenanigans. We went into The Dip in Eastbourne and been regulars at The Diplomat in East Kilbride, so there was a kind of a connection there — it must have called to us — and it was a combination of the two that made for the closing track on the album ['Down the Dip']"[73]. While spending most of his time manning the controls and working with individual musicians on overdubs, John knew there was malarkey going on. "The young lads from Scotland had their eyes opened by the 'punk stars' from London, and, of course, Bernie Clarke's capacity for drinking, philosophy and confrontation! There were goings on at the flat and in the local pubs. We'd start the day with a big breakfast — Dave liked to cook — and ended the day with some beverages and a joint or two."[74] Besides the fried breakfasts and booze, the band relied mostly on Pot Noodles and takeaway curries — a gut-rumbling assault that took its toll on Campbell. "I had an attack of Crohn's disease during the sessions in Eastbourne [an inflammatory bowel disease exacerbated by smoking, alcohol and fatty foods]. It was pretty serious and it meant I had to drop out of music for a fair while afterwards."[75]

Debauchery did have its benefits. The thick-headed camaraderie that grew over the month led to lifelong friendships, and "it meant there

---

[73] Owens, Campbell, ibid.

[74] Brand, John, ibid.

[75] Owens, Campbell, ibid.

was a real heart to the record" said Campbell[76]. John was essential to the formula, having the experience and amiable character to turn youthful intensity, unfamiliar musicians and a plethora of extravagant chords into a classic. "John knew a lot about Neil Young and liked to smoke a joint," said Roddy[77]. "I never met a more sympathetic producer...he really was great for me. I was young and he was very sympathetic, very kind, and he helped me make the kind of record I wanted. And I really wanted input from him, too, because I didn't know how to make records. I was so young, and in those days it was still quite a mysterious experience for me to enter a recording studio, and he made it easy. I think those guys [John and Bernie] did a great job."[78] For a break from the studio-pub-studio routine, John would take the band for a drive around Eastbourne and cruise along the coast road, listening to Neil Young and some of John's other Seventies favourites. Most important of all, from Campbell's perspective, was John's willingness to listen and not impose his own design. "John was open to ideas — if it sounds good then it's in. He managed to capture the feel of the songs and not make it what it wasn't. With other producers you'd think we were trying to make some kind of comedy record. But John got it. He had a way of listening and connecting with people."[79] The good times were punctuation to the heavy graft. The band were working on perfecting the formula of *High Land, Hard Rain* solidly every day, with much of the actual recording on tape taking place at night. The band started out with sketches of songs and explored ways to fill in the gaps of what the LP should be like as they went along: a ferment of experimentation that led to some baroque arrangements and creativity (like the reversal of the trumpet track at the end of 'The Bugle Sounds Again' and the cross-fade into 'Down the Dip', requiring manual splicing of the recording tape).

Throughout, there's a mood of night-time reflection, bittersweet Romantic melancholy. "The room was not very 'live' so the instruments

[76] Ibid.

[77] Irvin, Jim (editor), *High Land, Hard Rain, The Mojo Collection*, Canon-gate, 2007.

[78] Davis, Hays, ibid.

[79] Owens, Campbell, ibid.

were recorded fairly dry and had a presence to them," said John. "Most of the atmosphere, so to speak, came from the mixing process. We mixed quite a few tracks at ICC with the limited amount of gear they had, and some rented stuff to supplement that."[80] There's a Sixties Motown sound in there (if only in a Motown-via-Eastbourne seafront kind of way), a use of echo and reverb that evoke caverns of space and starlight. Not all of the choices have been seen as equating to good taste: the synthesised drums and percussion, the tom-toms. "There was too much reverb, but that was the Eighties," Campbell has said, also rueing a late bass note in 'Back on Board'. "It gave me a headache trying to follow all the chord changes."[81] The excitement of the moment carried the band through the long nights, a shared intensity and belief in making music that was not just pop. "For the solo [to 'We Could Send Letters'], John Brand handed me this Spanish guitar he'd brought and said 'make me cry!' That's true. I remember just improvising a solo in each take til we got a good one. Just me and John, in the dark late at night."[82]

I really remember, vividly, recording it and staying up all night till about seven in the morning, going to bed and getting up again to start recording. It was great. I remember when I sang 'Lost Outside The Tunnel' and it was like the last vocals I was doing. We'd been working there solidly for a couple of weeks and the producer was going, it's not right is it? And I was going, no, I'm not doing it properly. And then I was crying, just like a real wimp. It was great. Just standing there with tears on my face and them saying, anything wrong? It was really emotional. I was really crying. What a cliché! It must have been like that Neil Diamond movie, *The Jazz Singer*![83]

---

[80] Brand, John, ibid.

[81] Owens, Campbell, ibid.

[82] Roddy Frame commenting on *Tim Burgess's Twitter Listening Party* for *High Land, Hard Rain*, 3 May 2020.

[83] Hewitt, Paolo, 'Aztec Camera: I'm Gonna Live Forever', *New Musical Express*, 7 January 1984.

In the early mornings, the band would often go straight from a night spent in the hole of their stuffy studio to the open expanse of the beach, walking down to the sea.

*

The inner sleeve image and back cover of *High Land, Hard Rain* provide other intimations of the wandering night-time mood. Roddy is the angel-headed hipster under city lights, drawn to an illuminated advertising hoarding of a scene from Ancient Greece, where women are standing under rays of timeless sunlight wearing togas. As if it's all he could find that was beautiful. The more prosaic reality was that it was an advert for Estée Lauder's new Greek Island make-up range for spring 1983. But for a Romantic, even this commercial contrivance could be an intimation of escape in the dark downtown streets. The photographer involved was another Scot, Peter Anderson, a regular jobber for the *NME* who photographed all the legends, like Mick Jagger, Madonna, Joe Strummer and Tom Waits, and who had an inclination for capturing the wrong side of the tracks on film, the black and white chiaroscuro of downbeat night clubs, messy bars and studio grunge.

The cover art, framed in a night-time shade of blue, was by David Band. A graduate of the Glasgow School of Art, David was part of Edwyn and Alan's noisier social circle. He'd designed covers for the Altered Images' singles 'Dead Pop Stars' and 'Happy Birthday', and was used by Spandau Ballet for the *True* album (1983). The same style of Eighties primitivism, bold outlines and colours, is there in the *High Land, Hard Rain* cover, but this time it took three months to put together, with David given the job of visualising lines of lyrics from six of the album tracks. Talking about the Aztec Camera LP, Radio 1 DJ Peter Powell asked David whether he needed to like the music to produce a cover. "No, not at all," he said, "but it helps to know what the band are about and to get on with them."[84] There was another connection to *Gregory's Girl* through David. "Basically, me, John Gordon Sinclair and David Band were completely in love with

---

[84] David Band interview, Oxford Roadshow, 11 February 1983.

Clare Grogan," said Spandau Ballet's Gary Kemp. "Nothing ever happened — in fact it was rather courtly. I don't think anyone wanted anything to happen. But we were certainly all vying for her attention." David also had the Postcard cheek. "I first met David when I was still at school and he was in his first year at art school," Clare Grogan remembered. "He worked in a jeans store in Queen Street at the weekends. I'd tried on a pair of really skin-tight jeans because it was that point in fashion and he said to me, 'Nah. Your bum looks too big in that,' so that should have been the end of the conversation. But it wasn't and we became incredibly good friends."[85]

*

High Land, Hard Rain is desperately Romantic. Off-a-cliff Romantic. The songs are a manifesto for going on the road with nothing except a rucksack and a guitar, heading for the mountains where the wild roses grow; the vision of an idealistic innocent with nothing to lose, everything to see and find for themselves. There's a Kerouac thrill to every track, as if it was possible for an old, tired and cynical world to be made new again. 'Walk Out to Winter', 'Pillar to Post', 'The Bugle Sounds Again', 'Release': Roddy's moving out and moving on. It's breathless and bracing stuff. "Packing my bags for the path of the free"; "Get your gear, get out of here"; "I'll learn to love the life of the 'could I, could I, could I'". This isn't temporary slumming either. Trusting wholeheartedly to fate, knowing that nothing will be easy on the road: "Chill will wake you, high and dry/ you'll wonder why".

The songs are like a documentary of an East Kilbride rebel's life, said Campbell. "That excitement. There was something raw and honest about it. He was writing songs that no-one else was doing, it was really different and unexpected."[86] Working in the studio, John saw Roddy as "a young romantic poet eager to express his feelings and find out about the

---

[85] 'Painting a bigger picture: David Band remembered', *The Herald*, 21 April 2012. David Band died at the early age of 51 from a sarcoma, a rare form of cancer.

[86] Owens, Campbell, ibid.

world. Like two other great Scottish songwriters I worked closely with at the beginning of their careers, Mike Scott of The Waterboys and Stuart Adamson of Big Country, Roddy's songs are particularly Scottish, influenced by a punk angst but with the unique lyrical and melodic beauty of the Scottish experience."[87]

Bowled over by 'Walk Out to Winter', the *NME* wrote it was: "One for the morning when the sun shines in and there's fresh milk in the fridge, money in your pocket…"[88] From the first trill of guitar the song has a uniquely hibernal sparkle. Roddy said he was "finding lots of nice chords for the first time and very into clean glacial tones…Durutti Column. Clean and wintry vibes. The opposite of bluesy valvey authenticity, I guess. Straight lines. String bending forbidden."[89] Said to be his favourite track on the album, it's a song about the end of punk, replaced by a new era of conformity, complacency and empty-headed pop. Where were the new rebels going to come from? Where was the alternative to the suffocating new consensus of what constituted 'success' inside Thatcher's kingdom? "Despite what they'll say, it wasn't youth, we hit the truth" — an uplifting song, made sunny by chords nicked from 'Ain't No Mountain High Enough', but down below there's a shadowy and icy prospect of uncertainty.

'The Boy Wonders' picks up on the importance of not falling under the spell of modern consumer capitalism and all of its treats and distractions, for staying with reality ("I'll give you a glimpse of the hard and the clean"), and has been referred to by Roddy as an "acoustic punk song". The shouty conclusion was inspired by an anti-pharmaceutical industry protest song. In 2020, Roddy still remembered "the exact moment I was walking up my street and thought 'I know… we need shouting!' Like the Fall. 'Rowche Rumble' kind of thing"[90].

---

[87] Brand, John, ibid.

[88] Singles reviews, 'Walk out to Winter', *New Musical Express*, 21 May 1983.

[89] Roddy Frame, *Tim Burgess's Twitter Listening Party* for *High Land, Hard Rain*, 3 May 2020.

[90] Ibid.

And in 'Oblivious' he seems to be playing with the analogy between love-in-waiting and other kinds of gaps between received wisdom and the truths of ordinary life, the grip of conventional attitudes ("Got different badges but they wear them just the same"; "They'll call us lonely when we're really just alone"). We drift unconsciously through the days when the 'one' might just be a street away. Because the world runs on webs of chance and coincidence, Romance (as well as insecurity and misfortune) awaits those with the will to open up and look further. 'Oblivious' is a late blossoming of Sixties counter-culture pop: the "different drum" playing "a different kind of beat" comes from Roddy listening to The Stone Poney's version of Mike Nesmith's 'Different Drum' while being driven along in Alan Horne's van. The song's guitar solo was intended to follow the arcing trumpet line of Love's 'Alone Again Or'.

The mood on the streets gets more reckless with 'Release', a song written when Roddy was 15: "All I could get to was a gun or a girl"; a polite, poetic attempt at his own version of 'Heroin'. "The Velvet Underground inspired me because they used all these beautiful chords and lovely melodies, great lyrics – and really built up in a frenzy at the end of a song. That's where I've sort of copied things like 'Release'. It had that bittersweet quality. They could do these really nice melodies, but there was always something in there that made the edge show a bit, which was good."[91] 'Back on Board' was the last song written for the album. The beatnik excitement is softened by some good-natured, easy-going spirituality (the original inspiration was an 'Amazing Grace' tea towel featuring a Scottish piper hanging up in the kitchen at home): "Get me back on board, pull me up with grace"; "Hey, honest to goodness girl, I'd kiss you with the lips of the Lord." Reverend Al Green-flavoured Scottish soul.

Arriving in the week when Bonnie Tyler (*Faster than the Speed of Night*), Spandau Ballet (*True*), Michael Jackson (*Thriller*), Bananarama (*Deep Sea Skiving*) and David Bowie (*Let's Dance*) were dominating the album charts, *High Land* was too eccentric to even be considered just retro. *Rolling Stone* thought the LP was "radical not only in its musical restraint but in its arrogant rejection of fashion", making comparisons with Love's *Forever*

---

[91] Gumprecht, Blake, 'Aztec Camera', *Matter*, September 1983.

95

Changes. It shares the same feel of being an outcast's subversion of the excesses of the mainstream, unexpectedly sharp and wistful. Occupying its own quiet corner of the musical world. "Young singer-songwriter-guitarist Roddy Frame's anxious boyish tenor and shy romantic melodies are... stirred by the wind-chime strumming of acoustic guitars, gently draped over simple rhythm and keyboard touches."[92] The *Village Voice*'s legendary music critic Robert Christgau flip-flopped between comparisons:

> At first I did the obvious thing and pigeonholed this as high-grade pop — richer and truer than Haircut 100 or even the dB's or the Bongos and ultimately feckless anyhow. Now I think it's more like U2 with songs (which is all U2 needs). For sheer composition — not just good tunes, but good tunes that swoop and chime and give you goosebumps — Roddy Frame's only current competition is Marshall Crenshaw, and unlike Crenshaw he never makes you smell retro. His wordcraft is worthy of someone who admires Keats, his wordplay worthy of someone admired by Elvis C.; he sings and arranges with a rousing lyricism that melds militance and the love of life. These are songs in which sweet retreat can't be permanent, in which idealism is buffeted but unbowed — songs of that rare kind of innocence that has survived hard experience.[93]

Comparisons with Neil Young, Jackson Browne, Paul Simon, Crosby Stills & Nash, Bob Dylan and the Velvet Underground were all mentioned in reviews: "Aztec Camera do not sound like anybody but Aztec Camera, a very young band...with the sort of influences you can point out, admire, maybe notice a similarity here and there in chord structure with those same influences, but otherwise enjoy."[94] *The New York Times* saw how far away it was from teenage chart material, describing Roddy as probably "the world's most mature 19 year-old". "He is a virtuoso whose sinuous acoustic-guitar lines suggest some of the better aspects of 1960's folk-rock.

---

[92] Fricke, David, Review of *High Land, Hard Rain*, *Rolling Stone*, 15 September 1983.

[93] Christgau, Robert, Review of *High Land, Hard Rain*, www.robertchristgau.com

[94] DiMartino, Dave, 'Aztec Camera: *High Land, Hard Rain*', *Creem*, December 1983.

And the songs he writes for the group are literate, clever and more — they have an air of yearning and gentleness that are beyond many of rock's angry older men."[95] The band would have been less comfortable with the verdict of *The Face*: "The title is a cheeky pastiche of mid-period Bob Dylan [*A Hard Rain's Gonna Fall*], but the allure of the songs within is principally melodic; snowflake acoustic guitar blizzards through which Frame's nicely gawky but often disarmingly mature vocals prod like nothing so much as Nick Heyward with backbone."[96] It was generally held that the LP constituted a bright flicker of the potential for a music less ordinary. "The fragile re-awakening of pop continues," concluded the *NME*[97]. The album benefited from coming in the wake of the radio-friendly sparkler 'Oblivious', which reached number one in the Indie Singles Chart in February 1983 (although listed by the *NME* as 'Its Oblivious' by 'Another Camera'). The *NME*'s reviewer thought the song was "admirably urgent", "even at times passionate about itself" and "would have been *the* single [of the week] if it had been given the full-scale titanic production it so richly deserves." It was beaten to the honour by Indeep's 'Last Night a DJ Saved My Life'[98].

Elvis Costello had also taken notice of the Young Turk by way of his wife Mary Burgoyne, who had been listening to a cassette of *High Land, Hard Rain* on repeat in her car. *The Face* had asked who Elvis saw as his biggest rival. "Er...Roddy Frame. If I was to take the idea of competition seriously like B.B. King said of Peter Green that he was the only guy who really made him sweat, then I would say it of him." *The Face* interviewer wasn't convinced. "I do. I think he's really very good! I like his songs and that Aztec Camera album is my favourite record that's come out this year! He's also very young. If he's that good at 19, imagine how good he's going to be when he's 25! I wasn't that good at 19. I wish I was writing songs then as well as him. You won't be able to listen to him by the time he's 25

[95] Pareles, Jon, *New York Times*, 2 October 1983.

[96] Dadamo, Giovanni, 'Aztec Camera: The Outsider Comes In', *The Face*, December 1983.

[97] Weston, Don, ibid.

[98] Hewitt, Paolo, Single reviews - 'Oblivious', *New Musical Express*, 29 January 1983.

if he's that good now. That's when you start to feel nervous."[99] Elvis, though, seemed to be niggled in subsequent interviews when the 'sweating about Frame' line kept coming up. He wasn't losing any sleep. But he did at least like Aztec Camera enough to give the band a leg-up into the USA, inviting them to support him on his next tour.

*

High Land, Hard Rain went on to sell around 60,000 copies in its first year. By (unfair) comparison, *Faster than the Speed of Night* sold more than 500,000, *Let's Dance* sold 10.7 million worldwide. There were moments of commercial success for Aztec Camera, more *Top of the Pops* appearances, slots on prime time shows like *Wogan*, and later in the decade, *Love* (1987) sold 300,000. But the first singles and LP had promised more, the almost limitless promise of a new Bob Dylan for the Eighties, a Scottish troubadour who would claim a global audience with his plangent anthems from the frontline of life in modern Britain, dissecting the fairy tale lies. "Something got lost," said Campbell. "You can't keep doing the same thing of course, but the second album didn't work the same way. We were buzzy for a few years and it never got better than that."[100] There was a difficult anti-climax. A rural hideaway, fever on the streets of America, problems with drugs and drink, culminating in 30 year-old Roddy checking himself into rehab in 1994.

It had all looked very different in 1983 when Frame-o was top of the list for A&R scouts. With its limited resources, Rough Trade had found itself over-investing in Aztec Camera, just at the same time as it was trying to make a star of Green and Scritti Politti. "I knew that our record company didn't have the money to make a £50,000 video, or hire expensive American producers. We just couldn't afford it," Geoff Travis has conceded[101]. With A&R at every gig trying to whisk him away for nights out,

99 Ramball, Paul, 'Interview: Elvis Costello, *The Face*, August 1983.

100 Owens, Campbell, ibid.

101 Taylor, Neil, *Document and Eyewitness: An Intimate History of Rough Trade*, Orion Books, 2010, p183.

Roddy was able to speak his mind. "I remember one of the guys at Rough Trade taking me into a room, like the headmaster's office — this ex-public school boy — and told me, 'I hear you've been slagging off Rough Trade.' I think I'd said something about their distribution in an interview. He went, 'Well, we're not in the business of making pop stars here.' And I said, 'I've noticed.' I was arrogant enough to think that my stuff was too good to be buried."[102] Playing a gig one night, Roddy recognised a Polydor scout in the audience: "When you do something with Orange Juice," he called out to them, "we might consider signing with you." WEA, the giant formed of Warner-Elektra and Atlantic — the label of Prince and Madonna — had big money to spend. The A&R was also smart enough to know it was better to take the young Scot out for fish and chips and talk about music rather than try to schmooze him at expensive restaurants. What they didn't realise is how little of his soul the money was buying. Roddy had been schooled at the Alan Horne Academy: "[you have to] let the record company know who's in charge and don't let them push you about. Like I didn't think there was any need to rush ahead and record a follow up to 'Oblivious' just because it was a hit, even though WEA would have liked me to."[103] Known as a singer-songwriter's label, looking after Joni Mitchell, Tim Buckley and Warren Zevon, as well as classic bands like Fleetwood Mac, The Eagles and Crosby, Stills & Nash, WEA sent him a welcome-to-the-label present of the complete Jackson Browne on vinyl. Roddy later told an interviewer that he'd thrown the whole lot out of a window.

The restless odyssey imagined by *High Land, Hard Rain* became a reality, but one stripped of the hoped-for Romance. Touring all over Europe, the band entered the Rock Transmogrification Machine. "We had this huge pink bus and roadies who looked like Vikings, with axes. By the end of the tour we all had long hair and came on swigging beer, wearing Union Jack tee-shirts. There were a lot of people who'd come along ex-

---

[102] Paphides, Pete, ibid.

[103] Roddy Frame interview, *Alternatives to Valium*, May 1983.

pecting to hear some poetry, and they were a bit startled."[104] Part of the change may have been a revolt against a love story that wasn't working out. "I knew her at school and just met her again for the first time in years," Roddy told Neil Tennant at *Smash Hits* in February 1983 about a girl who'd moved to France. "It was love at second sight. I said, 'When can I see you again?' and she said, 'In about two years'. Great, I thought, it's going to be one of those unrequited loves that brings out all those Orange Juicey songs in you. If it doesn't work out, the album might be called 'Death In Paris!'"[105]

Even when he was back home, Roddy was on the move. He bought a cottage near Marple Bridge, between Manchester and the Peak District (in-between the family home and London, but also in the middle of nowhere), which became a temporary roost for songwriting. *The Tube* went to visit him there: a modest, vaguely depressing-looking bungalow with an open fire and flying ducks on the wall (just like there had been in Alan's Postcard HQ in Glasgow). Looking more like a short-term tenant than a home-owner, the softly-spoken new star welcomed the film crew inside with his guitar, the fire crackling in the grate behind him, and played songs planned for the next LP. "The house was right at the end of this long windy country road, miles away from the train station. It used to take forever to get there. I remember once having 10 minutes to get on a train to America and I hadn't even packed. I threw all my stuff in a suitcase, pure Kerouac, and starting running across these fields, leaping over hedges and under barbed wire. All this in the middle of the night. Two days later I was in the middle of New York for the first time."[106] *The Tube*'s Tony Fletcher suggested Roddy might be a kind of modern day Henry Thoreau in his shack, but the Kerouac comparison feels closer to the mark. Anything homely and self-sufficient had been left behind in East Kilbride. "He cherishes the idea of constant movement, the ability to get up one morn-

---

104 Mathur, Paul, 'A Fine Romance', *Melody Maker*, 13 February 1988.

105 Tennant, Neil, 'Aztec Camera', *Smash Hits*, 3 February 1983.

106 Mathur, Paul, ibid.

ing and just *leave*," observed the *NME*[107]. But by now the restless energy was artificially stimulated by regular use of heroin, speed and marijuana, on top of a heavy Jack Daniel's habit. "I was very young and wilful and I used to get out of it all the time."[108] "I'm a total addict, it goes through me like a stick of rock, and after a few drinks I was a different guy."[109] Roddy has talked openly of his hazy, 'lost' mid-Eighties period but blurred the details, steering the conversation — reasonably enough as a musician talking to music press — back to the music. "I've never really been that comfortable," he revealed in an interview in 1999. "I do suffer from what the Buddhists call 'dhukka' which drives all artists, a discomfort that chases you into the arms of a song, makes you want to express yourself, the feeling that you're never quite at home. Edwyn and I and Paddy [McAloon], we always felt like outsiders which is what drove us to write that kind of music. I've never lost that feeling. Some people say that to settle down is the kiss of death for a songwriter. I think the trick is to embrace and live with the contradictions and ironies and paradoxes of being alive. That's the challenge, not to reconcile the differences beyond our reach. But I don't put myself in uncomfortable situations just to milk a few songs; I wouldn't treat my muse so brutally."[110] The heady glamour of living in the New World, the land of so many of his heroes, its cities, vast open skies and roads without end, were never going to be conducive to finding a level of peace. In an echo of Kerouac's Sal Paradise, Roddy recalls "running up and down the streets of Greenwich Village having these mad experiences"[111]. For new recruit Craig Gannon, the tour had the runaway oddness of a dream.

---

[107] Hewitt, Paolo, ibid.

[108] Shepherd, Fiona, ibid.

[109] Thomson, Graeme, ibid.

[110] Aiken, Kit, 'Roddy Frame', *Uncut*, September 1999.

[111] Thomson, Graeme, ibid.

Only a few months before I'd been at school, and now I was appearing on TV in one of my favourite bands, playing to huge crowds all over America. As Roddy and I still say to this day, we were so young and foolish, but at the same time we knew we were involved in something special. People like REM and The Violent Femmes would follow us around from gig to gig and we all got pretty friendly with them. We played at the famous Danceteria in New York and that same night Madonna was dancing and miming to her record on the roof, and she came into our dressing room while I was in there on my own. This was before she was a superstar, and I didn't know who she was or what she did until she told me, but we had a chat while she was doing her hair and makeup, and later that night we ended up at a party in a Hilton Penthouse.

For all the drink and drugs, these were still polite lads unsure of the etiquette of stardom. "We had an invitation from a fan after a gig one night, who said she'd cook us lunch the following afternoon," said Craig. "We must have thought it'd be a nice thing to do, so the next day we all turned up at the front door and then sat in her living room being served lunch by this girl and her mum! Bands would normally never do that kind of thing, but there we were, somewhere in suburban America, having lunch in a stranger's house."[112] In America, Roddy was also starting to write the songs for an album that would be the end of the honeymoon with critics.

The experience of recording the second LP, *Knife* (1984), would be different. WEA's marketing and distribution power was behind Aztec Camera. Mark Knopfler was at the control desk. This was the big league: no more playing around, no more have-a-go indie. "I was ready to sit down and do some proper playing, and Mark Knopfler was brilliant for that. This sounds so muso, but he was the first musician I came across who really understood it was all about getting the right guitar with the right amp and using the right mic. Not screwing around with the EQ, just recording things as they should be...It was tricky, because he is very much into his own thing. I was young and strident and there was a bit of a clash.

112 Gannon, Craig, ibid.

But I learned so much from him about playing, and playing guitar."[113] Roddy wanted to work as a serious musician. But for the music press, and fans of the early material looking for some indie spike and chill, the LP that resulted wasn't just mature but middle-aged. Nice MOR tunes; the edge-of-a-train-seat exuberance gone. "By comparison [with *High Land*] it was a bit sterile…Roddy always thought he could do more [than the minor indie bands], but he was moving further away from the magic that made him…the stakes had become too high," said Campbell[114]. If Knopfler was an MOR 'red alert' to reviewers, he wasn't any more popular with the rest of the band. For a start, he had no interest in bass players, according to Campbell. "Demographically, I think Roddy thought [involving Knopfler] would take him to an older audience but I think it was completely shit," Dave Ruffy argued. "At the time it was Aztec Camera and the Smiths. The Smiths carried on going; we went mainstream and were left wondering, 'what are we doing?' Knopfler was so rude. He'd call Campbell 'Stanley' [after Stanley Clarke, a jazz fusion band leader and bassist] when he's not that kind of a 'super' player at all. He didn't understand anything about punk rock ethics of minimalism. He called Malcolm Ross 'Eric' [Clapton]! Knopfler said he was making music for kids but he wasn't! The first Aztec gigs I did, young guys would come backstage in tears. It wasn't rock 'n' roll, it wasn't pop music, it was something different. Knopfler didn't get that. I've never really had this out with Roddy. He was a bit of a star by then and nobody was straight with him… I was Roddy's mate but I also had the management in my ear."[115] The *Knife* sessions set out the model for the future of Aztec Camera, not a band anymore, but Roddy plus session musicians. "It was all downhill from there," said Campbell. "He moved down to London. It was 'who gives a fuck', y'know? It was such a young start and after that he didn't really

---

[113] O'Brien, Lucy, ibid.

[114] Campbell Owens interviewed for *Classic Scottish Albums: High Land, Hard Rain*, BBC Radio Scotland, 2006.

[115] McKay, Simon, ibid.

know what to do."[116] Roddy had become big business, and businesses — both the record labels and the managers — like to focus on where they think the USPs are, how the offering and the message can be kept lean and simple and remunerative.

"Roddy Frame is a snob," claimed the *NME* in 1984. "What robs Aztec Camera of making much more of an effect is their stubbornness, their old-fashioned tastes. The live show, for instance, lacks drama, sparkle or action; it's routine in its format and never subverted by its content. It has no style, and deliberately so. For Frame, style signals emptiness. He doesn't understand that style, when used well, can add brilliantly to a group, that it's not just clothes, but action and attitude...He believes his songs are good enough to ride over these considerations. He reminds me of the mid-'70s and elitist distinctions between 'serious' and 'shallow'. He wants Aztec Camera to be a 'mainstream rock band', and somehow I don't think that's enough."[117] Most of all, Roddy wanted to be a great songwriter. So there was no *High Land, Hard Rain 2* because it would have been a fake, something contrived and meaningless. The Boy Wonder who'd lived in that East Kilbride world and written those songs now belonged to the past.

Writing the songs that have been true to his changing tastes and experience has meant Roddy and the band being reduced to a footnote in music history, skipped over by Simon Reynolds in his flagship book on post-punk (2005), a minor sub-plot to Simon Goddard's history of Postcard (2014), and ignored by the documentary on Scottish new wave *Big Gold Dream* (2015) (in favour of bands like Josef K, The Fire Engines and The Scars, who made far less impact but are considered more important, more 'authentic', because they didn't dally with major labels or the vulgar mainstream). Born a decade earlier, Roddy would most likely have secured his place as one of the all-time great singer-songwriters. But in his own time the industry pressures were more fierce, and the audience was increasingly sceptical when it came to the sound of sincerity. A modern culture based around irony and detachment have shaped more standardised

116 Owens, Campbell, ibid.

117 Hewitt, Paolo, ibid.

tastes and listening — determining which badges of cool are safe to wear. The world thinks it's moved on and grown up. Everything, after all, has to change. Just like the location of much of the cinematic romance of *Gregory's Girl*, the Abronhill High School in Cumbernauld: opened in November 1978, demolished November 2014.

*

Dad's pretending to do stuff in the garage. Mum is sitting on a patio chair outside, smoking, even though it's going to rain.

No-one will admit they're bored on Sundays, and so no-one does anything about it. We don't do religion. No-one goes to church. But why do nothing? The silence is infectious. We've caught it from the street outside, from the whole miserable town. The planet is dead with it. And it's even worse today when Sarah won't argue back, or get that face like an angry frog when I'm calling her a cow. I know she's just in her bedroom taking out and putting back all the stuff she's collecting for when she moves out, unwrapping them all, wrapping them back up again. The clink of crockery.

Me in the living room, waiting for tea-time. Even salad sandwiches in front of Songs of Praise *is something to look forward to. A spatter of rain has started on the patio doors. Nothing to do but wait and watch time passing. The time that's slowly made the wood chip wallpaper curl away from the wall by the door and around the light socket.*

There's a wooden stag with twisting horns on top of the TV. Been there for as long as I remember, from when I was a kid. Must be Mum's. The big green encyclopaedias with gold lettering must be Dad's. I can't remember anyone ever using them. It's all their stuff, I've just never noticed it before. A Jubilee piggy bank. A photo of me with long curly hair. Sarah in NHS specs. A padded book on the side says 'Holiday Album 1978'.

*

Roddy Frame didn't want to write the kind of lyrics where "mustn't grumble" was rhymed with "apple crumble". Songs on *High Land, Hard Rain* were intended to mean something coherent, to be more than advertising jingles. "What's the most important thing about your songs?" asked the *NME* in early 1984. "That they're honest," replied Roddy. "Genuine. That they come over as having emotion and affect people." He went on to talk about why. "That stupid rap about why did you get married when I'm your friend and you're 19 and we're both lads? [Wham's] 'Young Guns Go For It'! I really hate Martin Fry also. He sings things like that line about apple crumble. What is he? Is he tongue in cheek? If he has got a tongue in his cheek then it's about time he took it out of his cheek and said something real. He's just a bore…I can be quite moralistic but it's more like a feeling rather than thinking it out. I quite like the idea of no set morality, just your own morality."[118] Pop had become inauthentic and dishonest. In other words, Roddy thought the people who wrote the songs were acting in 'bad faith'.

Existentialism plays an essential part in the background of Aztec Camera's debut LP (as well as much of the material that followed[119]). It's a long way from Westwood to the 1940s Parisian café scene, black turtleneck jumpers and Gauloises, but existentialism made it into Eighties' indie both directly via Jean Paul-Sartre's books and second-hand through other cultural influences — not as a means of intellectual showing off or another way of getting distance from the popsters, but because it felt urgently relevant. Existentialism was a philosophy of defeat. Its origins were in the ideas of Martin Heidegger (Germany 1918), then popularised by Sartre (France 1940). Most of all, existentialism was a way of thinking that could help ordinary people wipe away the mess, the mess created by authority, the establishment and all of the unreliable received wisdom it tried to impose on the population. Don't take any notice of what teachers, academics, governments and all those learned books tell you, said the existentialists. Instead people should look to their immediate vision and take personal responsibility for what they found and what they believed. A revolt against traditional abstract philosophy, existentialism was a set of ideas that anyone could use; not about grand and universal theories, but life as it was experienced from moment to moment.

---

[118] Ibid.

[119] Vague existentialist attitudes and notions are a common thread to the Roddy Frame songbook: see 'The Birth of the True', 'Phenomenal World', 'Hymn to the Grace' etc.

In *At the Existentialist Café*, Sarah Bakewell provides a more articulate explanation of how an existentialist thinks. "'Existence precedes essence'…having found myself thrown into the world, I go on to create my own definition…I am my own freedom: no more, no less." They "concern themselves with *individual, concrete human existence*", they consider that "as a human I am whatever I choose to make of myself at every moment. I am *free*…and therefore I'm *responsible* for everything I do, a dizzying fact which causes…an *anxiety* inseparable from human existence itself"; "I always want more: I am passionately involved with personal *projects* of all kinds"; "By describing experience well, he or she hopes to understand this existence and awakens us to ways of living more *authentic* lives."[120] In the context of the shambles of Britain in the late 1970s and early Eighties, here was a positive, start-again outlook with counter-cultural credibility derived from the recent past and Sixties' student radicalism. It set out to expose the 'phonies', while rewarding a sense of personal, home-made morality; a rejection of security in the name of a more life-enhancing freedom.

One of Roddy's favourite reads as a 16 year-old was Sartre's existentialist novel *The Age of Reason* (1945), an intimate study of the everyday mechanics of freedom set among the cafés and bars of Montparnasse. But the earlier and stronger influence came from reading Colin Wilson. One of the Angry Young Men of Fifties' Britain, Wilson became a short-lived publishing sensation with his book *The Outsider* (1956), a survey of writers and artists who had lived on the margins of society (Franz Kafka, Hermann Hesse, Vincent Van Gogh, Vaslav Nijinsky etc), creating their own versions of the world in existentialist fashion. The PR backstory was golden. The press were told how Wilson had written the book while sleeping rough on Hampstead Heath, spending his days in the British Library. In reality this had been a staged episode from earlier in Wilson's life and *The Outsider* was mostly written while he was living more snugly with his girlfriend in a flat in Notting Hill. But the story helped sell the beatnik Wilson package and he went on to publish a flood of crime thrillers and science fiction, many with existentialist heroes. Roddy was a Wilson fan, of philosophical serial killer novel *Ritual in the Dark* (1960) in particular. He

---

[120] Bakewell, Sarah, *At the Existentialist Café: Freedom, Being and Apricot Cocktails*, Chatto & Windus, 2016, p34.

would have felt an immediate affinity with Wilson. They'd both left school at 16, both were working-class *wunderkind* with an innate belief they had some 'genius' to offer.

> "I've read just about all of [Wilson's] early books. And some of them are pretty hard to find. But I'd rather find them by browsing around than order them from a library or anything — it's a lot more fun. I recently picked up a copy of his autobiography for two quid on the Portobello Road and it was a signed limited edition of about 300, which was a great find…He walked into a pub once when he was really young, about 18, and this mystic old bloke walked up to him and said 'You're gonna be really famous'. And he just said 'I know' and ordered a drink. I love that story."[121]

Existentialism, as an ethos of freedom and authenticity, had leached its way into American post-War culture. When he was in Glasgow, Roddy liked to hang out at the City Bakeries (what he called the "bad beat café") and was a jazz-listening Kerouac reader. As novelist Iris Murdoch wrote, existentialist culture had been an intoxicating brew when it first came to the attention of the British in the Fifties via the US, a population used to parochial places where "'people play cricket, cook cakes, make simple decisions, remember their childhood and go to the circus', whereas the existentialists came from a world in which people commit great sins, fall in love, and join the Communist Party."[122] The simplicity of it was crucial. It was an anti-intellectual and inclusive way of thinking. "I hate cleverness for its own sake. All I really ever wanted to do was to write songs that got across to people in a very direct way," said Roddy[123].

*

---

[121] Dadamo, Giovanni, ibid.

[122] Bakewell, Sarah, ibid.

[123] Dadamo, Giovanni, ibid.

There's a latent relationship between existentialism and the night time, something that's more instinctive than explicable: something about the hours when the world has become a blank canvas, the streets have emptied, the lights of offices and shops have been turned out. All that places are for, all that they mean, is far less prescriptive and pressured when they're lost in the alien blue and grey shades of darkness. The duties of daylight are gone. Ordinary consciousness drifts and dissipates, and the spots and splashes of electric light, the glimmerings of neon, only add to the ambiguity, to the knowledge that rationality can collapse into mystery. Night makes everything equal. The truck depot, the exclusive hotel, the derelict flats, they're all the same. They share the same grace.

In winter, the night is a grand old warehouse, vast and empty; the scintillating night, mineral cold, the stars like stones. And then, in the honeyed spaces of summer, the night becomes a forest thick with mystery, an unearthly mass of buildings, street signs, foliage and tree trunks. Everywhere becomes somewhere to explore. A bench in a pool of streetlight orange, under the fluttering of orange-lime leaves, is now somewhere to meet and stay outside in the night air.

The night is a world of escape, and it's natural that *High Land* is a late night LP. The landscape described there has nothing to do with the pop idea of 'nightlife', the cram of pubs and kebab shops, lads cruising in their pimped-up Ford Escort, but made up of scenes from a more simple-hearted teenage universe. Out in the streets, Roddy is a night-walker, dreaming, planning rendezvous ("nighthawk calls again/ Meeting after midnight like we do"; "I've got all the love and beauty in the spirit of the night.") The night-time connection is there in the lyrics and even more in the atmosphere of the LP, a nocturnal space, distance, stillness and resonance.

Night walking has been a counter-cultural tradition since the 18th century. It was used for professional reasons by criminals and prostitutes, then adopted by Romantics like Coleridge, Wordsworth and Rousseau for its mix of transgression and rhapsodic contemplation: "The act of walking, for the Romantics, inscribed a coded rebellion against the culture of agrarian and industrial capitalism onto both the material surfaces of the city and countryside — the streets, the roads, the footpaths — and their social relations. The act of nightwalking, moreover, carved out dark spaces in the landscape, cityscape and psyche that promised an escape from the penetrating glare of the Enlightenment."[124] Nothing so grand was happening with Roddy. If you needed to get out of the house and had no money, then meeting on street corners was all you could do. The quiet hours of night-time were the opportunity for working on his craft, staying up with Jim Waugh's *Nighthawk* jazz show on Radio Clyde from midnight to 3am and becoming attuned to the musical and emotional complexities of Charlie Byrd and Wes Montgomery.

Roddy is part of the dog end of the Romantic tradition, having "overdosed on Keats", evidently receptive to the foreign qualities and inspirations of the night. Because here was a separate element to feel and breathe that encouraged a keen emotion and creativity ("I felt the rain and called it genius"). Night time was an existential place for making things new, not relying on conventional ideas of purpose and 'success' ("So here we go digging through those dustbins, giving things new names.") And making things new based on good choices. "There must be some kind of blind force, or life force, in evolution, which I suppose you can utilise," said Roddy. "A feeling of goodness that flows through everything and everybody. I do believe all beings are basically good, rather than everyone being born with a clean slate to be bad or good in life."[125] So not just playing songs to make money, to become a star, but an attempt at changing the script. Asked by a fanzine what he thought Aztec Camera had to offer listeners, Roddy replied: "Occasionally on stage we add magic to the world."[126] After meeting with the young band, *NME* writer Dave McCullough felt for himself how that magic might work: "I looked up at the planes as they swept in through the night, at the edge of Heathrow, with Slattery's engine humming in the background, waiting for the ice to melt on his windscreen. Every half a minute they came with their lights creating little puffed-out clouds of white dust around them, frightening and terrible. The man-made world; take me away from all this worldliness! But

124 Beaumont, Matthew, *Nightwalking: A Nocturnal History of London*, Verso, 2016, p229.

125 Dessau, Bruce, *Jamming!*, October 1984.

126 *Alternatives to Valium*, ibid.

I liked it with a perverse fascination. Aztec Camera will take on those lights in the sky, the monolithic world and win, I thought."[127]

*

Unconscious as it mostly was of existentialism, punk still shared the impulse to document dirty kerbside reality — and what followed in post-punk was a more self-aware and reflective version of this instinct. Post-punk has been called a "world-making" machine[128], a response to the dishevelled political, social and cultural scene of the late Seventies. The Fall were named after the Albert Camus's existentialist book of the same name. Josef K's Paul Haig talked about drawing on his reading of Camus and the proto-existentialist Dostoevsky. It was a moment in time when even French postmodernism — and the questioning of the nature of a reality made by language and the control of language — were considered viable subjects for pop lyrics. Prefab Sprout could talk about how "words are trains for moving past what really has no name" ('Couldn't Bear to be Special'); Scritti Politti could dedicate an entire song to the post-structuralist 'Jacques Derrida'. And not everyone saw the point of it. "They were talking about Derrida and Claude Levi-Strauss, structuralism and semiology. It was stupid," said Edwyn. "I don't think it was useful, as far as it didn't pertain to anything that they were trying to do musically."[129]

Embarrassingly serious. But then we shouldn't be distracted by our contemporary expectation that culture can be — and should only be — working at the level of meaningless entertainment. "As anyone young enough to remember that time knows, sex, drugs and materialism are piss-poor substitutes for pop music," Mark Simpson has argued. "Gloriously, terrifyingly, pop music was invested with far too much meaning and signi-

---

[127] McCullough, Dave, ibid.

[128] Butt, Gavin; Eshun, Kodwo; Fisher, Mark, *Post-punk then and now*, Repeater Books, 2016, p58.

[129] Ibid.

ficance by a whole generation of young people back then."[130] The world was still something that needed to be worked out, it wasn't yet the End of History, and the streams of alternative music were an important part of that argument. All bands start with someone sitting on their own in a bedroom wanting to creating something from nothing; excluded and alienated from the distant realms of politics, without the power of wealth, it was the only way to be involved in making their own world. For fans, hearing their little-known band being played on the radio, making the top 40, was something, a small validation of an ethos, a spirit and attitude to life. Lyrics to our five LPs might be sometimes callow and confused, but they shared an attempt at finding meaning and saying something that countered the zeitgeist (just have fun, and if you're not having fun, shut up). They were part of a Quixotic sally against the new and pervasive Eighties spirit. "It was a time of big ideas. If punk rock achieved anything it was to inspire young free-thinkers in every dank corner of 1970s post-War Britain," according to Orange Juice's Steven Daly[131]. They were "the smartest band on the island at the time. We had no affiliation with anyone – we just created our own planet."[132]

First of all, the job was to puncture the bubble filled with confused dreams of the race, competition and consumption. The Blue Nile's Paul Buchanan saw the problem every day: "I go to buy the papers and I have to cross this busy road. Everybody's driving like a maniac. I just don't understand it. Why are they so stressed? I stand there and worry about all of them…There's this momentum to society, and it drags you into it…"[133] The Blue Nile saw how the songs needed to be written from a position of awareness of the potential for bad faith, the existentialist concept of how people act in line with social expectations, adopting the kinds of values that are contrary to their actual instincts and beliefs. "We have to stamp all the self-deceit out of ourselves before we stumble on a Blue Nile song…In

---

[130] Reynolds, Simon, interview notes for *Rip it up and start again: postpunk 1978-1984*, Faber & Faber, 2005.

[131] Daly, Steven, *The Glasgow School* sleeve notes, AED, 2005.

[132] Aston, Martin, 'Orange Juice: Where Are They Now?', *Q magazine*, July 1992.

[133] Roberts, Chris, 'The Blue Nile', *Uncut*, August 2004.

a way, I turned to music because it was a way that you could get in touch with yourself. You could put two notes together and if it felt right to you, if it made you happy or sad, that was what mattered."[134] Most of all, The Blue Nile were idealists. They didn't want to make more grist for the music industry mill, they wanted to express something authentic, that could be a kind of metonymy: "Taking all those little ideas and big feelings and scribbled notes and rehearsals in cold tenement flats and walking home disappointed by the world and turning the whole thing into another better thing than any of us," explained Robert Bell[135]. In this way the music could radiate a positive effect, resonate with people's ordinary experience and send ripples of awareness and honesty out into the culture. "I didn't invent penicillin and I didn't save anyone's life, but I'm glad we did what we did," said Paul. "This isn't a moral comment at all, but I think in a society where we're constantly encouraging each other to buy things, whatever they're worth, it feels to me an extremely small but worthwhile endeavour to try and make something for the sake of making it beautiful than making it about profit."[136]

Meanwhile, the prevailing tone and content of pop music was a 'phony' pose. Edwyn: "I don't care if people say I'm a wank. I expect people to say that. I do care, but I'm still going to continue to be myself and say what I say. People are so self-conscious they won't give anything away, so they resort to pre-fabricated clichés. They need to lay their heart on the line or they end up writing a load of cheap crap which isn't real."[137] "The songs are completely personal," said Morrissey. "I flee from the word 'image' because it implies something that you buy and take home in a box. No, we're naked before the world. We just rip our hearts open and this is

---

[134] Hoskyns, Barney, 'The Soul of Scotland: Danny Wilson/The Blue Nile', *Sunday Correspondent*, October 1989.

[135] Bell, Robert (*Word* magazine), quoted in Brown, Allan, *Nileism: The Strange Course of The Blue Nile*, Polygon, 2010, p247.

[136] Paul Buchanan, interviewed for *Classic Scottish Albums: A Walk Across the Rooftops*, BBC Radio Scotland, 2006.

[137] Needs, Kris, 'Orange Juice: Fruit Of The Loon', *Flexipop!*, April 1983.

how we are."[138] Meanwhile there were the bands who were considered to be faking integrity, where passion was only another part of the image-making. Robert and Grant targeted Dexy's Midnight Runners as a "hippy sham". "There's only one person around who talks about passion in music and we all know who he is"; "Just [Kevin Rowland] standing there with the clothes and the profile...How people can still talk in terms of soul and commitment being the absolute charlatan that he is"; "I tend to trust passion more when it's in a quieter voice, when it doesn't announce itself"[139].

In the background there's religion. Not as a practice or dogma to follow, not even a conscious set of beliefs, but absorbed through family life in the get-togethers of Easter and Christmas, the teas and hats and talk of church visits; the mouldy-vanilla smell of Bible pages; the hand-me-down rules of what constituted truth and goodness. The Blue Nile trio were all Catholics and their sound engineer Calum Malcolm had been due to train as a priest. A friend of Paul's pointed to the religious angst at the heart of his music career, his use of the kind of questioning lyrics that could have come straight from Mass, a kind of catechism: "Someone like Paul, who has an extraordinary voice, who is a poet, who is absolutely the real thing, is also trying to be this ordinary Catholic man and there's a real beauty in that, because it's such a tiring pursuit. Everything has to be justified. Why do I have this? Should I have this? Do I deserve this?"[140]. The doubting never stopped. "Sometimes you get breaks that appeared to be good," Paul said, "in a material sense you think this is good, an opportunity, but the funny thing is it's taking you further and further away from your spiritual hopes."[141] Roddy and Campbell were Protestants (and God forbid if they ever got involved with Catholic girls, said Campbell).

Morrissey and Marr were born into Irish Catholicism, an embattled family Catholicism that was having to uphold its values while living in the modern Sodom and Gomorrah of Manchester. It was a brand of

---

[138] Shaw, William, 'The Smiths: Glad All Over', *ZigZag*, February 1984.

[139] Snow, Mat, 'The Go-Betweens: The Gentle Three-Headed Monster', *New Musical Express*, 21 August 1982.

[140] Brown, Allan, ibid, p77.

[141] Paul Buchanan, interviewed by RTE One, 2012.

Christianity fascinated by the theatre of human suffering, the public displays of martyrdom. Catholicism was filthy with myth. Like the story of St Simeon living on top of his pillar in the desert for 30 years; St Denis, who was beheaded but still managed to walk away, head tucked under his arm, still preaching; the saints who nursed the sick, drank pus from wounds, ate lice from bodies, cleaned floors of excrement with their tongues. In bubbly Eighties' Britain, what could be more self-lacerating than setting yourself up as an oracle of anti-social gloom, the prophet of celibacy? "The Smiths can be seen as a supreme effort of will: emerging out of the grey, deadening anonymity of Manchester with a passionate vision of the way things should be," wrote Jon Savage[142]. There was always a sense of urgency to the Smiths, of being the output from a mission of their own making: "Morrissey believes popular music is not a washed-up creative force yet; there's still plenty of things that need communicating and he's ready and willing to man the Morse key."[143] And to communicate with the masses, not just the converted. "That's the problem with the general public, they've all got such long faces...I think I'd like to appeal to the sector of the public that don't normally buy records and don't normally go to gigs."[144] Because Manchester was the kind of place where both religion and atheism were a dead end, where people "worry [themselves] soulless, forbidden to be romantic"[145], "where shame is cattle-prodded into kids"[146].

The message, again, was how people needed to find the wit and courage to make their own world, break free from convention, embellish and illuminate the skies overhead with a thousand different clouds.

*

[142] Savage, Jon, 'The Smiths: Deliberately', *The Sunday Times*, 8 January 1984.

[143] Black, Bill, 'The Smiths: Keep Young and Beautiful', *Sounds*, 19 November 1983.

[144] Deevoy, Adrian, 'The Smiths', *International Musician and Recording World*, October 1983.

[145] Morrissey, *Autobiography*, Penguin Classics, 2013, p4.

[146] Ibid, p11.

Love hadn't been the answer. Becoming authors of a new world, one that was more honest and poetical, just might be. There could be a fresh start. But to be a 'good author' of that new beginning it was necessary to have more than personal experience and instincts to draw on. They needed to have learnt from the writers and auteurs of the past.

3.

Dusty in here
The Go-Betweens, *Before Hollywood* (May 1983)

rant McLennan died from a heart attack when he was 48. Images of Grant, a square-shouldered man with the regular features of an American action hero, have stayed with us. He's been frozen in time by all the promo pics and album covers that live on as web ephemera: the straight gaze of a guitarist in a rock band. Bygone moments of nearly celebrity.

Grant was known around the Australian band scene for being nothing like the poster boy of first impressions. He was someone who needed to be made fun of, for being bookish, prissy and old-fashioned; for being serious-minded in a way that broke up the flow of Aussie banter. Grant didn't seem to belong anywhere or with anyone. That didn't mean he was lonely, said fellow outsider Robert Forster, but he was the "alone man"[1]. Like a character in film noir or a Bukowski poem — the rebel, drifting and self-sufficient — he was suspended in solitary routines, living in black and white. Grant was the man seen smoking at his hotel room window; sitting in an empty bar with a newspaper in the afternoons; waiting on a platform as the last train pulls away; going about the business of a quest that was mysterious to anyone but himself, like following footsteps to the edge of the moon. "People think there's an explanation for melancholy," said

---

[1] Stenders, Kriv, *Right Here: the story of the Go-Betweens*, 2017.

friend and one-time Go-Betweens band member Peter Milton Walsh. "There's no explanation for melancholy. A man can be given everything the world has to offer and still go on longing."[2]

Two songs on *Before Hollywood* are clues to the story that was going to play out for Grant, 'Dusty in Here' and 'Cattle and Cane'. They were made from childhood memories, innocent enough to casual attention, but violent with pictures from the past; like smashed cars left long abandoned on the side of a country road; strange as dreams where the most important things are lost or only part-remembered. They were songs written by Grant in London in 1982 during the Go-Betweens' journey into British post-punk indie, a descent into a dim underworld where there was no path to follow, no certainty of getting another deal and, meanwhile, no money to live on. But somewhere in all those cold mazy streets of the Imperial capital, under the long shadows of Victorian neo-Gothic towers, inside the chambers of record industry power, there might have been a way out.

*

Grant's otherness had its roots in the rural north of Queensland. He was born in 1958 in cowboy country: Rockhampton or 'Rocky', a nineteenth century Gold Rush city. He first knew the world as Cinemascopic vistas of dusty scrub, cattle and sugar cane, where the plains were subject to drought, flood and, every thirty years or so, a cyclone of *Wizard of Oz* proportions. The north had a culture that was alien to the majority of the Australian population and Robert was shocked when Grant's brother and cousin first came to visit, fresh from the ranch: "Here were two big-hearted teenage boys in pressed jeans, cowboy hats, western shorts and boots, up for fun in the city."[3]

Grant was six years old when — suddenly, hauntingly — his father died. Dr McLennan had been both a GP and a landowner and the McLennans were comfortable financially, but Grant, his younger brother

---

2 Ibid.

3 Forster, Robert, *Grant & I: Inside and Outside The Go-Betweens*, Omnibus Press, 2017, p59.

Lachlan and sister Sally, were left with another, unwanted legacy. Silences. A knowledge of loss. Things left unsaid.

The children were brought up in "a house of women"[4] on a ranch in the small coastal resort of Cairns, even further into the tropical north. Mango trees and yellow-flowering penda dotted the downtown streets. There were pomegranate and coconut trees, luminous parrots and cassowary birds, giant fruit bats hanging from branches like outsized Halloween decorations. And, submerged in a giant Blue Lagoon cocktail offshore, was the Great Barrier Reef. Fishing boats trawled the waters for marlin. Grant would come to think of Cairns as being more like Florida's island city, Key West, than Australia, somewhere set apart, cocooned and fabulous:

> city of heat that gave its children
> faith in the fable of coral and fish
> told them the world was something to miss…
> The salt in the wind moves over the mudflats
> Sticks to your skin and rusts up the lights
> Blows through the ferns that breathe in the dark…
> Burn in a river tangled with reeds
> While a crane on the water silently feeds.[5]

There was a cultural connection between Cairns and Scotland through its local traditions of singing Scottish folk songs — a provincial custom coexisting alongside the usual homely 60s diet of American TV. Best of all for Grant, *The Monkees*.

One of the traditions of a wealthy rural family like the McLennans was sending the children to boarding school. Grant was sent away aged 11, in short trousers, blazer and akubra broad-brimmed hat, to Churchie, the Church of England Grammar School in Brisbane. It was still Queensland, but a thousand miles from home (the same kind of distance as that between London and Naples or London and Algiers). A boys-only school,

---

[4] Lyrics from 'Unkind and Unwise' on *Spring Hill Fair* (1984).

[5] Ibid.

founded in 1912 on an ethos of building character ("the making of men"), Churchie is one of Australia's wealthiest independent schools. 'Alis aquilae', the School's motto, 'on eagle's wings', was taken from a passage in the Bible stressing the muscular value of spirituality: "But those who wait for the Lord shall find their strength renewed, they shall mount up on wings like eagles, they shall run and not grow weary, they shall walk and not grow faint."

Grant arrived to find an assembly of redbrick neo-classical buildings, arches and colonnades, an expanse of green lawns and sport fields in a quiet suburb ringed by the Norman Creek. Living here, independently and as a member of a young élite, was an adventure. "As a kid I remember being very impressed by Brisbane," Grant said. "It meant the Gabba [cricket ground], because I was interested in sport at school. It meant bookshops; it meant anything that Cairns wasn't, Cairns just seemed so hot and boring to me at that stage."[6]

It was an experience that also meant exploring the bitter romance of being alone: he was the eldest son away from home, the boy with no father, a stranger in the big city. Being the outsider can be an intoxicating thing. There's the freedom to think and feel without the clutter of expectations, norms, duties and responsibilities, the time to grow a poetic relationship with the world. Quiet dawns. Long hours of twilight. Moonlit nights. "I recall a bigger brighter world," Grant sang in 'Cattle and Cane', "A world of books/ And silent times in thought". And at Churchie he had his own room to do it in, the first of a long series of places that were the harbour for a drifter and his outsider identity. There would be no holiday postcards or jokey posters pinned to the walls of his student rooms; no collections of empty beer bottles, quirky mascots or trashy magazines; no compromises to comfort. Whether on campus, sharing a London squat or renting places in Brisbane, Grant's rooms retained their spare masculinity throughout his life. Occasional visitor Peter Milton Walsh remembered: "[a] bed that was always made, plain white linen. Typewriter, table, magazines in a stack, lines as straight as a ream of paper. Vodka in the freezer, St-Rémy brandy on the shelf, next to it a box of crackers. Nothing

---

6 Stafford, Andrew, *Pig City: From the Saints to Savage Garden*, University of Queensland Press, 2006, p78.

but a rind of cheese in the fridge. Books, singles and albums in alphabetic rows. It was austere, clean, and spoke of discipline, a single devotion."[7] Earnest and intellectual but unstuffy, reminiscent of the rented rooms of Philip Marlowe, with that same sense of the inevitable sadness that can surround the life of someone still clinging to what might be perceived as being outdated ideals. According to Robert, Grant didn't have a serious girlfriend, someone who could share those places, until he was in his late 20s.

From Churchie, Grant's youthful Romantic gaze would have looked out over the river to the centre of the city, to a horizon of skyscrapers that were a range of dusty-blue monoliths in sunshine, mountains of lights at night. Even with its New World skyline, its industry and sprawl, Brisbane was still a city in the jungle. The disused wharves along the river were mixed with tropical mangroves, the air heavy with a sugary rotten-egg smell. The suburbs were filled with traditional Brisbane homes built on stilts to protect against termites and floods, with corrugated iron roofs and verandas. Every open space was a spout of unstoppable growth, prodigious palms and shrubs with leaves the size of elephants' ears, starred all over with flowers in all manner of lurid colours. The bush mountain god, Coot-tha, loomed over the city. "Above us the skies were deep blue — popcorn clouds skirting the afternoon horizon. Storms came on Fridays. Lightning-jutting beasts that pelted the city with an hour of tropical rain, washing it clean and giving to the vegetation the intensity of colour that was almost psychedelic," remembered Robert[8]. In 1974, when Grant was 16, the Brisbane river broke its banks and punched a way through the business district and surrounding areas of homes, forming a flood with depths of up to eighteen feet. He saw dead cattle drifting down the main streets, ending up being lodged in treetops and left to rot.

This was still Queensland's city, at the mercy of nature and stuck in a bubble of sub-tropical heat. It also had the old-world conservatism of a rural state. Ordinary folks sat around on their veranda to see out the long evenings in the suburban sprawl, the sun dying into bands of grey and

---

[7] Walsh, Peter Milton, 'There'll come a time one day', Riley Records blogspot, May 2015.

[8] Forster, Robert, ibid., p18.

purple; nothing much open after 6pm, the streets empty and police cars on the prowl. Fine for the lotus eaters, but the sleepy mood had something brooding and frustrated to it, a bovine disinterest that could become ugly. It was a contrast exposed by Grant in 'Streets of Your Town' (1988), a sweet, blue-sky carousel of a song that circles around to reveal sinister faces ("Don't the sun look good today?/ But the rain is on its way/ Watch the butcher shine his knives/ And this town is full of battered wives"). Brisbane culture mostly meant rugby league and lager. Young people who grew up in the city and had an interest in the creative arts, trained in medicine or other professions, were likely to emigrate to Sydney or London. Apathy stayed behind. Even the clothes were boring said Robert: "the tropical heat and the utility of clothing needed to withstand it tended to blur boys and girls together. Brisbane was never sexy"[9].

At the time it might have just looked like part of the Queensland shtick, but Brisbane was living through the most extraordinary period of its history. Joh Bjelke-Petersen was the state's 'Hillbilly Dictator' who directed traffic for the right-wing regime from 1968 until 1987, during which time Queensland became known as the 'Deep North'. With their constant presence and short fuse, the police were used as a weapon. They had no patience for people who weren't dressing conventionally, who weren't looking busy (or looking heterosexual). If Bjelke-Petersen was faced by dissent and protest, a 'state of emergency' would be declared and police would both up their visibility and level of aggression even further. When South Africa's Springboks rugby team came to Queensland in 1971, anti-apartheid protesters were cleared from the streets with force. But the policy failed to prevent outbreaks of opposition, so an irritated Bjelke-Petersen banned street marches altogether. Other initiatives included an attempt to ban gay men from pubs and clubs as "deviants"; and putting a stop to safe sex campaigns and sex education in schools during the HIV crisis. Bjelke-Petersen told one of his ministers that HIV could perhaps be used as a means of ridding the state of its indigenous population. Always looking to undermine the national government, even trying to establish Queensland as a separate country, Bjelke-Petersen was called by Australia's Prime Minister "a Bible-bashing bastard...a paranoiac, a bigot and fanatical". In spite

9 Ibid., p103.

of it all, his popularity continued to grow, and over the 19 year period he managed to triple the size of his vote. After recommending himself for the honour, Queen Elizabeth II knighted Sir Joh in 1984.

The Go-Betweens were made in this muggy, sometimes torrid anti-intellectual climate where fancy ideas from the metropolitan world weren't welcome. Bjelke-Petersen was a reassuring guardian of the old ways: a God-fearing gentleman-farmer whose inarticulate performances (he was famous for struggling to finish his sentences) played perfectly to old-fashioned prejudice. Because at least he wasn't trying to look clever.

*

Grant cruised through the state's education system. He started his BA arts degree when he was still only 17 — majoring in journalism and drama — and finished it two years later. He was helping to run the University's film venue and writing the occasional piece for the heavyweight Melbourne bi-monthly *Cinema Papers*. This included an interview with Queensland's chair of the film board of review, a body that made it possible to ban films in the state even if the federal board in Sydney had approved them. What qualifications did board members have for their role? asked Grant. What would a psychologist say about the actual effects of watching films? "He was a boy wonder. You can't imagine how far ahead of everyone he was," recalled Robert[10]. Films, literature, poetry. Grant had seen and read about it all, knew the classics, the arthouse rarities, the new wave. "He burned for the screen and wanted to be a reviewer or director, or both, like his heroes Francois Truffaut and Jean-Luc Godard."[11] Then there was a stumble. An application to the National Institute of Dramatic Arts in Sydney was turned down. He was too young. Being precocious was one thing, but where was all the academic achievement going to take him?

Forster arrived into Grant's life like an exotic bird blown in-shore by an unexpected storm, a "gigantic, glorious, preening flamingo of a

---

[10] Stenders, Kriv, ibid.

[11] Forster, Robert, ibid., p32.

man"[12]. While Grant was relentlessly independent, Robert was at home with his parents in a suburb known as The Gap, waiting for the day when he could bust out and fly. The Gap was spread over a long undulating roll of hills, rich with jungle greenery and strung with telegraph wires. One of the frontier suburbs similar to those of East Kilbride, the kind of place where working-class families counted their blessings but hoped for bigger things. On those Brisbane nights before starting the band, Robert would be spending his time watching TV, detective shows like *Callan* and all the sports. Sport was a big thing for the family — cricket, golf, football — and young Robert's chores would include collecting stray balls from the nearby golf course. "I remember spending twenty-one Saturday nights at home in a row – that was my record. My parents were going out more than me...I knew to break the chain I had to get up onstage."[13] According to one friend, Robert didn't have an adolescence, no period of rebellion and discovery until his late 20s[14]. Mr Forster was a factory worker, a fitter and turner, while Mrs Forster started out working as a PE teacher. At some sacrifice to themselves, the Forster's were able to send their bright young son to a private school, and, after all his academic and sporting success, he was expected to excel still further at the University of Queensland. "From being the schoolboy genius, I go to university and become the town dunce. My parents were very unhappy with me — it almost led to breakdowns of relationships with certain members of my family, because I was failing. The problem was, I was the first person in three or four generations of my family to go to university. And with no academic background, they couldn't understand."[15]

Grant and Robert turned out to be each other's answer. Whether it was the right answer or not, who knows? "Nothing in my life is numbered," sang Robert in a late Go-Betweens song, "In my life nothing is planned/ You might think you see purpose/ When what you're seeing is a

---

[12] Lee, Stewart, 'The Go-Betweens', *The Sunday Times*, 16 May 1999.

[13] Ware, Gareth, 'The Go-Betweens', *London in Stereo*, 21 February 2015.

[14] Interview with Clinton Walker, Stenders, Kriv, ibid.

[15] Nicholls, David, *The Go-Betweens*, Verse Chorus Press, 1997, p41.

band."[16] They met in 1976 in the drama classes held at the Avalon, an off-campus theatre where there was none of the order and mannered sobriety of the university lecture rooms. An unbuttoned place of larks and escape. "It was a jostling atmosphere in which Grant and I felt immediately at home, and our friendship began and blossomed here, amid the costume trunks, the works of Beckett, Genet and Ionesco."[17] Grant said the first time he saw his future band-mate he was wearing a loin cloth. "My class did *Hamlet*, and I played Polonius. And Robert's class did *The Rocky Horror Show*, and he played the monster. Typecasting, I thought!"[18]

There was Grant, with his Seventies middle-parting of blondish hair, already flyaway thin, looking short next to the gangling 6ft 4 inches of his elegant friend ("an affably bewildered plumber's mate alongside such a glamorous figure"[19]). They could have been the stars of the classic kind of mismatched buddy movie. Except that was just the myth. Robert was meant to be the louche showman, the drop-out who was as bohemian and offbeat as his vocals; the studious Grant was supposed to be "in bed by ten with herbal tea and books"[20]. They were different people, but not in the ways often assumed by media. True enough, from everything Robert has said about their years together, Grant was the rational one, his emotions under control and faultlessly correct, acting with "serenity and a crisp, businesslike attitude to things"[21]. It could be a prim kind of intelligence and a red rag to a bull in the rock circles he occupied. "Grant was preposterous," said Melbourne singer-songwriter Dave Graney. "We could not get enough of taking the piss out of Grant...He always managed to outrage us with his outlandish and fearlessly fey behaviour. Perhaps it was

---

[16] Lyrics from 'Too Much of One Thing' on *Bright Yellow Bright Orange* (2003).

[17] Forster, Robert, 'A True Hipster', *The Monthly*, July 2006.

[18] Stafford, Andrew, ibid., p79.

[19] Lee, Stewart, ibid.

[20] Forster, Robert, ibid., p297.

[21] Ibid., p256.

a persona built up from coming from such a succession of cow towns, maybe it was the boarding school…His soft and even speaking voice, which I could never believe, the way he would cock his head to the side when he was standing on his opinion (against all the surrounding mockery), his quick and easy laugh."[22] Grant was the type who would have preferred his social life to be filled with literary soirées, gatherings among the *philosophes*. He wanted to invite friends round for the kind of parties where they served cucumber sandwiches, said Dave Graney[23]. Grant was a conversationalist, alert and interested in people, the epitome of 'civilised'. And also a "proud snob" according to writer Andrew Stafford, who would bump into Grant in Brisbane record stores in the later years before he died. "We watched a man cross Boundary Street – shirtless, in shorts and thongs, a heavy beer gut hanging over his hips. Grant didn't bother to conceal his disgust. 'Look at that,' he muttered, shaking his head. 'What a *barbaric* country we live in!'"[24] "He was really protective about his books," remembered friend Pierre Sutcliffe. "The minute he left the room you'd put them all out of order, turn them upside down. And he'd get really upset if you used one as a coaster for a drink."[25] Even band members who borrowed a book had to be careful. "I have always read in the bath," said Lindy. "He came over one night — we used to rehearse every single night — and he screamed at me, 'What's that, what's that?' And I said, 'It's your book.' It was all wet, and there was no way it was going to dry properly. And I just laughed — I mean, I love books, but to me the more mucked up they get the better. But Grant is absolutely meticulous about his book collection, obsessional. He never did lend me another book again." (Lindy went on to suggest there was more to Grant's annoyance

---

[22] Creswell, Toby, 'Goodbye Fireboy: Grant McLennan 1958 - 2006', *Rock's Backpages*, May 2006.

[23] Stenders, Kriv, ibid.

[24] Stafford, Andrew, 'The Last Time I Saw Grant', *The Griffith Review*, August 2007.

[25] Stenders, Kriv, ibid.

than just the book — it was jealousy over her relationship with Robert, the obstruction to their friendship — but that's all to come)[26].

The book Lindy was reading in the bath was Thomas Pynchon's *The Crying of Lot 49* (1966). Pynchon's usual melting-pot of high and low culture, the product of Sixties' American counter-culture, was very Go-Betweens and very Grant: pop goes the intellectual. The short novel is a quest following clues and traces of the 'Trystero', a mysterious alternative postal service by which people "are truly communicating whilst reserving their lies, recitations of routine, arid betrayals of spiritual poverty, for the official government delivery system; maybe even on to a real alternative to the exitlessness, to the absence of surprise to life, that harrows the head of everybody American you know"[27]. One group using the Trystero service, by the way, is 'Inamorati Anonymous', isolated people addicted to falling in love. Pynchon would have understood Grant's situation as an outsider. As he wrote in a 1984 piece for the *New York Times* (which Grant may well have read): "Except maybe for Brainy Smurf, it's hard to imagine anybody these days wanting to be called a literary intellectual, though it doesn't sound so bad if you broaden the labeling to, say, 'people who read and think.'"[28] The eccentricities of his friend did at least make sense to Robert. "His place here is as a true hipster, in the 1940s and '50s sense of the word. Someone perched on the streets, in the saloons, on the lower side of life, possessing razor-sharp and deep knowledge of the cultural front – but never lording it in the traditional manner. Half jokingly, I once suggested he return to academia. He laughed the idea off, preferring to be the secret holder of wisdom 'on a barstool throne'."[29]

Robert always made the biggest impression because of his height, his striking looks and elegance. Made for a fashion shoot. Robert was also the more conventional member of the partnership. It was Robert who made plans for the band and thought about the practical details, the one

---

[26] Stafford, Andrew, *Pig City: From the Saints to Savage Garden*, ibid., p.92.

[27] Pynchon, Thomas, *The Crying of Lot 49*, Vintage, 1966, p117/118.

[28] Pynchon, Thomas, 'Is it O.K. To Be A Luddite?', *The New York Times*, 28 October 1984.

[29] Forster, Robert, 'A True Hipster', ibid.

who got married and had children, who did the fussing. "I was more calculating in life and art…My nature was the reverse of his: an easier approach, a more guarded heart."[30] The wild man was Grant. He was the wayward dreamer who resisted the inglorious demands of modern life. "Here was a man who, in 2006, didn't drive; who owned no wallet or watch, no credit card, no computer. He would only have to hand in his mobile phone and bankcard to be able to step back into the gas-lit Paris of 1875, his natural home," said Robert[31], who also wrote about the only time Grant drove a car. "Grant managed to guide the vehicle into a ditch. A look at the dashboard showed the problem. No petrol. He didn't know you had to put it in. He probably thought you could drive forever."[32] Back in 1983, Grant declared he would have been happy in the 18th century, "I could quite forget about the 20th."[33] The 18th century: home of literary salons, wordy coffee shop debate and gentlemen with a mammoth capacity for alcohol. Grant was himself a connoisseur of booze. He drank in ways he knew would provide the required effect when he needed it; a need that, eventually, became more or less continual. A favourite of his was the Long Island Iced Tea, a typically belting cocktail of five different spirits. Grant also invented the more functional 'Go-Between': take any glass, fill half with vodka, the other half with coke, add a slice of orange. Alcohol was one of his methods of Romantic escape, separating the poetic from the mundane and its melancholy memories, making the moon shine bright. Another method was heroin, which Grant used over many years, but sparingly, so that he would always keep a sense of control, remaining the conscious artist of his intoxication.

Two singer-songwriters in one band can mean trouble: separate forces that knock against each other and bring about a gradual decomposition. In the case of the opposing chemical elements of Robert and Grant there was a synthesis, the production of something more complex and

---

30 Forster, Robert, *Grant & I*, ibid., p93.

31 Forster, Robert, 'A True Hipster', ibid.

32 Forster, Robert, *Grant & I*, ibid., p61.

33 Barber, Lynden, 'The Go-Betweens: Mysteries of Exile', *Melody Maker*, 1 October 1983.

refined than their individual selves. It helped that it was friendship that made the band rather than the other way around. They both recognised something necessary to themselves in the other, that made them feel comfortable, that made them want to keep on talking and sharing their discoveries in music and film and books. They made their own private world where Robert was 'Bobbie'; where they'd hail each other with a big Cockney 'Al-lo!' (taken from the intro of an Ian Hunter LP they both knew); they'd read aloud bits and pieces from books, or letters from Grant's mother filled with bucolic details of life on the ranch, or from magazine interviews that confirmed the genius of Bob Dylan. A to and fro of dispatches from their own frontline of in-jokes and gossip. The chemistry worked because they appreciated the intensity of the other in a way that many other people didn't. "I realised his 'thing', film, wasn't just an enthusiasm," said Robert, "it was an obsession. And I knew that was exactly how I felt about music."[34] So rather than the usual posters around campus advertising for musicians to join him, Robert was determined to turn Grant into a musician, even if it went against the grain of Grant's enclosed nature. "It was better to play with a friend on your wavelength than a musician not on your wavelength. I'm going to teach my best friend an instrument — very unorthodox."[35] The connection was two-way. Visiting friends in the US in 1980 Grant was invited to join an already established band with a record deal, to have the chance of living in his dream city of New York. He turned it all down to return to Robert — with no deal, not even a drummer — to see what might happen with the Go-Betweens[36].

The world of anti-intellectualism they moved in meant the need for a secret language, making a treasure of culture. "Brisbane was culturally starved...Grant knew about film and I had a knowledge of music and books, and together we built ourselves a fantasy world of Paris and New York, and dreamed of culture."[37] Signs of an alien intelligence were al-

[34] Forster, Robert, 'A True Hipster', ibid.

[35] Stenders, Kriv, ibid.

[36] Vickers, Robert, 'Grant McLennan, 1958-2006', *Magnet* magazine, 8 February 2007.

[37] Lee, Stewart, ibid.

ways visible in their media interviews, the careful weighing of each word in their answers, considering what might be true rather than glib media sizzle. They shared an uncommon confidence even before the music press fell in love with them, when there wasn't much hope to cling to: golden boys who'd absorbed the rays of family admiration and kept the glow inside. Even when Robert started failing his degree courses, he was convinced it was because the system just didn't get him; and there's an arrogance to the way the Go-Betweens turned up in London expecting the music business to roll out a red carpet. The band was also a way of releasing their innate exhibitionism. Grant liked to be seen carrying LPs and copies of the *New Yorker* around campus; Robert dressed up; they both loved to start a mock sword fight that could spill out of their drama class and into the streets.

It was a friendship with depth and purpose, meaning they weren't inseparable 'best mates', extroverts surfing the years of good times and dewy-eyed confessionals. They didn't talk about everything. The death of Grant's father wasn't up for discussion, nor were Grant's casual relationships with women. They shared some houses in London but mostly weren't living together; Robert only remembered the two of them ever sharing one long car journey. There could be shyness before that private world could be re-entered once again. "It was the late-morning drive over to Grant's place," said Robert of their practice routine, "his mystifyingly frosty greeting at the door, then the 'Watcha reading? Watcha hearing?', state-of-the-Australian-cricket-team chat, until the guitars came out - 'This one's in G' — at which point the mood suddenly wheeled back to the warm camaraderie of the afternoon before and we'd sail off into the mystic with our first song."[38] Robert had the grace to often talk about his respect for Grant as a guru of the highbrow, but he was also conscious of the way Grant would sometimes look at him, "in wry amusement"[39], show a "sleepy-eyed superiority"[40]. Laidback Bohemians didn't have arguments,

[38] Forster, Robert, *Grant & I*, ibid., p298.

[39] Ibid., p307.

[40] Ibid., p32.

meaning some issues relating to the band "didn't get discussed, and festered a little, only a little," said Robert[41].

The long-running songwriting duel — like one of their mock-serious sword fights, bundling into a corridor and out the fire door — began in earnest with *Before Hollywood*. In their usual civilised way they had agreed at this point that all their output should be credited to 'Forster/ McLennan', and they should have an equal number of songs on an LP. Before a decision was made about the band they both had to agree to it. It was all very simple until it got messy. For the first four years of the band, Robert had been the songwriter. It was a role he enjoyed. But Grant was always writing — screenplays, novels — so why not songs? Very quickly it looked like the competition was going to be serious and at the time Robert was "deeply affected by it" said Lindy, because Grant was "going to write really great songs"[42]. This other Boy Wonder seemed to just turn up and succeed at everything. But it turned into the right kind of competition, a mutually generous experience that gave the Go-Betweens their distinctive mix of the sweet and the sharp, tart and cream. They worked separately on ideas. For Robert it was mostly a day job while still relying on the spontaneity and random flight of his muse, not taking anything from the classic rock and roll songbook, "not knowing the clichés"[43]. He'd come up with "one good bit" and the rest would somehow rush, flutter and settle into place. Grant was the nighthawk, making use of the carpet-ride surge over the rooftops of alcohol and drugs. Because of this, his songs also "seemed to fall together effortlessly," said future band-mate, bass player Robert Vickers. "He was a prolific and gifted songwriter, and I consider his consistency unequaled and his ability to marry a lyric of great sensitivity to a melody of great beauty unparalleled."[44] The partnership then came together to gauge the response of the other to each song, for it to be built

---

[41] Ibid., p193.

[42] Interview with Lindy Morrison, Stenders, Kriv, ibid.

[43] Christgau, Robert and Dibbell, Carola, 'The Parts that Got Left Out of the Robert Forster Interview', *Perfect Sound Forever*, February 2011.

[44] Vickers, Robert, ibid.

and refined again into a true Forster/McLennan creation. Their process became well-established, it was "always show and tell" said Robert[45], "our working method was no different to John and Paul's, knee to knee with guitars in a Liverpool front room circa 1960"[46]. Grant, in particular, would add guitar riffs to embellish and sometimes harden Robert's songs; he was the "riffmeister" on *Before Hollywood*.

Their songs are a kind of musical alchemy that can be too delicate and obscure to dissect. The elements are mostly simple in themselves, even amateurish, unmusical. There's a loose bag of bits: a gaunt guitar line, offbeat rhythms, a quirky tangent; melodies with the quality of grey sea-waves creaming onto a shore. Little is so smooth or easy or predictable that it becomes ordinary pop. And that is why the Go-Betweens didn't work as a commercial package. They weren't modern Hollywood. There was something more reminiscent of the French New Wave cinema about the writing: the naturalism, the edgy creativity, trying different angles and changes in pace, finding other ways to affect, engage and spark a response. A lean kind of beauty, and all the more beautiful for its awkward honesty.

*

"Grant and I very much liked Tina Weymouth [Talking Heads' bass player], and we also liked a show called *The Mod Squad* on TV, which had two guys and a girl. We just liked the chemistry. I think if Grant had have taken to playing drums, we would have had to get a girl on bass. It was like casting."[47] They still had their heads in drama class, thinking about the on-screen dynamics.

Robert knew Lindy Morrison as the brilliant drummer of Brisbane punk band Zero. He also knew Lindy wasn't happy with the band's drift from real instruments to drum machines and programmable keyboards. So she should have been a shoo-in. And yet it took a long time for Robert to ask Lindy to join the Go-Betweens. Lindy was six years older than "the boys" (as she called them, and continues to call them), and not committed to any material ambitions but to causes, the real-world battles of defending the people who'd been most vulnerable to the Queensland regime. With her degree in social work Lindy joined the newly-founded Aboriginal Legal Service, trying to keep aboriginals from being jailed for minor offences. Each night she'd go out on "pig patrols" to stop police picking up aboriginals who'd been drinking. The house she shared in the city was a hash-flavoured abode of hippy counter-culture, radical activists and ex-convicts living alongside musicians, jugglers, and out-of-work actors (like future Hollywood star Geoffrey Rush). As well as performing with Zero, Lindy was out on the streets taking part in agitprop theatre protesting against Bjelke-Petersen. Almost as tall as Robert, strong-minded, never reticent: girlish femininity combined with a languid long-limbed intensity; the steel only just under the surface. "[A] sheer force of nature, an Amazonian blonde...unshockable, confrontational and loud," according to good friend Tracey Thorn[48]. "Describing her quickly exhausted all possible weather metaphors," said Peter Milton Walsh. "Gales of laughter, gusts of enthusiasm, a storm of personality that broke in every room...SHE SPOKE, IF NOT LIVED, EXCLUSIVELY IN CAPSLOCK."[49] Lindy was never going to be the quirky token girl. She'd bowled Robert over. He liked her, and he knew Grant probably wouldn't. Robert and Lindy were a couple for a year or more (she had a thing for "intense nerdy men"[50], and was delighted by the idea that Robert was a virgin) before he finally tiptoed up to Grant, swallowed hard, and asked what he thought about Lindy joining the band. Grant felt it was a *fait accompli*, and for the first time Robert saw how his detached, dreaming friend could get angry. It didn't last long — Grant was too much of a gentleman and too distracted; Lindy was too valuable a talent, and they both liked the unorthodox image that was being created. So for the moment, Grant and Lindy bumped along, with the

---

[48] Stenders, Kriv, ibid.

[49] Walsh, Peter Milton, ibid.

[50] Thorn, Tracey, *Bedsit Disco Queen: How I Grew Up and Tried to Be a Pop Star*, Virago Press, 2013, p180.

debut Go-Betweens LP due to be called *Two Wimps and a Witch* (a phrase etched into the run-out groove of the *Before Hollywood* vinyl). "They seem less of a 'rock'n'roll group' than a small itinerant artistic community," suggested *Melody Maker* in 1983, "a close-knit group of friends who define themselves in terms of their separation from the music around them."[51]

A repeat of the same pattern of events came in 1986 with the arrival of violin, oboe and keyboard-playing vocalist Amanda Brown. She added musicianship and another level of colour and warmth to the music. It was also a new relationship — meaning, again, the ratcheting up of tensions within the band. The five-piece produced two more LPs and toured together with just an occasional sigh and raised eyebrow here and there. But all these tranquil, grown-up scenes contained the plot elements needed for the band's collapse and Grant's breakdown. Without it being spelt out, something wasn't right. "Historically, rock bands are supposed to have one star, or one and a half stars, but we had four or five stars," said Robert later in 1996. "Four or five very charismatic people. It's a theory that's been put to me a number of times. Strangely enough I never really thought of it. I thought when the band started that you'd try and get the strongest and the best team that you can get. So I always operated on that way of thinking. But I think in terms of show business, the focus on one person is a formula that is known to work."[52]

Amanda was a find: a classically trained musician playing in a café in Sydney with a boyfriend Robert and Lindy had known from their Brisbane days. She was also a picture of elfin beauty. Amanda joined the band and, slowly, inch by inch, became that first "real girlfriend" of Grant's. It meant a change in his worldview and whole sense of self; accepting that at some level he was now dependent on someone else; taking part in another way of living away from his bachelor room; and it meant losing the defences that came with independence, the distance and indifference. Might the lonely road, lit by its wan and thoughtful light, be leading finally to the burning orange windows of a home with Amanda? He wrote many songs for her, but none of them ever sounded quite settled or domestic: "There's

---

51 Barber, Lynden, ibid.

52 Condon, Dan, *The J Files: The Go-Betweens*, ABC, 12 March 2015.

a cat in my alleyway/ Dreaming of birds that are blue/ Sometimes girl when I'm lonely/ This is how I think I think about you…I know a thing about lovers/ Lovers lie down in trust."[53]

Then the lines were drawn: Robert and Lindy split as a couple around the same time as Amanda entered the stage. The break was managed in a typically dignified way — as it needed to be, given they'd made the decision in the morning and had to meet the same day for a soundcheck — but still, afterwards, there's a sense of stung resentment that had no place to go, turning into some complicated knots of feelings. Robert's subsequent late adolescence, when he made full use of his flamboyance and role as frontman of a cult band, didn't help. "There were times when, catching a quick look at my face in a mirror before dashing out, or in the curved windows of a Tube carriage while dangling one-handed on a strap, I'd think, Oh my god. That's you! I was ragged and running fast. A dandy underground rock star who'd pushed himself harder and harder through the decade."[54] Lindy-and-Robert never resolved itself back into a workable friendship. Even in 2006, at the Australian Music Prize: "Lindy [chose] the moment of the announcement of the award…to sidle up to me and tip a cup of poison into my ear. 'Whatever happened to that lovely young man who had so many dreams when he began his band and then lost his way?'"[55] Next: the differences in personality between Grant and Lindy were never likely to be resolved. Grant didn't want to be brought out of himself, spill his emotions and join the 'free expression' talk-and-share. Then: even Grant and Robert were starting to feel a loosening in the songwriting partnership that had held them together for so long. Grant turned up one day with a song Robert hadn't heard before, something fully-formed, a song he'd been working up and practicing with Amanda, and had already played to the LP's producer. It was 'Streets of Your Town'. No 'show and tell' for that one, and Robert was "pissed off"[56]. At

---

[53] From 'Love Goes On!', *16 Lovers Lane* (1988).

[54] Forster, Robert, *Grant & I*, ibid., p184.

[55] Stenders, Kriv, ibid.

[56] Ibid.

the same time, the romance between Grant and Amanda was evolving — except, Amanda was also close friends with Lindy. It was Lindy who'd made sure Amanda was in the band, invited her on tour before it was 'officially agreed', and who'd question Amanda over what she could ever see in Grant.

When the rumours began in 1989 that Robert was tired of the Go-Betweens after nine years of an LP and touring cycle, still with no breakthrough to chart recognition (unlike Orange Juice and Aztec Camera who'd had hits, and The Smiths who'd become legends), the barely visible crackle of fault lines through the band suddenly turned into fractures. The splits ripped apart into a yawning rift. Robert was talking about going solo, so was Grant. Then there was the idea that Robert and Grant would be a duo. Both Lindy and Amanda felt like they'd been dumped from the band. "They treated us like 'the ex-wives'," said Lindy[57].

"Lindy walked to the phone," wrote Robert in his autobiography. "She looked back at me after dialling and then turned in profile to talk. Her first words: 'Leave him.'"[58] It's the bleakest scene in the Go-Betweens' movie. Amanda confirms Grant's secret fear, that there'd never really been a way out from the melancholy places after all, just the same long road, the same rain. The day afterward, Robert found Grant "on the loungeroom couch with his face in his hands, rocking back and forth"[59]. Used to dealing with the world at arm's length, with a cool and watchful reserve, he was "the one of us without a survival technique"[60]. Grant decided to go solo because it might be a way to involve Amanda, even if it meant isolation from Robert. And so the 1990s are a spatter of projects, travelling, meeting different people. Robert got married. Grant went back to the old black and white routines. But now he's slouching around in sweatshirts and jeans, drinking more, meeting women in bars, still turning now and again to the release of heroin.

---

[57] Forster, Robert, *Grant & I*, ibid., p218.

[58] Ibid., p331.

[59] Ibid., p330.

[60] Forster, Robert, 'A True Hipster', ibid.

It's on a tour to support the release of a retrospective 'Best of' compilation in 1999 (The Go-Betweens as nostalgia act), that Grant tells Robert, unexpectedly, that he wants another try at the band. Again they had become each other's answer, and the period until 2006 is a golden one, the Forster/McLennan songwriting having lost none of its gorgeous melodic surprise.

> The last time I saw him was about two weeks before he died. The circumstances of the visit were the same as they'd been for almost 30 years: to play guitar together and do the catch-up with an old friend. He had a two-storey granny flat at the back of the house he lived in, and we played on a small deck there. A railroad track runs behind the house, and occasionally trains passed through the songs. We took breaks from the playing, and talked; we had such fun together. Talking. Always talking and gossiping – silly stuff we'd go round and round on.[61]

It was a new place Grant had bought in Brisbane on the back of the success of the *Oceans Apart* (2005) album, and because he'd found love again, with Emma, an actress. "I carried my instruments to the car. He was standing on the verandah. I noticed a bulging packet in the letterbox; it was an airmailed copy of the *New York Review of Books*. I called out that I hadn't known he was getting the magazine delivered again. He called back that Sal [his sister] had given him a subscription for his birthday. He then said one more thing: 'I'll lend you some.'...I drove off thinking about little more than negotiating the curve at the end of his narrow street, hoping that nothing was coming quickly at me from the opposite direction."[62]

Robert was back at Grant's two weeks later for a housewarming party. Emma was moving in. But Grant had excused himself when the first guests started to arrive, gone upstairs "for a lie-down" and hadn't returned.

---

[61] Forster, Robert, *Grant & I*, ibid., p326.

[62] Ibid.

"Grant led an internal life far richer than any external one that was possible to him, and that was the point: if the dream had not yet turned up, he possessed an eternal hopefulness that one day it would. Meanwhile, he would lead the life he wanted to, inside his head," concluded Peter Milton Walsh. He also suggested that Grant had always known there was a price to pay for his kind of Quixotic life. For being an island. Four years' after Grant's death, Peter told the story of the only time he'd seen Grant cry. One night Peter had been reading Grant a Bukowski poem, 'don't come round but if you do...' The poem closes with Bukowski's alter ego explaining to a former lover why they shouldn't worry if he didn't answer the door.

> I mean if I don't answer
> I don't answer, and the reason is
> that I am not yet ready to kill you
> or love you, or even accept you,
> it means I don't want to talk
>
> I am busy, I am mad, I am glad
> or maybe I'm stringing up a rope;
> so even if the lights are on
> and you hear sound
> like breathing or praying or singing
> a radio or the roll of dice
> or typing —
> go away, it is not the day
> the night, the hour;
> it is not the ignorance of impoliteness,
> I wish to hurt nothing, not even a bug...[63]

Grant was being so unlike himself, in tears, his faces in his hands. "For that moment — it came & went — he looked like a man whose fortune had

---

63 Bukowski, Charles, 'don't come around, but if you do', *Crucifix in a Deathhand*, Ioujon Press, 1965.

just been told," Peter wrote. "Or maybe someone who'd caught a glimpse of a feeling that might one day come knocking on his door."[64]

*

"Who's 'e?" says Brian, and I know he's looking at me. They say you should never look at Brian.

Brian is one of a group of them round the public bar who've been making loud jokes all evening. Red as a brick. Eyebrows like they've been drawn on. And now he's seen me looking back. I'd told Dean we should always stick to the saloon bar but he wanted to try it out.

Brian looks as salty and oily as a KP nut. And now he's both looking and talking: "You know what, if he's new, what happens? Thas right. He'll have to buy a round. Wha' you say — thas the rule — always has been. Yee—ss, don't gimme that."

All of them looking over now. It's hot enough already. The air's like a hot soup of fags and hairspray.

"You servin' twelve year-olds now then? Tell you what — I'll do you a favour son — I'll have a can of Tizer…"

They're creasing up over this one. Their wives are with them, laughing along.

"Leave him alone — ooh, don't!"

"Brian you wally."

"Dave — you'll have a what, a cream soda? Yeh, yeh, and for Chalky — make it orangeade, and better make it a small one, 'e's had too much already."

Dean's not looking at me now. He's been in The Bell loads of times before. He's wearing drainpipe jeans while I look like his little brother in my corduroy flares. I can't just pretend I'm not there, so I say — yeah — I will. I'll get them a drink. I'm so hot I can't even remember how much money I have left. Maybe I'm actually drunk. Dean bought a pint of Harp lager. I bought a pint of Harp lager. I had three pounds left at least from the fiver Dad had given me for my birthday.

A fiver. He'd forgotten to get me anything and came up to my room with that fiver instead, not saying much, not even wishing me a happy birthday because you could tell he was embarrassed.

---

[64] Walsh, Peter Milton, 'Who will remember your tunes?', Riley's Records blogspot, May 2010.

They all stared and Brian was laughing so much his face was all scrunch. I stood at the bar and they were all talking and laughing, all eyes and long yellow teeth, the bar counter shining pink and gold. The smoke and the perfume is even thicker around me and I'm looking at the fairy lights round the optics, a collection of piggy bank pigs, postcards and snaps of gangs of people, faces from years ago that I can just about recognise from those around me.

"Eh 'e's a gent this one, a real gent! You know what he reminds me of?"
I try not to listen.

"Look at his face. He's like a Ber-lisha Beacon."
"Oh Brian — " says a new voice.
Another: "Don't worry pal. He's a div."
They're naming drinks and I'm handing over the money. Serves Dad right if I waste it all.

"Wha' bout your girlfriend in the corner?" says Brian, pointing.
Dean really wishes he hadn't come with me now.

*

We don't have a mainstream of arts anymore, we have content. And content is a very different thing. More like a sixth element, everywhere and easy: films, TV, music, books and images that come with the kinds of digital interaction that have replaced letters, phone calls and time spent in company. The smart subscription platforms available for reaching mass audiences also mean content is cheap. The competition and financing of a global marketplace makes the streams of content in many ways perfect, in the sense of how they're made up of perfectly consumable pleasures. Quality standards are high. Film and TV content in particular has to meet minimum requirements to see the light of day, meaning it has to release hooks and spurs that dig into our minds, to be immediately engaging, lucid, thrilling and satisfying.

How different from the difficult old world of the arts, where artefacts were assembled in such manual and unpredictable ways, through processes hidden away in a half-light of recondite knowledge. In the medieval era, before the invention of print, books were priceless. The entire lifetime of a workshop would be dedicated to creating a single book, a volume bound in a cover of jewels and ivory. Books were a manifestation of God's beneficence. A library was a sacred place, an outpost of bright human knowledge in an otherwise overwhelming darkness of ignorance. Theatre and music were the stuff of seasonal, communal celebrations, shared memory and ritual.

The Eighties come some way towards the very end of this long tradition of the arts and the beginning of our great digital flood. There was the newly all-pervasive consumer economy of shops and shopping, but it was still being serviced in analog and linear ways. Expensive and fraught with clunky effort and dedication by consumers, still relatively un-private. Finding books that weren't current bestsellers or mainstream classics was a quest, it meant trips to out-of-the-way bookshops for a chance of feeling that quickening moment of seeing a special author's name on a book's spine. There always needed to be a journey involving time and patience, knowing that desires were likely to go unfulfilled in the dreary back rooms of second-hand bookshops and under the hot spotlights of the bigger chains, making a cursory trawl of the usual offerings, the revolving racks of Stephen King, Wilbur Smith and Jackie Collins.

Not that books were important culturally. TV was king, chirping away in the corner of every living room through every waking hour, as essential to a home as electric lights and hot water. And in the early Eighties it was still, by necessity, a shared experience. You watched the one TV set with mum and dad and the rest of the family, so the primary exposure to the culture of the time was heavily influenced by the situation on the settee. Evenings would be planned around limited TV schedules (1982 saw the introduction of a fourth channel in Britain — an unnecessary addition in the eyes of many) and the programme of viewing was in the hands of others. In 1983 that meant gathering to watch the hard-drinking, bed-hopping glam of *Dallas*; the bow-ties and showbiz glitter of programmes like *This is Your Life* and *Miss World*; followed by chilling rabies thriller *The Mad Death*, or a promise of nuclear armageddon in *The Day After*. For teenagers there was no way round the rectum-clenching moments of variety show schmaltz, sentimental goo, unexpected nudity or lusty, funny-eyed groping. A rapid exit was too obvious, and anyway, what else were you going to do besides watch TV? It also meant regular exposure to the news. The funereal tolling of the bells of the *Ten O'Clock News*, sombre-eyed newsreaders, and a window onto a world of IRA bombings, sex murders and an assembly of beaky, bristly, jowlish politicians, curious enough in themselves to make caricature seem redundant.

The biggest TV events of the year were films: *Superman: The Movie*, *Jaws II* and *Close Encounters of the Third Kind*. Because new films were a luxury. The industry's business plan at the time was based on restricting access to increase value, and there was usually at least five years between cinema release and a TV 'premiere'. While some expensive video players were being positioned proudly onto smoky tint-glass TV tables, buying pre-recorded videotapes themselves cost around £80 (or a whole week's wages for the average earner). Hollywood films and their extravagantly foreign posters on billboards and Underground walls were so far removed from ordinary British life as to be other-worldly, sensationally vivid with glamour and money. The disconnection was only heightened by the actual experience of visiting an early Eighties' cinema. One big screen and auditorium, crackly audio, the rows of mostly empty heavy seats with their raddled velveteen covers; the not very clean carpets and broken toilets; the fuzz of fag smoke.

The nature of listening to pop music is said to have changed in 1967. The first 33 rpm long-playing records of the Fifties and Sixties were meant only for the audiophiles and the extended pieces of jazz and classical music they wanted to hear in full, just as they might at a concert. LPs were for the "pipe-smoking uncles who were naturally worried about anyone playing trashy pop music on their jealously guarded radiogram", according to David Hepworth in *A Fabulous Creation: How the LP Saved Our Lives*[65]. Their record players were imposing, formal pieces of furniture, sometimes including a mirrored drinks cabinet stocked with sherry, Advocaat and Drambuie, and part of the apparatus of dinner party entertainment. Youngsters stuck to the dizzy pop moment contained within the 45 rpm single, what was faster, cheaper and all about this week's cool. Then, in 1967, there was the appearance of The Beatles' *Sgt. Pepper's Lonely Hearts Club Band* and the two separate worlds came together: an LP that was also a work of art, not a collection of singles but a sustained performance meant to be listened to as a whole. "As far as artists were concerned

---

[65] Hepworth, David, *A Fabulous Creation: How the LP Saved Our Lives*, Bantam Press, 2019, p xv.

these albums would ideally be treated as statements, much as new novels had been," Hepworth argues[66]. An LP could become the vehicle for the kind of heightened emotions and loyalty that had been saved for a much-loved book, kept in a pocket and filled with annotations. "It was a semi-precious object, a mark of sophistication, a measure of wealth, an instrument of education, a unit of currency, a banner to be carried before one through the streets, a poster saying things one dare not say oneself, a means of attracting the opposite sex, and, for hundreds of thousands of young people, the single most cherished inanimate objects in their lives."[67] An LP was also a sign of grown-up commitment to a band rather than a meaningless snog with a single. Hepworth suggests the glory days of the LP ended just 15 years' later, in 1982, with another commercial monster, Michael Jackson's *Thriller*. Making records changed again, this time from being an art to a more calculated science. That may well have been true for the mainstream labels searching for the formula to guarantee Return on Investment, but in our musical back alley of indie, the LP was still an artefact of distinction.

Sales of cassettes were growing and by 1985 had outstripped those of vinyl. Cassette tapes made it possible to keep on listening to music outside the house and give your life a film soundtrack, adding the pop energy and sheen somewhere like USA so obviously had and that Britain always seemed to lack. A new, smaller piece of kit than the tape player (a 'ghetto-blaster' or unless it should be allowed to be forgotten, what many were happy to call a 'wog box') was needed to fulfil the potential of the cassette: the personal player that became best known via the Sony Walkman brand. In 1981 the Walkman was still an oddity. *The New York Times* reported on the phenomenon of "waves of people walking about with little foam rubber circles on their ears and expressions of transport on their faces in a scene that was almost Orwellian."[68] Within a few years it had become a lifestyle essential — both for private listening at home and as an accessory

---

[66] Ibid.

[67] Ibid., p xviii.

[68] Ibid., p219.

of the fitness boom — following in the 'trendy' footsteps of Cliff Richard (who showed off his Walkman while roller-skating in the 'Wired for Sound' video) and Princess Diana (known to roller-skate around Kensington Palace listening to tapes of Elton John and Wham!)[69]. Cassettes were the beginning of a whole new universe of mixtapes, a finger held shakily over a stiff 'Record' button when favourites were due on the radio. You could make your own ideal LP, cut out the filler and produce a selection of favourites for sharing. In 1982 the US industry claimed home taping was costing $3.3 billion a year. Making tapes also played a part in changing attitudes to listening to music, encouraging an impatience to forward-wind to the hits.

Another innovation was the merger of TV and music formats. Driven by the launch of MTV in the US in 1981, the music video became a platform for global sales campaigns, and another way for blockbuster hits to distinguish themselves from the also-rans. It was another dilution of the listening experience, a dilution of the need for imagination or thought, encouraging a taste for unthinking thrills. Because a slinky, fast-cut, story-telling video would do a lot more for sales than artistry, experiment or a meaningful lyric. Producing music was becoming an ever more sophisticated enterprise. It was natural, then, that its strategy and resources would be structured around the creation of a machinery for chart hits, reducing risks to a minimum by moulding markets and managing tastes so that consumer needs — or, at least, their manufactured needs — would always be met.

*

The Go-Betweens were labelled as a 'literate' band. It became a cliché and an irritant. What did it mean? They knew how to spell? They had a "bed-sit bookishness", suggested Barney Hoskyns of the *NME* in 1983, "an allusive literary shell from which little seems to protrude. Their 'fast ballads' don't burst through, don't hit the ear, but seem lost in domestic cubby-

---

[69] Ibid., p210.

holes, stumped pleadings, circuitous poetics."[70] "That's bullshit," responded Robert. "We're obviously not vaudeville, which is what's required in this country for mass success, we're not jumping up and down on the stage. We're standing there playing our instruments. Somehow that's taken as if we spend all our time huddled over books. If we were bookish, we'd be off reading books, but we're in a rock-pop band, and being in a band takes you away from the seclusion that the word bookish implies. It really upset me because I see some truth when people say that we're very isolated because we came from a place that was away from the centre."[71] There was nothing cool about being introverted in the early Eighties, and the *NME* had drilled a nerve.

Many post-punk bands were bookish in ways that were in keeping with their gloomy, cold-eyed image. Ian Curtis (Joy Division), Howard Devoto (Magazine) and Paul Haig (Josef K) were affected by reading authors like Dostoevsky, Kafka, Joseph Conrad and Samuel Beckett. Pete 'Shelley' of Buzzcocks had changed his name from McNeish. The geezers from Subway Sect loved nothing better than a good literary caper: "We were really into libraries…We used to go round in this little Transit van, checking every library," said Vic 'Godard' (after the film director)[72]. According to Simon Reynolds, the essential piece of kit for a post-punk band was a "well-worn library card"[73]. There was also tendency among music journalists to leap on any reference to authors and literature in song lyrics as evidence of profundity, as reassurance of a depth to pop music that had been missed.

In the case of Grant and Robert though, they were as much authors as readers. Grant was always writing film scripts and poetry accord-

---

[70] Hoskyns, Barney, 'Ridiculous and Wonderful: The Smiths/The Go-Betweens at the Venue, London', *New Musical Express*, 15 February 1983.

[71] Snow, Mat, 'The Go-Betweens: Money Can't Buy You Love', *New Musical Express*, 13 October 1984.

[72] Reynolds, Simon, *Rip it up and start again: postpunk 1978-1984*, Faber & Faber, 2005, p26.

[73] Davenport, Neil, 'Tracey Thorn: My Rock 'n' Roll Friend – book review', *Louder than War*, 3 April 2021.

ing to sister Sally[74]. "[P]oetry was my first adventure," he said[75]. "When I grew up I wanted to be a screenwriter. That's what I've always wanted to do, and when this band finishes, which it must at some stage, I sort of hope to get into writing films or just general fiction writing. The ability to imagine and create your own world — that's one of the great joys of being in a band."[76] It was the auteur, the writer-director, who inspired him most of all. Charlie Chaplin epitomised commitment to a personal philosophy, to both an individual sensibility and an awareness of a society's cruelties, not just the show and the performance. Another hero was Hollywood's very first writer/director, the king of irreverent 'screwball' comedy Preston Sturges.

It wasn't only an intellectual interest. Grant was drawn to the look and feel of the artist lifestyle, the Romantic garret where there were no responsibilities except to those of a fickle muse: a high window, a desk of papers, moonlight forming a square on a bare wall. Life wasn't meant to be just for doing. "I'd drive over to his place to play guitar and he'd be lying on a bed reading a book," remembered Robert. "Grant never felt guilt about this. The world turned and worked; he read. That was the first message. He'd offer to make coffee, and I knew — and here's one of the great luxuries of my life — I knew I could ask him anything, on any artistic frontier, and he'd have an answer. He had an encyclopaedic mind of the arts, with his own personal twist."[77] Grant's bookshelf was known to include a collection of Blaise Cendrars, the avant garde modernist poet and novelist who was also a passionate reader and traveller. Lots of nineteenth-century French poetry, Apollinaire, Baudelaire, Verlaine. Less well-known poetry by Americans Frank O'Hara and Adrien Stoutenberg. Works by hard-drinking loner Malcolm Lowry. There's a glimpse of Grant's command of the field in 2005 when he was asked to list his favourite books. Instead of anything familiar he named Australian writers, first novels by

---

[74] Stenders, Kriv, ibid.

[75] Interview with Nick Cave and Grant McLennan, *Juice* magazine, 1983.

[76] Gumprecht, Blake, 'The Go-Betweens: Past Hope, Past Care, Past Help?', *Matter*, April 1984.

[77] Forster, Robert, 'A True Hipster', ibid.

young women (like Delia Falconer's *The Service of Clouds)* and *Totem,* a series of love poems by Luke Davies[78].

Robert's list leans towards the witty and picaresque. Jane Austen's *Pride and Prejudice,* Kerouac's *On the Road* and *A Confederacy of Dunces* by John Kennedy Toole; but it also includes the *Collected Poems* of Anne Sexton, a tragic figure who wrote openly in 1960s America about her private demons: depression, alcoholism, drugs, incest, masturbation. Sexton was a particular influence on Morrissey[79]. Robert wasn't just a casual reader indulging in a high-minded past-time. There were writers he had a passion for, like James Joyce, Oscar Wilde and Christopher Isherwood. He unnerved the Brisbane rock scene with his first single for the Go-Betweens, a homage to librarian 'Karen', the lady so adept at helping him find Hemingway, Genet, Brecht, Chandler and Joyce on the local library shelves. Not the stuff of guitar anthems.

The band itself was named after the 1953 LP Hartley novel (made into the film with Julie Christie and Alan Bates in 1971), an evocation of a lost Victorian age where lovers take advantage of a boy's innocent help to carry on an illicit affair. Hartley was a complex character, a reactionary who preferred the company of nobility but had "affairs with servants, gondoliers, chauffeurs, and assorted rough trade, one of whom tried to murder him"[80]. Hartley eventually drank himself to death.

Robert was as much interested in the lives of writers as their output, what it took to be a creative artist, the ardour, hope and anticipation: "Those spine-tingling days or months when they know they're going to make the jump to fame and fortune that will change their lives forever."[81] He admired the courage of artists like Oscar Wilde, "someone who'd walked to the edge, thrown his arms triumphantly to the sky, and jumped

---

[78] Sandall, Simon, 'Robert Forster and Grant McLennan list their favourite books', *readersvoice.com*, 6 May 2005.

[79] Ibid.

[80] Lee, Hermione, *Penelope Fitzgerald, A Life*, Vintage, 2014, p255.

[81] Forster, Robert, *Grant & I*, ibid., p89.

off"[82]. Robert had an early inkling he would become a writer when he discovered that his unusual middle name 'Derwent' actually came from a tutor who'd been used by the family long in the past, and who was the son of Samuel Taylor Coleridge. "Destiny had tapped, a pat to encourage stirring feelings I had of being someone with a gift for words."[83] Robert's lyrics are dotted with writer characters, always working away at a film or book — they're also more highly-strung than Grant's, dramatic, angst-ridden, full of quirks.

Robert and Grant were only fairly elementary musicians. They wanted to be master songwriters instead, using music as a way to convey moods and stories, modes of looking and feeling, and a rock-pop band was always meant to be the siege ladder that would allow them to be taken seriously as author/auteurs: "we had a number of other ideas we were going to unleash upon the world once the band was famous, which our 20 year-old minds figured would be in about three years. It was the Orson Welles theory: get famous at one thing, and then bring on everything else you can do."[84] There was going to be a Forster/McLennan film, a jewel heist starring James Garner; and a Forster/McLennan book, *The Death of Modern America: Bob Dylan 1964–66*. Their last scriptwriting collaboration was for a mistaken identity gangster film, *Sydney Creeps*, written in the storeroom of an old cinema in Brisbane in the late Nineties. Without the fame, the other creative projects never happened. There were only the usual false starts and drawers full of unfinished novels and scripts.

Since 2005, Robert has combined music with criticism, writing regularly for *The Monthly* in Australia, and produced an autobiography, *Grant & I*, which has the easy art and humour that make it one of the best of its kind. There's an absence of score-settling and self-aggrandisement, more of the simple sunshine of a Monkees song. But it also makes you wonder what a Forster/McLennan autobiography would have been like, taking turns over chapters, and what a rich brew would have resulted.

---

[82] Ibid., p184.

[83] Ibid., p15.

[84] Forster, Robert, 'A True Hipster', ibid.

*

The five LPs share this writerly character. There are no standard pop lyrics because they're trying to write poetry. It may be green poetry, but it's warm with lived experience and sincerity; with imagery that comes from places seen fresh; where ideas are meant and the anger is real. Their reading of literature meant 'ordinary' experience was heightened and refined by 'high culture', leading to an everyday Romanticism — not from gazing over perfect lawns, spires and mountains but corner shops, warehouses and rows of terraced houses.

Their inspiration often came from a legacy of popular songwriting treated as fine art: Edwyn was a student of Cole Porter and Noel Coward; Marr and Morrissey wanted to be the new Leiber and Stoller; Robert saw himself in Tin Pan Valley — the artisan workshop of Irving Berlin and George and Ira Gershwin — on *Before Hollywood*: "Who's your tall friend?…The Valley of Tin Pan/ Is where he belongs." The songwriting style comes from an attempt to reflect some of the more nuanced and affecting qualities of literature. There's a common introspection and self-examination. Worst of all for those wanting pop music to know its place, it could be smartly intelligent. "As Morrissey himself demonstrated incontrovertibly, Thinking Too Much was undoubtedly the most degenerate, the most anti-social habit any teenager could pick up," wrote biographer Mark Simpson[85].

The influence of literature was recognised, the writerly style was conscious. "To me, theory and semiotics were no use to songwriting," said Edwyn, "the only thing that was any use was just decent literature — plot lines, characters, the way people use language." It wasn't about trying to sound smart. "Costello's lyrics can't hold a candle to the best of Vic's lyrics [Subway Sect]. It's not that witty to be punning all the time."[86] A favourite novel of Edwyn's was JD Salinger's *Catcher in the Rye* (1951). When it came to the second Orange Juice album, the LP was released via production company 'Holden Caulfield Universal' after the lead character. "Well, I

---

[85] Simpson, Mark, *Saint Morrissey*, SAF Publishing, 2004, p25.

[86] Reynolds, Simon, Edwyn Collins interview notes, ibid.

just thought the novel was so evocative of adolescence, we'd take a little dig at ourselves," decided Edwyn. "It was meant to be self demeaning, it was meant to be quite wry."[87] Maybe, though, it's more than a joke, more a nod to a deeper sympathy with the novel's disappointed Romanticism. In *Catcher in the Rye*, Holden has a half-mad intensity, his nerves are all on the surface. Through his eyes, the pretence and compromises of the "crumby" adult world are exposed, and there's a clash between the kind of good instincts that amount to a personal morality and the bitter reality that goodness in itself won't get you anywhere. Holden knows that all the "swell girls" will end up with the "Guys that always talk about how many miles they get to a gallon in their goddam cars…Guys that are very mean. Guys that never read books."[88] It's the same kind of clash that's seen in the lyrics of *You Can't Hide Your Love Forever*, where the awkward, giggly hopefuls encounter the hard rules of Eighties' love affairs. Like this Holdenesque moment from 'Tender Object': "Sick inside and my eyes to the ground/ Looking for a sign to set me free/ In my chic cold misery"; and times where emotions are expressed with a novelistic intricacy: "I say I'm not sorry/ To cast you off discourteously/ When you talk so realistically/ The thrill of love is gone for me" ('Dying Day').

Edwyn's grandmother was the one to introduce him to a wider literary world, to the less well-known Russian writers of the nineteenth century, like Lermontov (and the doomed Romantic cynic of *A Hero of Our Time*), and Goncharov (whose idler *Oblomov* suffers terminally from a state of 'dressing-gownness'); as well as twentieth-century science fiction satirist Yevgeny Zamyatin (*We*); Americans like F. Scott Fitzgerald (*The Great Gatsby* and *Tender is the Night*), and Richard Brautigan, the counter-cultural performance poet best known for *Trout Fishing in America* (1967). Edwyn's fellow songwriter James Kirk was influenced by more obscure sources ("I was fascinated by the Romantic movement in art and literature, and more particularly where they interface with the Scottish Music Hall"), manifested as a watery medievalism and re-imagination of the pale knight of the Pre-Raphaelites: "Through wooded glades on my trusted steed/ All rushing

---

[87] Bohn, Chris, 'Hate can be positive', *New Musical Express*, 2 October 1982.

[88] Salinger, JD, *The Catcher in the Rye*, Penguin, 1994 edition, p111.

through the trees" ('Wan Light'); "The clarity of my eyes/ Shines both in memories of past victories/ Fine scenes shining white, shining white" ('Felicity'). The band's wordy wit encouraged some over-reaching, according to Steven Daly. "The thing with Orange Juice was that print was our medium. We always talked a good record. Making them was another story."[89]

Orange Juice lyrics were a lesson for the Smiths. You could skew the norm, be self-deprecating, witty and camp but also poetic. Morrissey was ready and waiting. "Writing, as far as I'm concerned, is a human necessity – like having to brush your teeth. It's really that simple."[90] He was unusual in being, most of all, a lyricist. "Books were always more important to me than music. But I always believed the two could be combined quite successfully in a way that hadn't been done before. I felt lyricists in popular music were just a bit too traditional; it was like a profession, with a collection of words that had to be used. You know, the moon-June-spoon school of songwriting. It's become important to me to write words off the accepted track."[91] Morrissey had been in training for years for the role of literary pop prophet. He'd been writing scripts for Coronation Street — how priceless would those pointedly acerbic episodes now be if Granada TV had accepted them? — as well as all the blurb for his New York Dolls fan club. He was a chronic letter writer. "I am reliant upon the postage stamp, and tactlessly revealing letters are catapulted north and south — anywhere a considerate soul might lurk."[92] In our realm of digital communications, emails and messaging have to contain instant purpose and impact, they shriek and bully and wink for a response. Letters in the early Eighties had been the place to be expansive, for a patient prelude followed by enquiries into the life of the recipient. Only then would there be the set-up of the story, confessionals, digression and a conclusion. They were an invitation to meandering conversation. The gentle pace of the letter form allowed for emotions to be worked out along the way, for subtlety

---

[89] Aston, Martin, 'Orange Juice: Where Are They Now?', *Q* magazine, July 1992.

[90] Savage, Jon, 'The Smiths: Deliberately', *Sunday Times*, 8 January 1984.

[91] Trakin, Roy, 'Not the Jones: Morrissey', *Musician*, June 1984.

[92] Morrissey, *Autobiography*, Penguin Classics, 2013, p116.

and doubt, for the most personal of reflections and revelations to be drawn out by the act of writing.

Morrissey's mother was a librarian who encouraged him to read Thomas Hardy and gave him a present of the *Complete Works of Oscar Wilde*: "I swam in books as a child". He learnt to be discerning and critical. "Thomas Hardy's *Far From The Madding Crowd* set me alight, but *The Mayor Of Casterbridge* didn't. And I feel that about so many people that I've liked, apart from perhaps Shelagh Delaney [playwright and screenwriter]."[93] Screenplays resonated even more than books for Morrissey if they captured that golden moment of Sixties' New Realism and working-class revolt against the Establishment, like Delaney's *A Taste of Honey* (1958), *Saturday Night and Sunday Morning* (1960), or *A Kind of Loving* (1962).

> "I think the time when those films emerged was a time when people were only prepared to be very real about things. For the first time in British films we had people who were speaking in very down-to-earth voices. Before that everybody had a very clipped, theatre-school way of talking. And for the first time also you had very real images, and it wasn't just a Hollywood pantomime…That period was very brief, however, because very soon after we went back to the whole escapism bit, which I never ever liked, and today's film industry is dead because of that."[94]

Morrissey was aware of how much his reading, his absorption into a complex vision of literary fiction, may have thrown his entire sensibility into disorder: "it gets to the point where you can't answer the door without being heavily analytical about it."[95] Reality couldn't match the heightening of vision and charmed coincidences of literature, where hidden depths and sensitivity could be the most important currency. "In your formative

---

[93] Hoskyns, Barney, 'These Disarming Men: The Smiths', *New Musical Express*, 4 February 1984.

[94] Ibid.

[95] Ibid.

years you're led to believe that lots of magical things will happen with other people — which doesn't actually happen," he said[96]. One particular short story by Oscar Wilde, 'The Nightingale and the Rose', struck Morrissey to the quick. A nightingale purposely impales itself against a thorn in order to make a rose. The flower is picked by a young student to give to someone they've fallen in love with, but the gift is rejected because another suitor has offered them the more worldly offering of jewels. The rose gets thrown away. "Armed with a deeply unhealthy interest in language, wit and ideas Morrissey succeeded in perverting pop music for a while and making it that most absurd of things, *literary*," according to Mark Simpson[97].

Compared with the other four LPs though, *The Smiths* is probably the least literary of them all. Morrissey's story-telling rarely manages to go further than his petty trials and travails, their injustice, and his immediate and contrary responses to them. His rose keeps getting tossed out. While the irony and humour works, bookishness could sometimes make Morrissey self-consciously articulate. There's something in his interviews of the effort and insecurity of Leonard Bast in *Howards End* trying to impress the Miss Schlegels over tea and cake. It can make him appear painfully heavy-footed. Like this from an interview with *The Face*: "I am very concerned about what they said because at least one of them is a *sworn enemy* who would get no small quotient of pleasure from wilfully misinterpreting my activities, I'm afraid to say."[98] Morrissey's attitudes to literature can seem overwrought. He once told *Smash Hits* he found it impossible to read a "single line" of Oscar Wilde's "without swimming in tears"[99].

Morrissey's subsequent writing career — and it was always his stated ambition to write books and a screenplay — has undermined his reputation. His song lyrics are glimpses of possibility, but Morrissey went

---

[96] Fletcher, Tony, *A Light That Never Goes Out: The Enduring Sage of The Smiths*, Windmill Books, 2013, p78.

[97] Simpson, Mark, ibid., p13.

[98] Kent, Nick, 'The Smiths: Dreamer In The Real World', *The Face*, May 1985.

[99] Rimmer, Dave, 'The Smiths: Hits And Myths', *Smash Hits*, 16 February 1984.

on to show all of his hand in a mostly magnificent but flawed *Autobiography* (2013), (why did no-one at Penguin have the nerve to stand up to him?); and a novel, *List of the Lost* (2015), that demonstrates all the dangers of self-belief that's been able to grow without checks and filters. Many writers have late-night moments when they believe what they're writing is strange, never-seen-before genius, that they've unleashed an enthrallingly kinetic assault of language. Then they read it again and see it's not James Joyce, it's not Thomas Pynchon, it's just bad. Maybe even as bad as this from *List of the Lost*: "Eliza and Ezra rolled together into the one giggling snowball of full-figured copulation, screaming and shouting as they playfully bit and pulled at each other in a dangerous and clamorous rollercoaster coil of sexually violent rotation with Eliza's breasts barrel-rolled across Ezra's howling mouth and the pained frenzy of his bulbous salutation extenuating his excitement as it whacked and smacked its way into every muscle of Eliza's body except for the otherwise central zone."

Roddy Frame's lyrics for *High Land Hard Rain*, with all their twists and puns, were the product of intensive bedroom scribbling. If anything they led to something "too intelligent" said Campbell Owens[100]. "I do spend a lot of time on them. Something like 'We Could Send Letters' — the lyrics to that were written, then rewritten and rewritten. I've almost got a book at home called 'We Could Send Letters'."[101] *High Land* includes nods to poetry, the overdose on Keats ('Release'), and to TS Eliot (the "Hollow Men who never got the groove", lacking soul, on 'Down the Dip') and to the spirit of *On the Road*. He's very conscious of quality control on his debut to make sure he avoided "the poor excuse they peddle as their prose" ('The Boy Wonders'). As we've already seen, Roddy was immersed in Colin Wilson and his mission to communicate a personal and accessible take on existentialism. "What I love about [Wilson] is that he's one of the most original, progressive authors I've read, but his style is so direct. And he writes everything; he writes seedy sex novels, murder stories, spy stories and he always manages to get his ideas to come through all of them very

---

[100] *Classic Scottish Albums: High Land, Hard Rain*, BBC Radio Scotland, 2006.

[101] Gumprecht, Blake, 'Aztec Camera', *Matter*, September 1983.

clearly…[the critics] mistook his confidence and the need to get things done for arrogance."[102]

Similar to Grant and Robert, Paul Buchanan was a frustrated writer. He'd taken a degree in literature and medieval history, had worked for Glasgow theatre groups on their press relations, but ended up putting his energy into the Blue Nile because he believed he "couldn't write a good book."[103] Each of the group's LPs had been five years or more in the making because they involved careful, line-by-line, moment-by-moment composition rather than the pouring out of more tunes: "I regarded the records more like books," said Paul[104]. In his appeal to a lover on 'Stay', he writes "a new book every day, a love theme for the wilderness." The video for the single, an early directing job for Anton Corbijn, shows the band taking turns to sit at a writing desk to pen the lyrics, ignoring distracting showers of A4 paper. Everyday things become more than themselves on *A Walk Across the Rooftops*, small details evoke an entire situation and mood in a writerly way. Like these lines from 'Easter Parade': "birthday cards and silent music/ Paperbacks and Sunday clothes…In hallways and railway stations/ Radio across the morning air". Words chosen carefully to soak the reader with the sad nostalgia of single moments, the black and white pictures of New York's Easter Parade on Fifth Avenue, Fred Astaire and Judy Garland from the 1948 film of the same name; with images of a silvery Hollywood dream and its ticker tape celebrations. Dusty sunlight in office bureaus filled with typewriters. In his use of what Ezra Pound called the "luminous details", Paul was following in the Imagist tradition popularised in the early 20th century. And in this way the Blue Nile created miniature inhabitable cities, combining forms of expression that could be less limited than language and so more universally affecting: "Somehow or other, the music sort of gets in between your sentences and expresses something that with language we can still find difficult, maybe it's soul. And I'm not saying language can't do that. Sometimes it can. But you hear

---

[102] Dadomo, Giovanni, 'Aztec Camera: The Outsider Comes In', *The Face*, December 1983.

[103] Brown, Allan, *Nileism: The Strange Course of The Blue Nile*, Polygon, 2010, p121.

[104] Paul Buchanan interview, *Ireland am*, TV3, 2004.

a great song, and you're thinking 'I felt that.'"[105] They were songs intended to have enough character and presence to stand up and walk for themselves. "All you're left with is the songs; they kiss you goodnight, and you kiss them goodnight. You pour a lot of love into them, and hope they chime with somebody else's feelings, whether it's Hollywood stars, or the man waiting for the bus."[106] Paul's style was learnt from hardboiled detective novels, like those by Elmore Leonard and James Ellroy, with their short, seemingly emotionless sentences; commonplace scenes, humdrum things; the mundane made emotional. The album title itself, *A Walk Across the Rooftops*, was inspired by the sordid city streets and suburbs of Philip Marlowe and Sam Spade, and there were other American influences, from the wild men of counter-culture like Charles Bukowski and Walt Whitman. In this way America became imprinted onto the lyrics: the tall buildings of the big city, "automobiles", "exit signs and subway trains", where the "candy girls want candy boxes", and escape comes when it's time to "saddle the horses".

*

Now we're drunk and Brian's sitting with us.

"So — let me tell you about this bloke. He's got his 25th wedding anniversary coming up and his wife's vairy partic-lar. Doesn't want any rubbish for the entertainment, y'know. So e's all stressed aboud it, ringing everyone he knows and there's nothin. E's walking back to the station from his posh London office one evening and e's had enough."

I'm kind of listening. Lager makes everything as warm and soft as the pub curtains. I'm a baby in a womb of swirly brown velveteen chairs and orange and burgundy-flowered carpet. And I'm also kind of watching Elaine. Cat-eyed under her bob fringe. I only know it's 'Elaine' because that's what they've called her, the people at the table opposite.

"He's walking back to the train station past this community centre place, a tatty old place, and he hears this music. It's the most be-yew-tiful thing e's ever heard — he can't believe it, piano music like somethin from heaven. It's a rap-sody. Heaven! Goes in,

---

[105] Kelly, Jennifer, 'At the Source of the Blue Nile: an interview with Paul Buchanan', *Pop Matters*, 30 January 2013.

[106] Brown, Allan, ibid., p7.

and he thinks, what, eh? There's just this rough lookin feller sitting at an old piano. Like a tramp he is. He stands with him and listens while he's playin and he can't believe it. He's amazed by it. So the bloke asks him what's that song called, it's magical. And the feller says — yeah, yeah, nice isn it? I call it 'Bend over darling, I'm goin to do you up the arse'."

Brian sucks on his fag, his face scrunching hard.

Elaine looks over to our corner. She's seen me looking and I don't care. Eyes meet and stick for one dangerous moment.

"'Well — er, er, hmmm, thas a very unusual name isn't it,' the posh man says. Doesn know what to make of it. But the music. God, it's so be-yew-tiful he's got to have him, he doesn't have to mention the names of the songs does he? 'You tidy yourself up, come wearing a suit and tie on the night, and I'll pay you whatever you want'. Deal's done."

Looking again. Can't help it. Sugar and trouble when she looks back.

"It's the night of his big posh do, his wife all dolled up in her best frock and pearls. Got his posh friends all there and this bloke starts playing on a great big grand piano. The music's okay, but to be honest, nothing special, y'know stuff you'd get anywhere, like in a supermarket. The bloke's promised everyone this special night of music they'll never forget, and they've just got this bit of piano. So he goes up to him and says 'what's happened? it's not the same as I heard the other night'. 'Well, I've got to be honest with you,' says this piano feller, 'I really need to have a wank, I've got to have one.' He's desperate isn he? 'I'll just go to the toilet and when I come back everything'll be good'. Off he goes, and you know what? It's true. Now all of a sudden the music's brilliant and everyone's lovin it, all this gorr-geous music."

One more look and that'll mean she's definitely seen me. Tonight, something will have happened, at least one time.

"But after the next song is finished the bloke rushes over, cos something else isn't right — cos — cos — " Brian's turned purple. "'Look!' he says, 'the music's wonderful. But —' he says. 'Do you know, your flies undone, your cock's hanging out and there's semen all down your trousers?' 'Oh yes! don worry' says the ol piano feller, 'I'm going to play that one for you later...' he said 'I'm playin it for you later!'"

She gets up and they go. Doesn't look back.

*

The Go-Betweens started out in a world of salad days, playing gigs by the side of swimming pools, at barbecue parties and student refectories; once even at a pineapple plantation. In a Brisbane gig scene dominated by heavy metal and prog rock they were a sunshine band from the golden West, sharing something of the sounds of The Byrds, The Mamas and the Papas, Creedence Clearwater Revival and Jonathan Richman's Modern Lovers. Most of all they wanted to be like The Monkees. It was going to be perfect, thought Robert, "you hang around a house, you write great songs, you have wacky adventures, you meet strange characters, there's lots of laughter"[107]. Even when they tried to get serious it wouldn't stick. The first band name chosen by Robert was 'The Godots' from the Samuel Beckett play ("The band everyone's been waiting for"). But for their first perform-ance this was tidied up on the posters to something that sounded more like a groovy beat combo, 'The Go Dots'. The horseplay was all happening off-duty, and in their early shows they weren't always having much fun. As Nick Cave suggested while in conversation with Grant, "you always kind of exploited the nervous, sensitive artist thing. I'm not being unkind, but uncomfortable and awkward on stage, that's what the Go-Betweens were kinda about." Grant had agreed. "I felt I was impersonating someone. It took me a long time to feel comfortable."[108] They were never likely to blend into the Brisbane punk scene. Most band members, they discovered, were: "honest to God crooks who lived by stealing cars and robbing chem-ists...the way we looked and played made them treat us like some sort of odd pet." They only ever had one glass thrown at them, said Grant, and that was a liqueur glass. "Even the people who didn't like us threw wimpy glasses!"[109]

They conquered Brisbane in those early years. The next chapter was meant to be set in New York, said Robert.

For Grant and I, it was our spiritual home, the 'Promised Land', straight-up. Everyone that we ever liked seemed to pass through there.

---

[107] Interview with Robert Forster, *Live! Queensland* band exhibition, 12 June 2013.

[108] 'Grant McLennan and Nick Cave', GQ magazine, 1993.

[109] Pye, Ian, 'On the Brisbane Beat', *Melody Maker*, 26 June 1982.

Though we liked Australian and European things, New York was the real myth and beauty. Where do I start? The late '50s, commuter trains, people coming into NYC drinking martinis and popping tablets and working in skyscrapers. The Lovin' Spoonful, Bob Dylan, Truman Capote, Marlon Brando, James Dean, Warhol. It goes on and on and on. It was a place of myth, and we thought about it a good deal before we got there. It was like Rome and it was like Paris, wrapped up in film and books and magazines and songs.[110]

The more practical, low-budget option turned out to be London, the other global centre for the record industry. They didn't have a single label contact to try. They were just going to turn up and run from one big record company to the next with their guitars, wow the bosses with their understated genius and settle in somewhere around a log fire drinking tea from china cups, slurping from their saucers. But as soon as they arrived in London in 1979 the dream soon lost its charm. The capital of the old Empire was just another industrial city suffering from years of decline, it was dog-eared and broken. Between 1979 and 1982 unemployment rates in London were higher than the national average and its population was shrinking. Tourism, seen at the time as being the most likely saviour of the capital's economy, was stuck in a slump[111]. They flew in from Brisbane to find a small, tired country, where even the London trees and parks and squares were greyish, their colours subdued, plants stunted, cringing against the cold and grimy air. Much of the city was derelict, "a flat, never-ending, maze-like village" looking like "the shabbier parts of Brisbane"[112] and the boys didn't like the idea of "walking the eerie council estate parks and entering piss-stained lifts"[113], "lewd sex-worker cards spill-

---

[110] Canino, Gary, 'The Go-Betweens', *Bomb* magazine, 2015.

[111] Beckett, Andy, *Promised You a Miracle - Why 1980-82 Made Modern Britain*, Penguin, 2015, p147.

[112] Forster, Robert, *Grant & I*, ibid., p64.

[113] Ibid., p151.

ing out of telephone booths"[114]. "The economy is at the worst it's been I think since the 17th Century," said Grant at the time, "public services are deplorable, no one really seems to enjoy living there…It's a country which I think doesn't know the word imagination anymore. They seem to have sucked everything they can out of the pop form, which is something the English have always traditionally understood. But I find most of their music now very sterile and I wouldn't recommend anyone go there unless they're interested in corpses."[115] They didn't take to Londoners either. "We don't really loik the English…Part of me is glad that Thatcher is in power in this country, because she might screw and dry up the English people to the point where they'll have to turn around and just open up and be more human and friendly."[116] Their quiet confidence ran out. Doors stayed closed to the two expectant young Australians, sitting poised in so many office waiting-rooms, under the eyes of secretaries: Grant and his "relaxed amiability and intense seriousness", Robert's "straightforward manner it's easy to mistake for glumness"[117].

It was only by accident that their first trip to Britain led to anything. Edwyn was dropping off copies of 'Falling and Laughing' to the Rough Trade shop when he spotted the 'Lee Remick' single. He'd heard the Go-Betweens on John Peel's Radio 1 show and his ears had pricked up when he heard the band was in town. The Go-Betweens hurried up to Glasgow to meet the transparent-spectacled-one, sample some of Alan's razor wit and become a Postcard band — just for the one single as it turned out ('I Need Two Heads'). They played in Glasgow and Edinburgh, nowhere else in the UK, and returned to Brisbane sheepishly, in an ambiguous position. London was firmly shut to them, they'd gone back empty-handed. But they were still part of the Postcard thing, receiving an upswell of attention they could at least see happening from a great distance, if only through the wrong end of the telescope — news only arrived second-hand and weeks

---

[114] Ibid., p309.

[115] Condon, Dan, ibid.

[116] Watson, Don, 'The Go-Betweens: Up From Down Under', *New Musical Express*, 26 November 1983.

[117] Ibid.

late via the British music press. It was a false start. Just like their debut album recorded in Australia, *Send Me a Lullaby*, it was a hopeful experiment that lacked a script and direction, that was expected to somehow work out but was never likely to. The romance needed a shove from someone with the combination of know-how and idealism to make it work out. Again, that meant Geoff Travis and Rough Trade.

*

Geoff had a *Dice Man* moment in 1974 while he was teaching at a girls' school in London. "I walked out to the bus stop and waited for the bus to come and take me to work. When it hadn't arrived after a while I thought, I don't know if I really want to keep doing this. I decided to wait five minutes and if the bus came in that time I'd get on it and go to work and carry on with the course and maybe my life. If it didn't arrive, I'd chuck everything in. It didn't arrive."[118] Geoff was one of the Seventies' radicals fascinated by the possibilities of collectivism and co-operation, who rejected the comfortable options made possible by his family background and Oxbridge degree. He'd lived on a kibbutz, moved from squat to squat, seen the tail-end of American beatnik culture and bought a whole shop-load of cheap vinyl from the thrift stores. All the drop-out adventures were resolved eventually into a little record shop collective at 202 Kensington Park Road that was opened for business in Christmas 1975.

Geoff's anti-establishment style was velvet smooth. "Tall and gangling. And he had that famous Afro. A piercing gaze. Very softly spoken," remembered Geoff's early Rough Trade collaborator Vivien Goldman. "One of those intelligent people who know they don't have to shout about their intelligence...very fair and very committed, very obviously socially committed. Idealistic."[119] To get anywhere in the record business, Geoff needed to be more than nice. The record industry hadn't built an empire on being fair-minded, it was a business more based on

---

[118] Taylor, Neil, *Document and Eyewitness: An Intimate History of Rough Trade*, Orion Books, 2010, p37.

[119] Ibid., p28.

confidence tricks and sharp practice where artists and performers were given the razzle dazzle and made to sign away their creations. Seventies' chart-topper Gilbert O'Sullivan, as one example, earned just £500,000 from label revenues of around £14.5 million. Labels would often be fined for campaigns aimed at rigging the all-powerful Gallup charts (sales figures were taken from just 275 shops around the country, a workable number that could be targeted with aggressive promotions, given free posters and t-shirts)[120].

Geoff was driven by the possibility of a business based on both good music and integrity. "We were happy in our own little world — there was a logic and beauty to it," he said. "And the real world's taste is so terrible."[121] He made it work, first of all, by being able to pick out genuine quality and originality from the hodge-podge of gigging bands who just wanted to be the next Clash: bands like the Smiths, Everything But The Girl, the Jesus & Mary Chain, the Strokes; by working closely with his artists on the behind-the-scenes mechanics of operations, getting them to hump boxes if necessary. Crucially, Geoff had his own distribution network. The Cartel was separate from the industry giants, an alliance between Rough Trade and Small Wonder in London and Red Rhino, Probe and Revolver out in the regions. "This is what people forget: back then, the records used to sell. Nowadays, you'd shift maybe two thousand if you were lucky. Back then, anything halfway decent sold from six to ten thousand," Geoff said[122]. The success of indie operations led to the first independent singles and albums charts in January 1980, making sure non-mainstream acts selling decent numbers could still be visible.

In early 1982, two and a half years after the first abortive British odyssey, the call came from Rough Trade, "one of the hippest labels on the planet"[123]. Having heard potential in *Send Me a Lullaby*, Geoff agreed to

---

[120] McSmith, Andy, *No Such Thing as Society*, Constable, 2011, p77.

[121] Hepworth, David, ibid., p201.

[122] Taylor, Neil, ibid., p107.

[123] Stenders, Kriv, ibid.

license the Go-Betweens debut album and finance a follow-up that was to be recorded in Britain. "This was a fucking *dream*," said Lindy[124].

*

Before Hollywood was written over the course of that summer. This time London didn't seem so alien. They settled in and the days and nights of song-writing and rehearsing contained an unexpected felicity. Like new trickles of grass and wildflowers blooming in the cracks of the city's dirty grey pavements and asphalt.

Still the band had no money to live on and that meant putting up with a muddle of squats and sharing places on a budget until the LP was out. It also meant trying to eke out some money as a little-known band playing clubs that were enduring their own hard times. "They don't give you any money, they don't give you any beers, the club's generally a real pit," said Robert. "You know, it's the middle of winter and they turn the heating off after about half an hour of the audience arriving," Lindy recalled. "So the audience are waiting for you to go on and they're all shivering. You go up to the promoter and say 'turn the heating on' he says 'Oh no, we've only got a little bit of oil left and we need to keep it for tomorrow'."[125]

Squatting was a hit-and-miss business. They would have been lucky to find heating or hot water, and there was always the danger of gatecrashers looking to get their own share of the facilities. "When we first arrived we were moving around a lot," recalled Lindy. "Rob and I had been squatting in Hampstead until we were kicked out of there. We ended up trying to fight them in the courts and lost. Fulham Palace Road was the best living conditions we had in our whole ten years in London. It was a huge home and I don't know how we managed to get the rent so cheap. Were they were laundering money or something? The Birthday Party [including Nick Cave] had rooms in the house as well. Kind of unworkable in

---

124 Ibid.

125 Nicholls, David, ibid., p119.

the end. They never did any cleaning."[126] Lindy was already doing enough cleaning work. "I was the only one of us who ever had a job. First time I was in London, earlier in the 1970s, I'd worked as a nanny to Georg Solti's kids, went with the family to Italy. It was really interesting to see rich people's houses by the Thames, and it was exciting to see that kind of life."[127]

Those penniless days together were remembered as a special time by all three. There was no money to spend on going to the cinema or pubs, so they ended up mooching around their shabby-genteel Georgian squat when they weren't rehearsing. Huge, elongated rooms that swallowed up their few bits and pieces of temporary furniture; high ceilings and tall windows letting in the watery London sunlight; unreal, echoing spaces. They'd inch their way out onto a sooty flat roof to create their own im-promptu sun terrace. Or they'd walk the empty daytime streets around them. The band lived surrounded by the upright, dignified architecture of homes designed in the Regency and early Victorian period to meet the needs of newly affluent middle classes during the housing speculation boom. Quiet places. Neglected. Moss in gutters and between the paving stones. The pillars, wrought iron balconies and private gated parks that had once been an exhibition of confidence and moral certainty. Now they were just streets being made to go on living through an age of reduced circumstances, temporarily embarrassed.

For the Go-Betweens, a gang of drifters needing a place to hide out for a while, the summer days were slow and easy and full. "It was a won-derful summer. It was all fun and exciting for me — just a careless and irresponsible time," said Lindy.

I was very happy to be out of Australia, which was stifling for me. Lots of drugs were being taken in the house, by us and some of the Bad Seeds too. The drug of choice for Grant was heroin and for me was always pot. Robert and I shared a huge room and we spent a lot of time working, he'd be writing and I'd be working on drum patterns.

---

[126] Morrison, Lindy, Skype interview, 11th March 2019.

[127] Ibid.

And there was a huge amount of reading. I was into Bloomsbury: Nancy Mitford, Victoria Glendinning's biography of Edith Sitwell. I always loved Simone de Beauvoir, and I remember loving Montgomery Clift's biography. I don't know what the boys were reading, probably Jeanette Winterson, Sylvia Plath, that kind of thing. Robert would be listening to a lot of Coltrane, Ornette Coleman. There was a huge jazz influence at that time — maybe because of Laughing Clowns [the Sydney band fronted by Ed Kuepper of The Saints] and their interest in jazz. There'd be Dylan, Iggy Pop.[128]

And this, another vignette from Lindy, captures some of the quiet pleasures of that moment in time.

In the early lean London days, Grant had lucked in for a couple of weeks and was staying in a flat with a television that worked AND a video player. He rented *The Misfits* (directed by one of his favourites, John Huston) and invited me over to watch it with him one chilly sunny London afternoon. We sat in silence as the dramatic tragic film unfolded and after it finished he fussed around making tea in a china pot and served to me at my chair in a china cup and saucer. We tentatively and quietly discussed the meaning of the film. As was usual, he stressed the importance of the role of the director and the writer [Arthur Miller] while I put the case that is was the actors that had made the film so wonderful.[129]

Robert's memory is different when it comes to the location for much of the summer. He puts them in St Charles Square, a tree-lined avenue in Ladbroke Grove and another grand terrace of mansions, crumbling steps leading up to the portico. Another four storeys of dejected former splendour. There was cheap rent because the owner who lived in the basement was friends with Geoff and the house was up for sale. "It was fairytale stuff — three musicians run away from home, break into a

---

128 Ibid.

129 Creswell, Toby, ibid.

deserted mansion, and are allowed to stay for one magical summer. We slept and worked by curtainless windows that looked out over gardens and rooftops, the moon within arm's reach above our sleeping heads."[130] Robert went to the newsagent for a paper each morning. They'd spend afternoons playing tennis, making trips to libraries and bringing back carrier bags full of books "to devour over long lazy days"[131].

The Go-Betweens had also begun to hang out with the Rough Trade crowd. They could afford to go and see their label mates play gigs because they'd have their names on the door. Lindy would make onion soup for Roddy when he came round to visit. Green, the star of the moment because of *Songs to Remember*, would be seen around the offices with his guitar and "a genius-in-residence sign flashing over his head"[132]. The boys played for the label's cricket team, The Old Roughians, watched occasionally by Joe Strummer (until Grant was banned "for nearly killing someone with a fast ball."[133]) There were nights out with Tracey Thorn and Ben Watt of Everything But the Girl, who remembered how the Go-Betweens were part of an Australian gang in London, "whose idea of fun is to arrive in a cab and go home in an ambulance."[134] Robert, said Tracey, was "tall, handsome and taciturn". He always had his head in a book. Tracey also found him oddly theatrical. When the four of them went on holiday together in Sussex, Robert took to wearing a long cape he'd bought at a village jumble sale[135]. The best part of Rough Trade for Lindy was Geoff himself, her doe eyes widening further in his presence: "I'd have done anything to be in his circle. He was this brilliant, unattain-

---

[130] Forster, Robert, *Grant & I*, ibid., p108/109.

[131] Ibid, p185.

[132] Ibid., p108.

[133] Taylor, Neil, ibid., p154.

[134] Thorn, Tracey, *Bedsit Disco Queen: How I Grew Up and Tried to Be a Pop Star*, Virago Press, 2013, p179/180.

[135] Ibid., 180.

able man"[136]; "incredibly intelligent, Jewish, handsome, gentle, intuitive."[137]

It wasn't the best of summers for Geoff's business. Rough Trade was starting to suffer from being in a market overloaded by start-up indie labels and new record stores. The shop had moved to larger premises at Blenheim Crescent, going deeper into Notting Hill, and that had meant more people on the payroll and more costs. Geoff was having to get tougher about how a 'good' enterprise could compete in a bad world.

*

Before Hollywood was the making of the Go-Betweens sound and identity, a great leap forward in quality from the band's debut. It was the product of a special coincidence of circumstances: first of all, a warm English summer, where even the grubbiest of streets, rundown shops and rusted railway bridges had been transfigured by rosy fingers and a balmy heat. Robert famously described the Go-Betweens as having "that striped sunlight sound", seeming to define them in terms that related only to Australia. But the particular sunlight sound was first made in Britain, not the wilting tropics but boreal places, where sunshine is felt as a blessing and a relief. At least for one summer, London was luminous and dark-sparkling, a space where the Go-Betweens' memories of the past were given the air, distance and contrast enough to be articulated in an emotional way, as a sound that expressed the momentary glitter of times past.

Another important circumstance was the close proximity of other former or current Rough Trade bands. Orange Juice and Aztec Camera were showing what could be done. The British scene both worked as models of possibility and confirmed their sense of otherness, and both were motivation for the band to keep working and creating: "In some ways it's really valuable, because you react against the complacency there and the

---

[136] Morrison, Lindy, ibid.

[137] Condon, Dan, ibid.

boredom. It pulls what strength you've got inside you out," said Grant[138]. London provided a position of perspective for Grant, who "never really felt Australian"[139]. There were no guarantees of rewards, not a career, but earnest creativity. Here were the conditions for a determined artistry, fragile hopes of recognition — the kind of environment found in the early days of film-making in America.

Old Hollywood and the lives of classic Hollywood stars and film-makers were a fascination for the band. Robert wrote a letter home from London early that summer, talking about how hot the weather had been and how he wants to make sure the new LP has some "conversational drama" about it. Then his attention drifts.

> Princess Grace's death is very upsetting, it seemed only a minor accident. I think James Stewart could die soon. To know he's still alive and to see his old films from the thirties, that time in between is a wonderful life for him to look back on. But so much of Hollywood is dying, did you see that series Hollywood? There was one episode on Hollywood in the beginning, the building of the sets, the sun of California and the people who worked early Hollywood. Early Hollywood is a great period of history, a combination that's perfect, of huge casts, stars, intellectual directors and hack directors.[140]

There had always been a sense of affinity among band members with the uniquely glamorous character of this lost age. One of the first names considered for the band was 'The Hepburns', after Katharine. "Robert was dreaming of another time that was more innocent, what it would have been like to have been in LA," said Lindy[141], before Hollywood became a commercial machine, the homogenisation of process and output. They shared a longing for a time when the other-worldly glamour was real, not

---

[138] Ibid.

[139] Nicholls, David, ibid., p125.

[140] Ibid., p121.

[141] Morrison, Lindy, ibid.

drummed up for the sake of publicity; when success could be sudden and romantic, not just paid for. This was exactly what the Go-Betweens wanted: to be the kind of exceptional talent that comes from nowhere and breaks all expectations and conventions.

The marathon of writing over the lonely London summer stirred up feelings of loss. What had been left in past, like the years of Hollywood, Brisbane, home and people. "It was a long goodbye to the country of exile," Peter Milton Walsh has written of the songs, "a kiss blown from a train window. It was not simply despair but, like something by [film director Michelangelo] Antonioni, the most beautiful kind of despair."[142]

"Robert would spend his days writing songs," remembered Lindy. "He was always writing, and he'd find it hard."[143] Robert was striving to hit that note of drama. What comes out is restless self-examination, the thwarted man. "My head fits/ Into my hands/ I roll it around/ And nothing comes out"; "It's thunder town they'll do/ What they can to hold your down".

"Robert is in some ways more unsure of things than I," suggested Grant. "I think that nervousness and unsureness might come out in his music and his lyrics. I tend to be more sentimental in some ways, I'm interested in poetry a lot more, I think, as well. To try and be clear — that's what I learned from writing poetry. I think the great poets are very clear. It should be concise. It should be just like crystal."[144] For the first time, Grant started to look back to personal memories in his lyrics. And immediately he came upon his father. 'Dusty in Here' is where the album is stopped in its tracks by sudden, choking recollection. Stands still and looks around, seeing how we never quite leave the past behind us. It's not one particular place that's "cold and dusty", everywhere is haunted by pervasive loss. In this state of anxious, preternatural awareness, nothing is normal or entirely innocent: "In the dark/ When shadows have their way/ A finger's a chimney/ And the moon's on fire". The laws of physical nature are too

142 Walsh, Peter Milton, ibid.

143 Morrison, Lindy, ibid.

144 Gumprecht, Blake, ibid.

simple to account for the strangeness of things, for moments like these when ghosts are watching, with a presence so strong that Grant has to experience the loss of his father all over again. "You won't write, no you won't write/ That's all I ask, that you just write/ And you say no, that you can't speak".

Side two opens with the Go-Betweens most celebrated song, 'Cattle and Cane'. Grant is a boy again, coming home from Churchie to the Queensland outback. He wrote 'Cattle and Cane' for his mother, maybe the only way he could broach the subject of the past, to make a nod of recognition to the shared pain of memory without succumbing to sentimentality, and he would sing it to her down a phone line because the cattle farm where she lived couldn't get the 240 volts of electricity needed for a record player. "Singing about cane fields and livestock and stuff in 1982 brought a lot of warmth to me. It was a strange town and we were trying to work our way through the London music scene. And that song some way carried sunshine in it. It came so easy and I was using someone else's guitar."[145] It was a guitar borrowed from Nick Cave while he lay comatose from heroin in a flat in Shepherd's Bush. Cave complained afterwards that he was never able to play anything on it, that Grant had stolen the guitar's only tune. There might be sunshine in 'Cattle and Cane' but the childhood memories are still elegiac: the unspeakable poignancy of having left his father's watch to ruin in the shower, the air full of cinders from burning fields. The song's meaning is made explicit in the single phrase "memory wastes". "[M]emory can be a wasteland where you wander around and live the rest of your life," explained Grant[146]. The juddery drum rhythm is unsettling. It's so unusual no-one's been able to pin it down: a mix of a 5/4 time signature with 2/4, 7/4 and more conventional 4/4. Maybe even a 13/8 — something more likely to turn up in jazz fusion. Whatever it is, it confirms the song isn't meant to be serene nostalgia. It was seen as the best kind of challenge by Lindy. "Rehearsing was fun. The guys weren't aware they were asking for strange times, it's just the way it turned out. Other drummers would have strangled that out and gone back to conventional

---

[145] 'The Acoustic Stories', *That Striped Sunlight Sound* DVD, August 2005.

[146] Nicholls, David, ibid., p126.

times, but I enjoyed that circular, skewed feel. It was the best drumming I ever did because I was left alone to create the beats I wanted to."[147] Oddly for such a personal song, 'Cattle and Cane' was completed by a footnote from Robert, asked by Grant to contribute his riff of impressions for the run-out: "I recall the same/ A reply/ A plan you once had/ Time out of mind and that time was bad/ So I knew where I was/ Alone, and so at home."

The melancholy and loss is also there in 'Two Steps Step Out' ("Tried faith and drugs and gold/It didn't work, I couldn't fill the hole"), there was only love left, and that was a long, maybe impossibly long road ("I'd walk a hundred miles/ a thousand miles, a million miles").

*

"We had to make a classic," said Robert in 2016. "Our first album was not a classic album, and you don't know how many chances you're going to get."[148] All those years had passed and still it was *Before Hollywood* that Robert believed to be the best Forster/McLennan set. "It's a beautiful record. There's a timelessness to it."[149] The route to vinyl is a familiar one from the last chapter: John Brand, Eastbourne, Bernie on piano, the band sharing bunk beds in the studio's one-room residential quarters.

"We'd never really worked with a producer, and we talked with Geoff Travis about our fantasy candidates, people like Lindsey Buckingham [Fleetwood Mac] and Robbie Robertson [The Band]. But John Brand walked into our rehearsal room, taped us, then walked back the next day with the songs written out and with arrangement ideas; no one had ever done that with our music…Aztec Camera walked out the door and we walked in, and John made two classics."[150]

---

[147] Morrison, Lindy, ibid.

[148] Mulvey, John, 'Robert Forster, Album by Album', *Uncut*, 18 January 2016.

[149] The Go-Betweens, *Tell Tales*, Beggars Banquet promotional cassette, 1996.

[150] Mulvey, John, ibid.

"Once again back at ICC with all the limitations of time and equipment," said John. This time he was working with an older, more experienced three-piece who were less distracted by the Eastbourne nightlife. They'd toured and the songs had been rehearsed over and over again in London, so recording was easier. "*Before Hollywood* already had a conception, the band knew how they wanted the songs to go for the most part. They needed guidance for a lot of the arrangements, but mostly I was responsible for finding the sound and the balance of the instruments, and again [like *High Land, Hard Rain*] we created a great atmosphere with the dryness of the studio. Outside of the studio in the flat they were more studious I guess. Both Robert and Grant spent the long hours of 'off time' reading and writing. A lot less partying." The bigger challenge was cohering the output of two songwriters: "Their songs are very different and they were both entirely responsible for the way their own songs developed. Both were sensitive souls in their own way, Grant's songs are obviously more melodic, Robert's more rhythmic. This stemmed from their individual singing abilities and styles. There were some challenges for Lindy — the time signatures were often very complex — but they were well rehearsed and she got through the backing tracks without too much blood!"[151]

Geoff Travis knew the Go-Betweens had a commercial indie LP inside them and Brand was brought in to find a balance of melody and edge, emotion and anxiety. "My role was to deliver a more rounded album I guess. We had a lot of fun experimenting with guitar and drum sounds, with different amps and heads."[152] There were many straggle ends to tie together. The songs on *Before Hollywood* are frayed with little detours, unexpected turnings, snatched glimpses of vistas; often there's a jazz-like structure, the use of repetition for creating tension, a break into melody. "John Brand caught all the fire, all the angles and the beauty we had, and added to it," said Robert[153].

Lindy finished the drum tracks early. "I could wander around Eastbourne, which I loved. I went up to London to get some pot for John

151 Brand, John, Email exchange, 11 June 2019.

152 Ibid.

153 The Go-Betweens, *Tell Tales*, ibid.

and the band, but I ended up getting robbed at Victoria Station. I lost the money and the pot. Highly embarrassing. The saddest thing was that on the first day we arrived in Eastbourne I had a toothache. Rather than interfere with plans, I got a dentist to just pull it out. It's only recently that I've had an implant, I just got used to having the gap. All done so I wouldn't fuck up the recording."[154]

Eastbourne's autumnal mood was fitting. Their special summer had come to an end in a place made slow by long memories, where the evenings were drawing in over the nineteenth century promenade. "I thought it was romantic," said Grant, "I do like the faded glamour of the English seaside."[155] Robert added: "We were 24, 25, it was the time when you'd just start the flickerings of reflecting, looking back...it had just started to dawn on you, a whole other set of emotions."[156] The photo on the LP cover was taken in a shop on Fulham Palace Road. A brooding portrait among some remnants of past, unknown lives. It's reminiscent of Bob Dylan's *Bringing It All Back Home* (1965), ("Must have been something the boys thought up," said Lindy, "I didn't know."[157]) The sequencing was supposedly based around another American classic, the Beach Boys' *Surf's Up* (1971). According to this thinking, 'Dusty in Here' is positioned like 'Disney Girls'; 'Ask' is the rowdy 'Student Demonstration Time'; 'Cattle and Cane' opens side two like 'Feel Flows'.

The subject of *Before Hollywood* was: "Childhood, lost love and lost utopias," argued the *NME*. "The Go-Betweens yearn for the elusive, the perfection that may once have been but never will again...a rare masterpiece"[158]. Edwyn wrote the review for Melody Maker: "A monumental record...very, very insidious [sic]. On repeated plays I find it very, very

---

[154] Morrison, Lindy, ibid.

[155] Ware, Gareth, 'The Go-Betweens', *London in Stereo*, 21 February 2015.

[156] Ibid.

[157] Morrison, Lindy, ibid.

[158] Snow, Mat, 'Absolutely Sweet Betweens', *New Musical Express*, 26 March 1983.

moving."[159] While the reviews were strong, the lack of pop immediacy meant there were obstacles. Some liked the complexity, some not. "A little static for rock and roll," wrote Robert Christgau of *Village Voice*, "but as poetry reading goes, quite kinetic."[160] "It's as if they write sweet songs, Postcard ditties, then impale them to the ground with lead stakes. Instead of flowing, the songs writhe under dead beats," complained *NME*'s Barney Hoskyn[161]. But he was contradicted by fellow *NME* writer, Don Watson: "Now the slightest voice of early Postcard comes up with perhaps the most brilliant expression of its promise. The message that comes through The Go-Betweens' glisten is that this is no time to be disheartened. This is a time rather to grasp for the few grains of brilliance that still sparkle in the sand-heap...On record they reach for intangible strands of feeling and catch fine cobwebs of melody, entrancing with light strokes of surrealism, catching the heart with their immaculate deceptions."[162]; "*Before Hollywood*, their masterpiece to date, stands as undoubtedly one of the most underrated of the year – a hard centred exploration in the art of melody unique in a time of soggy pop dropsy."[163]

As Grant explained to *Melody Maker*, just ahead of the recording sessions: "I think we are a pop group, but we're the most unusual pop group there's ever been. Although we work with melody, we sometimes work against it, and that's like one of the cardinal sins of pop music."[164]

*

---

[159] 'Singles Reviewed by Edwyn Collins of Orange Juice', *Melody Maker*, 12 March 1983.

[160] Christgau, Robert, Review of *Before Hollywood*, www.robertchristgau.com

[161] Hoskyns, Barney, 'Ridiculous and Wonderful: The Smiths/The Go-Betweens at the Venue, London', *New Musical Express*, 1983.

[162] Watson, Don, 'The Go-Betweens: King's College, London', *New Musical Express*, 4 June 1983.

[163] Watson, Don, 'The Go-Betweens: Up From Down Under', *New Musical Express*, 26 November 1983.

[164] Barber, Lynden, ibid.

Grant was in Trafalgar Square in 1983 when he first heard Radio 1 play 'Cattle and Cane'. "I felt like the Beatles must have felt hearing 'She Loves You' on the radio the first time!" he said. "An incredible buzz. It still happens – if you've got a song and it's on the radio, it reminds you of that feeling when you were a kid listening to the radio."[165]

There weren't to be many moments like this. When Lindy had made her trip back to London she'd got a lift with Geoff. "He said he'd been listening to commercial radio and realised he'd been way off. He needed a more commercial band. I should have seen then we were going to be dropped."[166] That commercial band turned out to be the Smiths, Geoff's vehicle for putting his foot down and burning rubber away from the limitations of indie, the debts of his shop and the disorganisation around him. From then on, Rough Trade would work according to a business plan. Dave Harper was at Rough Trade at the time: "The Go-Betweens had been on an upward trajectory and got eclipsed totally by The Smiths, and it got very bitter. 'Fucking Geoff won't return our calls, we're going round in this shithole van and it's not really happening' [the quote isn't attributed — but sounds like Lindy]."[167] The Smiths were a curse to them. "We were very proud to be on Rough Trade, to be part of that stable," Lindy says. "But it all changed when the Smiths signed. It used to be fun, just a mess, people everywhere, smoking pot. Then one time we went in and everyone was at their desks, really quiet and no fun. Ignoring us. What's happened? 'The Smiths are coming in,' they said. That was the change in culture. The Smiths were a bunch of arseholes."[168]

Another cliché the Go-Betweens were never able to shake off was their lack of commercial success. "The Go-Betweens produced records of quiet brilliance and got nowhere. Sting sang about a sodding turtle and became a millionaire," said *Select* magazine reflecting on the injustice of

[165] Mills, Fred, 'The Go-Betweens: Their Back Pages', *Harp*, June 2005.

[166] Morrison, Lindy, ibid.

[167] King, Richard, *How Soon is Now — The Madmen and Mavericks who made Independent Music 1975-2005*, Faber & Faber, 2012, p213.

[168] Morrison, Lindy, ibid.

the Eighties' marketplace[169]. As Tracey Thorn claimed, they were "seemingly the best-reviewed band of all time"[170] and that still meant nothing when there were no 'hits' and smallish audiences at gigs. The Go-Betweens had to move from label to label and were sometimes left without a deal. Touring was expensive and the 'tour support' from record companies was only an advance on cash that had to be paid back from future sales. It meant the band's income was always being strangled. "For the next twenty-six years we received no record royalties outside Australia for *Liberty Belle*, *Tallulah* or *16 Lovers Lane* — until Beggars [Banquet] wiped the remaining twelve thousand pounds of debt in 2015."[171] The year after *Before Hollywood* was released, Grant said they were "negotiating with Alcoa Aluminium to write jingles"[172], and was only probably joking. Even after hitting a new high of recognition in 1986 with the *Liberty Belle and the Black Diamond Express* album, Robert found himself walking around with plastic bags over his shoes to keep out the wet from the London streets.

Fame didn't ever matter to Lindy, who's sick of being asked about it. They had been a success on their own terms. They'd been themselves, had the chance to be creative and been appreciated by the discerning. "The same recurring question — it's why I stopped doing interviews. I was never interested in fame. I always understood how we fitted in, we were too quaint, too unique to be big. A woman on drums was never going to work in Australia, it was better in the UK…but still."[173]

The boys were asked, again, how they felt about their lack of success by the *NME* in 1984.

Robert: "We've known all these groups, from Orange Juice to the Birthday Party, Aztec Camera, the Smiths, and bang! six months later they're very successful. It's very interesting because you can see the

---

[169] Nicholls, David, ibid., p14.

[170] Thorn, Tracey, ibid., p180.

[171] Forster, Robert, *Grant & I*, ibid., p207/208.

[172] Gumprecht, Blake, ibid.

[173] Morrison, Lindy, ibid.

route of how it happened because you're so close to it. Everyone else around us seems to be stars…"

"It's all right," soothes Grant. "In the reflected light we look the stars!"

Robert: "We're the friends of the stars!"

Grant: "We run out and buy their Chinese meals…"[174]

*

You could have your own vision, separate from the mainstream. That was all working out okay. You could have a sense of purpose informed by a cultured, precisely-formed kind of beauty. But was anyone else ever going to hear the subtlety and sensitivity involved? With so many problems in the world, could the music be used to change anything?

---

[174] Snow, Mat, 'The Go-Betweens: Money Can't Buy You Love', ibid.

4.

What Difference Does it Make?
The Smiths, *The Smiths* (February 1984)

*L*ike a Victorian factory in a moorland vale at night, lights burning in every window, the print works are an ominous sight. Townsfolk who sleep innocently in their beds are shut in against the goblin nightwork of the industrial estate and its juddering, thrumming, maddening din; the chambers made claustrophobic by choking smells of ink and wax where hot metal workers tend constantly to arcane machines, feeding them with lead, working the keys, banging at slugs to keep the words in line.

This night's job is worse than any other. The words have a madcap intensity that might at any moment turn the slugs into runaway trains, swarms of metal snakes with all the determined sense of nonsense.

Morning comes like convalescence after an illness. The silver skies of England are mustard-streaked with cloud, skies that are fleet and chill, promising another day of muddle, sun one minute and rain the next. Elderly delivery lorries, the drudges of the roads, make their way out from the depot with boulders of paper goods to trade for another day along with their own greasy currency of mud. The places they're heading for are nowhere convenient for a delivery, just boltholes in brambles of sprawl, the ribbons roads and lean-to estates with nowhere to park without causing an obstruction, no spaces for turning, no place to stop for a fag.

Newsagents were some of the the last remnants of the old British way of shopping: heavy ill-fitting doors and bells, opening with a shove onto an extravagance of mundane pleasures. Every inch of space is a rainbow of noisy brands and old stock laid out in a thick carpet over the counter and shelves, a confusion of *Woman's Weekly*, pocket-money toys, knitting wool and jars of pear drops; stuffed in alongside them, signs of the new world of computer magazines and Wispa bars. There's something for everyone in those caves of sugar, gloss coatings and polypropelene. A morning copy of the *Daily Mirror*; Silk Cut and a Mars bar for lunch time; a quarter pound of cola-cubes and candy cigarettes for the kids, a box of Terry's Carousel to watch telly with. And for the teenager who doesn't want pineapple chunks anymore, who wants the whole sad commerce of civilisation to burn, there's the *New Musical Express*.

Morrissey was born on the morning of 14 May 1983 in the warm, finger-dirtying pages of the *NME*. It wasn't his first press interview, but the first with a music paper that would play a large part in the making of his reputation. An article with a headline written at the only moment in time when the band was less well-known than the bags of crisps. Cath Carroll wrote 'Crisp Songs and Salted Lyrics' about her interview with Morrissey, the "colourful Mancunian" who was immediately understood to be more than just a spokesperson for a no-synths four-piece. He was going to lead his own invisible insurrection of a million minds: "Smithsville could be anywhere, a timeless zone where high school and low-life collide. They're the young generation an' they've got something to say. Hey, hey it's The Smiths...The Smiths extend a gracious hello to even the squarest squares."[1]

Morrissey had made embryonic appearances in the music press as author of mini gig reviews for *Record Mirror*, written under the pen name 'Sheridan Whiteside'. Whiteside was the lead character in classic Broadway comedy *The Man Who Came to Dinner*, a confrontational egoist. Sheridan spoke his mind, however inappropriate his vinegar wit might sound to the ears of polite company. A long correspondence with the *NME*'s letters page was a demonstration of the Whiteside-manner that Morrissey had under cultivation. "Go and see them first and then you may have the audacity to contradict me, you stupid sluts," concluded one epistle in defence

[1] Carroll, Cath, 'Crisp Songs and Salted Lyrics', *New Musical Express*, 14 May 1983.

of Buzzcocks[2]. Morrissey was desperate to write for the music press, and the *NME* in particular, to be part of that circle of contradictory voices, its spite and sarcasm, its ability to translate indie music into something more than just an entertainment product. "The British music press is an art form," said Morrissey in 1983[3]. And looking back in 2007: "The *New Musical Express* was a propelling force that answered to no one. It led the way by the quality of its writers — Paul Morley, Julie Burchill, Paul DuNoyer, Charles Shaar Murray, Nick Kent, Ian Penman, [Barry] Miles — who would write more words than the articles demanded, and whose views saved some of us, and who pulled us away from the electrifying boredom of everything and anything that represented the industry...the torrential fluency of its writers left almost no space between words, and the *NME* became a culture in itself."[4] He eventually realised the *NME* didn't want him as a writer. He'd been "greeted with disinterest"[5] and the thwarted journalist turned to an alternative route. "The artist must educate the critic," said Morrissey at the start of his performing career in 1983, quoting his beloved Oscar Wilde[6]. Writing the words — both for the music and about the music — was a way of magicking the genie from the limitations of its industry bottle, releasing a sense of purpose into the wider world. Because while making music was a start, he believed that making music meaningful — even Messianic — was the more worthwhile ambition. By 1985 Morrissey would be on the cover of *NME* posing as Jesus Christ.

The Smiths made studied, divinely elegant indie guitar music; exactly the kind of tasteful but bruising sound that an *NME* critic would dream of making for themselves. What really made the Smiths the longed-for crossover act, both foxily cultish and mainstream, was Morrissey. Inter-

---

[2] Long, Pat, *The History of the NME: High Times and Low Lives at the World's Most Famous Music Magazine*, Portico Books, 2012. p160.

[3] McCullough, Dave, 'Handsome Devils', *Sounds*, 4 June 1983.

[4] Morrissey, 'I abhor racism and apologise — for speaking to the *NME*', *The Guardian*, 4 December 2007.

[5] Interview with Morrissey, *David Jensen Show*, BBC Radio 1, 26 June 1983.

[6] Interview with Morrissey, recorded as part of ICA's Rock Week, London, 5 October 1983.

views with the *NME*, *Sounds*, *Melody Maker* and others became his means of imparting a worldview that turned the prosaic business of vinyl releases into something more like opening up a subscription to a public cause: the confirmation of how modern life could be empty and dismal, unfeeling and unkind; a predicament accompanied by a piquant melange of bitter-sweet emotions as both protest and compensation. Morrissey and his Smiths would smash away the superficial and unpleasant until all that was left was a sense of a workable identity, something solid and defiant. No longer lost in petty fears, boredom and letdowns. The *NME* became known by the scoffers, lamely, as the *New Morrissey Express*, because of the number of cover features he was granted in the early Nineties. "[W]e put Morrissey on the cover whenever the occasion demanded and many times when it signally didn't," wrote *NME* staffer Stuart Maconie[7]. "The result was the same, the paper flew off the shelves. In fact, and this is curious, the *NME* when adorned with the (usually shirtless) Morrissey regularly sold more copies than the current Morrissey single that the piece was pegged around."

The interviews and their revelations were a ritual and a tease. From the beginning, Morrissey knew the media razzle was an illusion (and more Paul Daniels than Merlin). Publications like the *NME* liked to stir up a cauldron of emotions. Fascination, adoration, loathing, love and sex were all in the steaming pot. In the case of the Smiths, the role of the music press in delivering information on what was happening in the music world, independent criticism and discussion, seemed to become by comparison an irrelevance. Morrissey was a phenomenon animated by the sudden acceleration in commercialisation; a music press that wanted to be taken seriously; by his ability to horrify the tabloids. It was a time and a place when he could be unbearable.

In the end it was always likely that Morrissey would dwindle to become a curiosity of indie. The quality of his work — the lyrics, the voice, the intensity — were all still there, but he was having to swim in a water other than his natural element of Eighties' cultural angst.

---

[7] Maconie, Stuart, *Cider with Roadies*, Ebury Press, 2004, p233.

*

In the early part of the decade, the *NME* was the soapbox for indie. Musicians might read *Melody Maker* for the classified job ads, metal fans preferred *Sounds,* but the *NME* was the one to break news from the weirder frontiers where some crazy-headed eccentrics were rising up. It was just another phase in the life of a music newspaper that was first published in October 1946 and stayed on newsagent shelves until 2018. The *New Musical Express* was originally a professional publication aimed at crooners and jazz players who played in clubs and bars with the big bands, made for an age when musicians were bohos: louche, cigar-chewing grifters with week-old oily-hair and frayed suits. The whole lot of them praying to get a place on an American tour.

Melody Maker (1926-2000) was the incumbent to the throne of top music paper, the establishment. In the Fifties it was *Melody Maker* that thad been the more open-minded when it came to the proletarian noise of rock and roll. Struggling to compete for sales, *Sounds* (1970-1991) was always looking to find its own niche, encouraging editors to take a punt on new trends, throwing itself into punk. *Record Mirror* (1954-1991) made its name by running the first features on the Beatles and the Rolling Stones, but lost out in the battle for readers with *Smash Hits* after it turned to a similar mix of chart pop and lip-glossed comedy from 1982 onwards.

By the end of the 1970s, the *NME* was a languid and long-haired character, stretched out among the dog-ends of decadence. Secretly hoping someone would come along and clean up the mess. The Carnaby Street office was a place for popping amphetamines to wake up, smoking weed to wind down, lunchtimes at the pub, then heading out for the serious business of a night on the tiles. Rather than bother with going home, writers would sometimes choose to go back to the office and sleep in the muggy record review room, a windowless cubby hole. With no receptionist, musicians like Joe Strummer, Elvis Costello and Paul Weller would wander in and out. Readers would come along too, for a rant or a chance to hang out with the big name journos. "At the *NME* no-one gave a fuck about what you did as long as you did your job," said Charles Shaar Murray. "It was rock 'n' roll, not children's television."[8] They were a "free-floating raft of misfits" according to Danny Baker. "We used to push the desks back and play football in the office. Charlie Murray used to be furious whenever the ball came near him because he always hated sport."[9]

For young hopefuls with a typewriter living in the desolation of the British suburbs it was the most glamorous writing assignment imaginable. That's why when the *NME* advertised for a staff writer in 1976 there were 1,200 applicants. Among them were Neil Tennant, Jonathan Coe and Sebastian Faulks. 17 year-old Julie Burchill was one of the few chosen, recruited along with Tony Parsons to meet the *NME*'s need for "hip young gunslingers" to cover the punk scene. According to Stuart Maconie, an *NME* staffer from the late Eighties onwards, Burchill said that "one day she was a schoolgirl in Bristol, the next she was sitting on Chrissie Hynde's knee and snorting amphetamine sulphate in the back of the Sex Pistols van as it drove along Oxford Street."[10]

There was a chillier side to the *NME* environment: steely competition to win the approval of the editor, to show you were 'in' with the coolest bands, as well as an unattractive class divide between university graduates and the rest. Women were usually only taken on for secretarial roles and record companies were comfortable sending round naked girls 'dressed' in balloons to deliver copies of new releases. The danger of *NME* burnout was epitomised by Nick Kent. "For one article on Keith Richards in 1974, Kent spent 40 sleepless hours in the company of the Stones guitarist, fortified by what Richards called 'the breakfast of champions', a mix of heroin and cocaine."[11] Like a restless phantom, skeletal and high-strung, Nick Kent was running out of ways to find his kicks. Its glory days over, the Rock and Roll Highway had turned out to be leading to feelings

---

[8] Long, Pat, ibid., p76.

[9] Ibid., p84.

[10] Maconie, Stuart, *ibid.*, p218.

[11] Long, Pat, ibid., p130.

of emptiness, isolation and nights fretting and fumbling around the edges of sanity.

A new order was introduced by editor Neil Spencer. Sexism and rock hedonism were out, 'right-on' politics, multiculturalism and feminism were in. *NME* was going to be anti-Thatcher, anti-corporate business and anti-racism. Nihilism was ousted by an astringent commitment to taking on the establishment, and the *NME* became the only explicitly left-wing publication sold in the newsagents. By 1985 it was an important part of the Red Wedge movement formed by Billy Bragg, Jimmy Somerville and Paul Weller, campaigning to encourage more young people to become politically aware and vote Thatcher out at the next General Election. Neil Kinnock was given a cover spot, features discussed the Socialist Worker's Party, *NME* reporters went out onto the streets to talk to the "dispossessed youth" of Britain's cities who found themselves "surplus to industrial requirements" and consequently "sold their arses to strangers"[12].

Neil Spencer also wanted to change the office culture. "I recruited a lot of female writers and tried to create an inclusive atmosphere," he recalled. "But a lot of the writers that I brought in were either ignored or propositioned or people called them names. You also had a cadre of homophobes. Almost obsessively anti-gay."[13] "The women were supposed to be in the back cooking the brown rice while the men sat around smoking dope and discussing how heavy Dylan's lyrics were or whatever," said writer Ian Penman. "Danny Baker was going through the *NME* photo archive one day and he found this photograph of Charlie Murray in the mid-'70s. Charlie was holding this inflatable plastic Led Zeppelin PR thing, this plastic zeppelin, between his legs. Danny ran off 40 copies on the Xerox machine. Charlie was really not amused."[14]

Another significant change for indie was a swing of the telescope towards the regions. The *NME* readership was mostly outside of London anyway, and there was new interest in getting contributions from stringers, the kinds of people who spent their nights in some the most obscure

---

[12] Tyler, Andrew, *New Musical Express*, 26 February 1983.

[13] Long, Pat, ibid., p137.

[14] Ibid.

corners of the gig scene among the Walsall psychobillies and Torquay's hardcore skiffle pubs. A more regional network meant more attention to bands from places like Glasgow and Manchester.

The *NME* wanted music to be treated as a serious art form. One tactic was to appropriate some of the excitement and buzz generated by French postmodernism among students, the kind of coruscating philosophies that were a toolkit for deconstruction, that needn't justify their value or even have to make much sense. It was an editorial policy that opened the door to antic, anything-goes intellectualising. Prose written with a knowing smile. "It was gloriously provocative but at times very long-winded and egocentric writing, inspired by French philosophers Michel Foucault, Roland Barthes and Jacques Derrida and the work of the Frankfurt School of dissident Marxist social theoreticians," according to *NME* historian Pat Long. "Whether this approach had any place in a weekly music paper is a moot point, but suddenly the pages of *NME* assumed something of the atmosphere of the staff common room of the philosophy department of a small provincial university."[15] The difference being there was no arbiter, no peer review. Paul Morley had worked in a bookshop as a teenager, getting high on the thrill of writers like Marshall McLuhan to build himself up for delivering prose with "an intoxicating fizz — adjectives and assertions bubbling through alliterative, multi-clause sentences, with shoals of commas barely keeping order", while somehow still managing to keep "a precocious authority"[16]. Not everyone was impressed, including the Go-Betweens: "'Dollar is the most avant-garde group in the world'. It reads well, certainly – it's outrageous, nobody else is thinking that. Paul Morley's…just trying to drum up something around himself…a journalist who wants to attach himself to a generation like Tom Wolfe does."[17] When Barney Hoskyns took on a commission to interview Morrissey in 1984, he was armed and ready with references. The result was a

[15] Ibid., p139.

[16] Beckett, Andy, *Promised You a Miracle — Why 1980-82 Made Modern Britain*, Penguin, 2015, p184.

[17] Snow, Mat, 'The Go-Betweens: The Gentle Three-Headed Monster', *New Musical Express*, 21 August 1982.

piece structured around quotes from Roland Barthes, Nietzsche, Jean Genet and William Morris, drawing on Karl Marx's theory of alienation and Sigmund Freud on sexual neuroses. No form of pop was safe from hyper-analysis. Ian Penman's interview with the lead singer of Kid Creole and the Coconuts began with a quote from Barthes and went on like this:

> The August Darnell world – as manifested in a lot of Dr Buzzard's Original Savannah Band and all of Kid Creole and the Coconuts – is a looking glass world, a somewhere far away peopled by metaphors. But you don't need a map to find this island, because its mythology is built around that very real, most easily found (and lost) of places – love. Sexual love, romantic love, high life love, hedonistic love, hardship love whatever, wherever or whoever...There's a whole new lyrical country here just waiting to be discovered. It is cavalier, cinemascope and carnal. It's a subliminal carnival, a bit of a circus, a sip of a cocktail: amorous, clandestine, physical, light-headed and heavy-lidded. The dance of love – do you know the opening steps? You awful flirt![18]

And here, Cynthia Rose explaining the secret of Aztec Camera:

> Rarely is the 'singer-songwriter' allowed any natural patience to heed the rushing waters of emotion and experience; and in the current singer-songwriter boom, it seems axiomatic that some studio mojo be quickly corralled to embellish every half-baked twitch of such artistes' minds with exotic aural perfumes and the most expensive glitter. Result: an overly familiar frame within which resonate to the point of real tedium those overarching (and often class-coded) vocals which bespeak Young White Male Angst. Not so Roddy Frame who's sussed that in its heaviest hour each soul is of a separate mind, that each bears his or her own burden and that each such mind *is* its own division. Among other things, he numbers sickness as an unhealthy diversion and war-for-

---

[18] Penman, Ian, 'Kid Creole — a classic NME feature from the vaults (1980)', *The Guardian*, 6 March 2012.

business-reasons as a token that any populace so divided cannot *stand* to be too well lest it be held accountable for its own miseries.[19]

Mark Fisher was one reader who felt he'd been drawn into studying post-structuralism and an academic career by the *NME*: "There was a kind of contagion of autodidacticism, and the music press formed part of what was in effect an alternative education system."[20] Naturally then, the *NME* started to broaden its scope to reviews of films, books and TV, interviewing Woody Allen and Steven Spielberg, and positioning itself as having a pair of alternative spectacles for the whole cultural landscape.

However playful the intentions may have been, the *NME* was a diet of lentil gruel compared with the sweet mousse of pop and its tutti frutti commodity of vinyl and cassettes now on sale everywhere from WH Smith and Woolworth's to Boots the Chemist. Being such a stark alternative to the surging spirit of the times meant the *NME* went into decline. Sales of the *NME* peaked in 1981 with 270,000 copies of an issue marking the suicide of Ian Curtis; by 1985 sales were half that number. The number one was now *Smash Hits* (1976-2006), the glossy weekly with pull out posters and sing-a-long lyrics that flew with the busy wings of the pop zeitgeist. Being pushily commercial made it even more cool. "*Smash Hits* became sort of an MTV in magazine form," said Barney Hoskyns. "The primary focus was on pop groups that looked good and were colourful and the treatment of them was quite superficial. It was very much a reaction to this legacy of pseudo-intellectual deconstruction of pop culture that you got at the *NME*."[21] Irritatingly, *Smash Hits* started out at an office just down the road from the *NME* with former *NME* editor Nick Logan in charge. It was a risk for local newspaper group, the East Midlands Allied Press (soon to be better known as publishing giant EMAP); but by 1979 it was an experiment that had started to sell 150,000 copies a week. *NME* found much

---

[19] Rose, Cynthia, 'Aztec Camera: Knife', *New Musical Express*, 29 September 1984.

[20] Butt, Gavin; Eshun, Kodwo; Fisher, Mark, *Post-punk then and now*, Repeater Books, 2014, p14.

[21] Long, Pat, ibid., p144.

of the charts to be like the back of a sofa, full of tat and fluff that nobody would miss. *Smash Hits* raved over each discovery and the optimism was contagious. "People OD'd on the gritty social realism of punk and they wanted fun pop and bright colours and *NME* couldn't do that," Charles Murray said. "Poor Neil [Spencer] had the misfortune to preside over *NME*'s identity crisis and a larger one in the rock community."[22] Paolo Hewitt arrived in 1983. "The readers didn't know who Roland Barthes was and they didn't care. You had *Smash Hits* taking off and we didn't know what to do with people like Boy George and Simon Le Bon and Duran Duran. There were no rock acts and the *NME* was flummoxed. Meanwhile *The Face* was covering drugs, fashion: I used to read *The Face* rather than the *NME*"[23].

The *NME*'s staff was broken into factions. There was still the class divide (Barney Hoskyns spent his youth at a public school, Paolo Hewitt in a children's home). And now there was also the black American music fans versus the indie fans. "I remember a meeting where we were seriously debating whether to put Paul Young on the cover or Tom Waits. It really didn't seem clear which was the right choice…It was an identity crisis."[24] The confusion was everywhere. The reach of the *NME* meant everyone from the British Army to Woolworth's and sports car manufacturers were buying advertising space, as well as the kinds of dinosaur rock and chart pop acts that didn't sit well opposite the counter-cultural prose and Microdisney reviews.

Within the commercial marketplace the *NME*'s position was uneasy, but it remained a mighty behemoth to the indie labels and their fledgling bands. The *NME* was much more than its circulation figure. It was the kind of 'keeper' paper that was passed around student halls, sixth-form common rooms, bars and clubs, and a large underworld of the record-buying public, a Bible for niche audiences of music listeners alienated from the mainstream. Green Gartside claimed to have been a subscriber from the age of eight. Pat Long has argued that it was "one of the most import-

---

[22] Ibid., p146.

[23] Ibid., p149.

[24] Ibid.

ant and influential magazines on the planet...[with] an influence on British culture out of all proportion with the size of its readership...[it] changed the nation's cultural DNA forever"[25]. Loyal readers had a personal relationship with the paper, like it was an older friend who had all the right vinyl as well as some inspiringly reckless attitudes to life. The *NME* stage-managed the perceptions of a generation. It was Paul Morley, for example, who prompted attention to the Postcard bands, who caused the A&Rs to descend on Glasgow. Labels like Zoo, Factory and Rough Trade didn't have the schmoozing potential of the majors but they did have the essential advantage of being the underdogs. As the guardians of musical integrity and anti-big-business values they were natural allies — and it meant they were allowed a degree of latitude.

Indie bands would let journos join them on their nights out, not as a calculated PR tactic to deliver copy but certainly in order to get some kind of attention. Why not? Barney Hoskyns and Mat Snow were occasional members of the notorious Australian gang in London with the Go-Betweens, the Birthday Party and the Triffids, and were always — in this company — the lightweights. "I never shot up," said Mat Snow. "I can't stand needles to this day...We'd all wander around in a pack trying to score from various places, then there'd be evenings where somebody's fixing up in the bathroom and there was lots of lying around and listening to records and talking vaguely."[26] Who knows how much these relationships helped lead to the effusive reviews of what — especially in the case of The Birthday Party — could make for a discomfiting listen. *NME* writers, mostly, were like privileged tourists entering the darklands of an edgy, grey-skied Bohemia. Taking taxis and charging drinks to expenses. It was no real surprise that the original king and queen of punk, Parsons and Burchill, would decide to take the kudos and run, buying a nice family home together in leafy Essex while dismissing the punk scene as a mistake. Parsons would go on to write a regular column for the *Daily Telegraph*.

Our five bands had to be careful with the music press and learn quickly how to play the game. Not all of them arrived fully-formed like

---

[25] Ibid., p9.

[26] Ibid., p157.

Morrissey, fit to burst. "Suddenly we are in the Interview Situation," wrote Dave McCullough on meeting Aztec Camera for the first time in January 1981. "The three new Postcards (they had only known Horne a week) sit trembling before me almost as much as I tremble. They each smoke with a fixity of purpose that creates a strange symmetrical unity of smoke clouds. Their cigarette ends topple over on to the carpet without them knowing it. I laugh half in nerves too but half in excitement of recognition: this band is great and young and they don't even know it!"[27] Lines of communication weren't always that clear. "'We're not wimps though. Just romantics. There's a difference,' says Roddy, grinning at Campbell, who grins in return. Then the both of them grin across at me. I don't really know what all this grinning's in aid of, but I grin back just the same," wrote the *NME*'s Dave Hill in 1982[28]. By the time he was interviewed by the *NME* again, this time by Kirsty McNeill, Roddy had turned laddish, downplaying anything that might be heartfelt about the lyrics, and allowing himself to be photographed standing on top of a beach hut waving a kilt on a stick. 'Tartan Tearaway' was the headline[29]. He didn't trust the music press to really get the distinction between wimp and Romantic. The Blue Nile would fumble their way through interviews with minimalism and mystery. "Listening to The Blue Nile's music is like floating in the Mediterranean on a summer's day," wrote *The Face*. "Talking to them about it is like doing the breast stroke in treacle."[30]

The other main channel to public attention was John Ravenscroft, a DJ given a snappier name for radio. It wasn't easy to win recognition and find a way onto John Peel's Radio 1 show, and consequently the rewards were greater. Being chosen for that week's collection meant other radio DJs might start playing your single, the music press and A&Rs would take you more seriously, fans would start multiplying all around the dreary suburbs, swapping tapes and turning up to gigs. Every week the show was

[27] McCullough, Dave, 'After the Fall…Aztec Camera', *Sounds*, 3 January 1981.

[28] Hill, Dave, 'Aztec Inca Contract At Last', *New Musical Express*, 4 September 1982.

[29] McNeill, Kirsty, 'Tartan Tearaway', *New Musical Express*, 11 June 1983.

[30] Brown, Allan, *Nileism: The Strange Course of The Blue Nile*, Polygon, 2010, p112.

receiving thousands of cassettes from both the bigger labels and the strange and spirited universe of DIY hopefuls. In their careful management of the launch of the Smiths, Rough Trade chose the John Peel Show for early session recordings rather than another Smiths' fan David 'Kid' Jensen (who would have brought much bigger listening figures). John Peel was a brilliant curator of everything hardcore, flailing-limbed, splodgy and drawling, and his obtuse wit and lugubrious enthusiasm was all part of a package that turned him into an unlikely 'national treasure'. He was the underground tunnel to Radio 1 airplay, a station that spent the Eighties being dazzled by its overground popularity and culture of celebrity DJs, summer roadshows and the chance to be on the telly fronting *Top of the Pops*. "Radio 1 used to sound like Surrey to me," recalled Eighties historian Andy Beckett. "Perhaps it was the disc jockeys they used in those days, with their creamy car-dealer's voices and their discreetly tabloid opinions; or the on-air pub quizzes and snooker, where female contestants were flirted with and spoken to slowly; or the endless suburban doze of the afternoon programmes; or the sense, if you cared about pop music, that the records played were nothing but restaurant muzak to the DJs – to be talked over, cut short, looped repeatedly, forgotten about."[31] He didn't mean John Peel. "If it wasn't for John Peel, there would be no Joy Division and no New Order," said Bernard Sumner[32]. But that sounds more like gratitude than a considered truth. John Peel didn't make the indie movement happen. He didn't write 'Love Will Tear Us Apart', didn't experience the bitter ashen taste of living on those Manchester streets, the uncertainties, emptiness and frustration. He played the records. He didn't lobby Radio 1 bosses to give his alternative leanings some airtime, it was a job. Radio 1 gave John Peel the opportunity, the space and the privilege of playing a personal miscellany. His taste was always eclectic and affected by some singular predilections: the first to play the Fall and the Cure but also 'Young Guns' by Wham! He played a lot more of Clare Grogan's Altered

---

[31] Beckett, Andy, 'They Both Hated DLT', Review of Simon Garfield, *The Nation's Favourite: the True Adventures of Radio 1, London Review of Books*, 15 April 1999.

[32] Cavanagh, David, *Good Night and Good Riddance — How Thirty-Five Years of John Peel Helped to Shape Modern Life*, Faber & Faber, 2015, p26.

Images than Orange Juice. And Edwyn was suspicious. "He's still very much an old rocker. He's very macho, very sexist and all those old clichés that liberal people use. You only need to listen to him on the air — mimmicks Peel's voice — 'How I'd like to spank that little schoolgirl's bottom'."[33]

*

Dad has put flowers in a glass thing he's found at the back of a cupboard. He's got the wrong plates out, the big ones, for people to put their Mr Kipling cakes on. He's even done pineapple chunks and cheese on sticks. So there's a food mountain in the kitchen the EEC would be interested in, all because Di and Derek and the girls are coming over in their Ford Cortina. The first time they've been over since Mum left.

I'm sent down to Chapman's at the other end of the estate for a jar of Maxwell House because Adrian won't do it, and that means taking Mum's bike. Every time I have to ride that bike I feel like a monkey on a tricycle, my skirt flaps up to my ears, my knees bump the handlebars. Faces appear at windows. Small boys run down the road after me like the circus is coming.

Then I have to go into Chapman's shop, the only place open, and make small talk about the old days. It's the smelly place where I used to go every week for my paper round. The window is still covered in hand-written orange and green starbursts. Pint of milk 15p! Mothers Pride 25p! Mr Chapman doesn't bother much with changing his stock and the fruity whiff of veg is enough to make you vom. You can tell what he had for last night's dinner from his moustache and his tie. And he still thinks it's okay to look at my boobs.

By the time I get back the Cortina is in the drive. Dad won't sit down, walking back and forth from the kitchen for no reason. Everyone's watching telly. Derek and Di are on the settee with cousin Rebecca, her hair newly crimped; and crimped in a bad way. Adrian's on the hard fold-up avoiding conversation by pretending to watch Bull-seye. Cousin Rachel is looking unstable and unhappy on the pouffe in her pink leg-warmers and a jumper the size of a tent.

Great columns of dust divide one side of the living room, a wall of sunlight, with the other.

---

[33] Pye, Ian, 'Juicy, fruity, cheap 'n cheerful', *Melody Maker*, 17 January 1981.

"Have you been watching that Channel 4?" asks Derek with a glint in his eye, really hoping we have. He wants to talk about poofs and lefties.

"Not really," says Dad. *"Haven't got much time with my new job you know."* What does he mean? We sit in front of telly every night. Terry and June. Blankety Blank. Cagney and Lacey. *He just wants to talk about 'being in sales'. All I know about sales is that it means the garage is full of tins of pet food.*

There's some relief when Arnold's turns up in the road and toots his horn. The girls go out to get sweets. Doesn't Adrian want to go with them? asks Di. Face like he's eaten a worm. No-one knows what he wants.

*

According to a research paper in the British Medical Journal, the suicide rate in Great Britain doubled the month after Margaret Thatcher became Prime Minister in 1979. It did the same following the General Election in 1983, and again in 1987[34]. Hope was a fragile thing in the Eighties.

Mrs Thatcher remains the bogeyman of the decade — but to what extent was she responsible for creating this kind of despair? Many famous quotes are apocryphal. Thatcher's "there's no such thing as society" isn't one of them. Her handwritten notes went further, arguing there was "no such thing as a collective conscience, a collective kindness, collective gentleness, collective freedom"[35]. In other words, in the Thatcher worldview, there were only competing individuals who were responsible for themselves, their personal ambitions and fortunes. It was a vision based on a belief in herself as the model of possibility, how a very ordinary "grocer's daughter" could raise herself above humble origins to become Prime Minister. It was an example she came back to again and again in her speeches and interviews: how anyone could 'better' themselves, so long as barriers to achievement, the drag from muddled values and state-funded safety nets, were removed. *Let Our Children Grow Tall* was the title of a 1977 book of her selected speeches.

---

[34] Turner, Alwyn W., *Rejoice! Rejoice! Britain in the 1980s*, Aurum Press, 2010, pXI.

[35] McSmith, Andy, *No Such Thing as Society*, Constable, 2011, p5.

But there had been nothing ordinary about Margaret Thatcher's background, no grounding in 'normal life'. Her grocer father was an active participant in local government and school governor; home life was sombre and serious-minded; she was extremely focused on her school studies (winning her a place at the University of Oxford); and had what might be reasonably described as a monomaniacal political career. Not normal life but that of a narrowly-focused workaholic and very few people indeed could be like her. It was Mrs Thatcher's good fortune that the Victorian spirit of her outlook had suddenly become very modern. Perfect for the already wealthy, the newly-monied middle-classes and anyone willing to sweat and chase for more. Nothing was owed to those who hadn't made the best of their opportunity, no special favours should be given to the 'weak' in the name of making a 'better society'.

Decades of effort to bring about more social equality in Britain were reversed. Between 1949 and 1979, the share of wealth owned by the top 1% in the country had fallen from from 6.8% to 4.7%. By 1989 the 1% had reclaimed 7.1%. By 1990 the top 10% of earners were being paid three and a half times that of the bottom 10%[36]. The number of people considered by Government to have inadequate income to live on, at 'supplementary benefit' level, had remained static at around two million between 1960 and 1977. By 1983 this had increased to 8.6 million, up 43% since 1979[37]. The shake-out of both traditional industries and professions meant being jobless wasn't only a threat to the young and low skilled. In the year after Thatcher was elected unemployment rose by almost a million, by a further 700,000 the year after. It was a shock for: "middle-aged men, unprepared for the indignities of the dole office, the scrutiny of officials behind grilles, the inching, shaming queues," wrote Andy Beckett. "On the BBC1 nine o'clock news, lists of major redundancies were sombrely read out every night during the early 1980s, as if they were wartime casualty figures."[38] At the forefront of the response to unemployment wasn't a strategy of supporting industry and employers, but talking up the

---

[36] Ibid., p6.

[37] Hudson, Ray and Williams, Allan, *Divided Britain*, Belhaven Press, 1989, p23.

[38] Beckett, Andy, ibid., p57.

possibilities of more individual responsibility and making the leap into entrepreneurship.

No matter how loathsome the ideology — an outlook that has been responsible for exacerbating if not creating the most serious problems of the 21st century, such as unsustainable economics, social inequality, poor mental health, climate change — attributing the direction of a decade to a single person is unreasonable. Margaret Thatcher was both the victim and beneficiary of economic and social forces she had little control over. There wasn't really that much Thatcher in Thatcherism. She was a strong leader, gutsy, persistent, principled. But like all high-profile leaders she was mostly only a vehicle for other people's ideas, someone who was trying to manage a set of wicked problems that were well beyond her control. Her radical liberal ideology was inspired, and given the chance to be implemented, by a much wider movement of think-tanks, economists and media opinion-influencers. She was only hanging on to their coat tails. It wasn't her fault if there was a swell of opinion favouring a more assertive and confident way of thinking after the failures of the Seventies. Thatcher can't take the credit for the economic boom that finally arrived either, and, arguably, it was a boom that could have come earlier and prevented a good deal of human misery. North Sea oil was a gift to a new administration appointed just in time to gather returns of £3.8 billion in 1980-81 and £6.1 billion in 1981-2[39]. Encouraging council house occupants to buy their homes was another one-off windfall: £692 million in 1980-81, almost £2 billion in 1982-3[40]. Global recession and the use of new technologies in agriculture had led to lower food prices, easing the pressure on prices of goods in general. The sheer state of Britain in decline, its mass of derelict property and land, meant a tantalising panorama of opportunities for speculators. Derelict areas like London's Docklands were a new paradise for property tycoons. In other words, it is the essential nature of economic cycles that an upswing in financial prospects was always likely — whatever monetary and fiscal policies were pursued.

---

[39] Ibid., p215.

[40] Ibid., p227.

Thatcher's ideas had germinated in a fine-looking, red-brick Georgian home above a grocer's shop in Grantham that was sturdy, staid and redolent of a stiff sense of purpose. She wanted to re-build the nation around these kinds of old-fashioned values, where mother was at home looking after the family, there was hard work, thrift and moral standards. They were principles that had taken shape on hushed Sunday afternoons after the roast dinner had been enjoyed, when the family was resting in order for their work to begin again on the Monday; the hours spent looking from high windows over little shops to the town's church and its medieval spire; waiting for the family's bone china cups to be brought out for tea, the silver sugar bowl and tongs all on a tray.

The PM's mission was ultimately made to look like a piece of whimsical dreaming by the realities of Eighties Britain. Her policies only encouraged the disintegration and dirtying of ideals. There was a sudden increase in the population's dependence on the state (by 1983, dole payments were costing taxpayers £5 billion a year[41]); being jobless had become an ordinary state of affairs. More women were either choosing or needing to go to work, and the traditional family was breaking apart. There was a decline in deference. A new acceptance of sex and violence in media. The growth of an unscrupulous business culture. A booming financial services sector based on unheard of levels of risk-taking (re-directing customer's money into bonuses). A creeping addiction to spending, hire purchase and credit card debt.

Mrs Thatcher has been blamed for the decade's aggressive materialism, but it's not as if she'd wanted it that way. She was only pleased the old British 'way' of nationalised industries, unions and other lingering social collectives was breaking down — and that she was being re-elected. It was a rough time to be in politics. You had to slap or be slapped, said the new king of political advertising Maurice Saatchi. There was a hardening of dogma, and the divisions between the Conservatives and Labour weren't only over details of official policy or approach but could be brutally personal. Opposing manifestos were a clash between fundamental philosophies of life, a butting of heads over what was sanity and what was madness and there was little middle ground, only a landscape of carica-

---

[41] Sampson, Anthony, *The Changing Anatomy of Britain*, Hodder & Staughton, 1982, p426.

tures. The Conservative voter was crowing and slimy. A hard-faced snob whose home was their castle. The Labour voter was a grim, flat-cap wearing relic — or, maybe a worthy, pale-faced vegetarian. Any other political persuasion might be well-intentioned but was woolly and out of touch. The polarities meant a great deal of shrieking in debate, media headlines and on roadside billboards. Leftish policies and ideas that would now be considered perfectly sensible were, in this earlier context, treated as screaming lunacy, the end of civilisation.

The story of 'Red Ken' is one illustration. Labour's Ken Livingstone became leader of the Greater London Council (GLC) in 1981. He was a charmer in a scruffy jacket, tie askew, who lived in a bedsit after having split up with his wife. He preferred to take the bus rather than use the official council leader's car. A hard-working, down-to-earth activist, Livingstone also knew how to get a headline. This irritating combination of administrative power in the English capital and easy relationships with journalists made him a top target for attack by the new coalition of neoliberal interests. Rupert Murdoch's *Sun* newspaper called him "the most odious man in Britain"[42]: because Livingstone had turned down an invitation to the Royal Wedding (as someone who didn't believe in the monarchy he thought it would be hypocritical to be among the revellers, so he went into the office to do some work instead); he'd said police racism was a factor in that year's rioting (now a well-established truth); ridiculously, he wanted to bring in free public transport for London's pensioners; he'd even argued the IRA weren't just "psychopaths" but had a political motivation (a position that would lead to progress towards peace and power-sharing in Northern Ireland). The *Daily Mail* ran an article in which psychologists concluded he was a dangerous fanatic, all of his thinking explained by the fact he was an "attention-seeking hysteric"[43]. Livingstone was more of a hate figure than Thatcher ever was, physically assaulted in the streets and bombarded with hate mail. In reality, rather than the Red of popular imagination, Livingstone hadn't even read much Karl Marx. He was a Sixties free-thinker fascinated by the potential for real-world politicking to change

---

[42] Beckett, Andy, ibid., p145.

[43] Ibid., p152.

everyday lives for the better, to give people freedoms other than the illusory ones of consumers. The visible demise of socialism — a term that had begun to droop with associations with everything that was ugly and decaying in Britain, the melancholy industrial landscapes, the unions and strikes, the angry men in unfashionable clothes — meant anyone or anything related to socialism caught the eye. Opposition to the political and commercial dynamism intent on turning Britain into a land of free markets was scattered and weak. Even the usual kind of youth fervour was withering according to commentator Peter Everett: "There is still idealism among the young and it takes many forms, from militant vegetarianism to attending concerts in support of the Labour Party, but its minimal by comparison with support for CND in the early sixties or even the Anti-Nazi League in the late seventies."[44]

A new alliance was formed by Government with the police, an alliance that would become increasingly important as the decade went on. One of the first manoeuvres of the new administration in 1979 was to force through a delayed pay increase for police forces of 45%. It was controversial because other essential public services employees were to get nothing on the same scale, and Labour had previously tried to stagger the increases. But for tactical reasons Thatcher pushed the expenditure through, immediately positioning her Government as a friend to the police chiefs. A radical agenda was coming and the forces of law and order needed to be fully behind the governing party, no matter what. Police had to do more than fulfil a job function, they needed to be willing in spirit to be officers defending an ideology, to focus their attention actively onto citizenry who didn't fit the new scheme of things. In 1981 this included the re-introduction of the Vagrancy Act of 1824, allowing police to stop and search anyone they 'suspected' of committing a crime. What was known by police as the 'SWAMP 81' initiative — reputedly taken from a speech by Thatcher referring to fears of Britain being "swamped by people from a different culture"[45] — led to 1,000 people being stopped and searched in the borough of Lambeth over the course of just six days. These were the

---

[44] Everett, Peter, *You'll never be 16 again*, BBC Publications, 1986, p157.

[45] Margaret Thatcher speech, reported on *World in Action*, Granada TV, 1978.

changes in police activity that would lead to the summer of rioting. Racism among police officers was typical, expected, even fashionable, according to an investigation by the BBC's *Panorama* programme. A young cadet was confident enough in the racism of police culture to have written the following in a college essay: "Blacks are a pest. I don't have any liking for wogs, nig-nogs or Pakis. They come over here from some tinpot country and take up residence in our overcrowded country."[46] Police aggression was needed to break the miner's strikes of 1984 and 1985. Forces took on a quasi-military role that went well beyond what would normally be expected from preserving law and order. The violent beatings doled out by police cavalry at Orgreave in 1984 cost South Yorkshire Police half a million pounds in compensation and costs[47]. Then came the Public Order Act of 1986, which made it illegal to cause what could be interpreted as "harassment, alarm or distress" in public places, thereby criminalising any protesters who became inconvenient to the Government. So crowds could be assumed to be illegitimate. They weren't expressions of a shared passion or identity but 'mobs' — an instinct among police that culminated in horror and tragedy in 1989 and the death of 96 Liverpool football fans at Hillsborough. This was the place our bands called home, a society in transition, sickly and convulsive, with little of the orderly progress the word 'transition' might suggest.

The violence of the political and economic landscape was only one dimension of the national anxiety. In 1979 the Thatcher government gave the go-ahead for 160 American nuclear missiles to be stationed at Greenham Common. Britain had become, according to one investigative reporter, America's "unsinkable aircraft carrier"[48], and a primary target for any pre-emptive strike from the Soviet Union. It was accepted by Whitehall that US military strategy included a presumption that the most likely nuc-

---

[46] Jones, Margaret, *Thatcher's Kingdom: A View of Britain in the Eighties*, Collins, 1984, p270.

[47] Jones, Owen, *The Establishment And How They Get Away With It*, Penguin, 2014, p128.

[48] Campbell, Duncan, *The Unsinkable Aircraft Carrier: American Military Power in Britain*, Michael Joseph, 1984.

lear conflict would be small-scale and take place solely within Europe[49]. At the same time, the election of fellow neo-liberal Ronald Reagan to the presidency of the US in 1980 had encouraged heightened rhetoric and determination to be ready for a Third World War if necessary. British Army recruitment advertising in 1981 pictured a Russian tank careering through the streets of Kabul. The ad proposed the all-too-possible scenario that the next stop for the mechanised Red Army would be Germany[50]. The Cold War was insidious. There would be new scares about potential conflict from one week to the next. Nightmares of a post-nuclear attack wasteland were the tentacles of a beast that never showed its face, tentacles that had a wide-reaching influence on the psychology of societies across decades. In his book *Bomb Culture* (1968), Jeff Nuttall argued that much of post-war youth culture, the careless rock and roll hedonism in particular, had been shaped by fear of imminent apocalypse[51].

The Falklands War in 1982 was a reminder that all the abnormality of war, the nationalism, jingoism, the threat of conscription, could very quickly become an accepted part of life again. Even closer to home was Northern Ireland, the running sore of military rule, the murder of neighbours, revenge killings, deaths of hunger strikers. The trigger fingers of soldiers patrolling the streets of Belfast and Londonderry were twitchy.

*

So bands were political. If opposition to the Thatcher government was weak and incoherent, if the only visible response to hardline policies was a stronger and more market-oriented corporate pose, bigger smiles and smarter haircuts, then it was time to think beyond elections and stand up for causes. "Post-punk was post-everything, really…except, oddly, sincerity," wrote Ian Penman. "Everyone was brittle with it."[52] Socialism

---

[49] Beckett, Andy, ibid., p157.

[50] Ibid., p86.

[51] Nuttall, Jeff, *Bomb Culture*, Paladin, 1970.

[52] Thorn, Tracey, *Bedsit Disco Queen: How I Grew Up and Tried to Be a Pop Star*, Virago Press, 2013, p134.

was a given, the standard anti-Thatcherism. But specific causes were an easier way to get up noses of the Establishment. Bands who supported Rock Against Racism were also likely to sign up for events around nuclear disarmament, gay rights, the striking miners, Amnesty International. Because standing up for causes was somehow all of a piece, a combined assault on complacency, assumed superiority and the growing public disinterest in anything outside of the acceptable 'normal'.

For Green Gartside, music and politics were inextricable. "I had always wanted to make music but it wasn't my place growing up in Wales, there were no bands. One of the things that got me, made me political in the first place, that started me thinking, was just the general impoverishment — culturally and materially — in South Wales at the time. It was a desperately oppressive thing. That's why music and politics seemed to be that important to me."[53] By the middle of the decade though, the trend for musicians backing causes was starting to look like a lifestyle choice. "This year I've picked three issues," said Paul Weller, "new trade union rights, CND and International Youth Year."[54]

Roddy Frame's conception of politics had nothing to do with either fashionable causes or late night beer and sandwich committee meetings. It was a rush of blood to the head. Excitement at the sight of people gathering on the streets. "How we'd storm the palace," dreams Roddy on 'Release', "meet me at the gates." Half the city is on its feet in a spontaneous outbreak of support for the good and the true; aflame in the crowd, he grabs "a red, red flag for a souvenir"; "Sack the world and make a red parade/ Burn the banks down while the bugles played" ('Birth of the True'). His lyrics are shot through with a vision of wild-eyed revolt, the romance of giant-killers ("We clicked our heels and spat and swore we'd never let it die,"). It's instinctive and non-intellectual, filled with an age-old sense of good versus evil (the people against the combine, the 'thing') which would have been imbibed from living in a working-class home ("The vampires made a killing, filled their pockets up with shillings/ saying 'someone has to pay'"). The b-side to one of his most commercial releases

---

53 Butt, Gavin; Eshun, Kodwo; Fisher, Mark, ibid., p174.

54 Everett, Peter, ibid., p155.

in 1988, 'How Men Are', was his version of worker's anthem 'The Red Flag'. "Politics simply means knowing what is wrong and what is right, simply to see what is ideological in the light of what we see round us," Roddy told one magazine in 1984. You didn't have to play the politics game. Truth could be sensed, be something emotional — the answer to any wrong-headed system was in ordinary people saying no. "The idea of Free Enterprise is a complete farce. Someone setting up a factory and having ten people working for him who makes five pounds a week while he makes ten pounds a week is totally wrong. The wealth of a country should never become the sole property of a minority of individuals... It is quite an encouraging sign to see ordinary people pelting the police with rocks."[55] He was willing to take action if there was likely to be a concrete outcome. When the Government moved to 'starve out' the striking miners by freezing the assets of unions providing strike pay, Roddy raised £19,000 from arranging a concert at Brixton Academy. Orange Juice played their last ever gig at Roddy's fundraiser. A few months earlier they'd played at a GLC event in Crystal Palace. "More boogieing," commanded Edwyn. "We can overcome this Thatcher Government!"[56]

"Well, our band was born out of a fascist state," explained Robert Forster to an *NME* journalist unaware of the slide in Australian politics. "No, you may laugh, but it's true. Brisbane, where we come from, is exceptionally right-wing. It's run by fundamental Christians and rivals the Southern states of the USA for racism. We've been at concerts where the Special Branch has come in in overalls and taken all the gear away."[57] Being in a band in Queensland was anti-social behaviour in itself, an instant way to mark yourself out as a subversive, loud and annoyingly overground. The Go-Betweens' lyrics don't stray explicitly into political language, but in a similar way to the Blue Nile, the band made a cogent statement simply by committing themselves to artistic creation. Every LP is a manifesto of integrity, because they at least didn't use their university studies to become

[55] Dessau, Bruce, 'Roddy Frame', *Jamming!*, October 1984.

[56] Aston, Martin, 'Orange Juice: Crystal Palace Bowl, London', *Melody Maker*, 6 October 1984.

[57] Bohn, Chris, 'Hate can be positive', *New Musical Express*, 2 October 1982.

management consultants or fund managers. When politics enter the scene at all for the Blue Nile, it's as shadows from the giant cogs of the world machine. Lyrics to 'Heatwave' and 'Rags to Riches' were written by Paul Buchanan after seeing news reports of the Israeli army's siege of Beirut, for example. Paul himself spent time working for an agit-prop theatre group in Glasgow, 7:84 (named after the fact that 7% of the population in Britain at that time owned 84% of the wealth. The group lost its Art Council funding in 2006).

The Smiths are assumed to be the most political band of the decade. They were a sprout of protest in every interview, their politics redolent in all of their 'might as well stay-at-home in a cardigan' look and feel. Except it wasn't just a world-weary languor in the face of stupidity that the Smiths were advocating. "You *have* to be interested in politics these days. If you're not you're a completely lost individual. Whereas, years ago, politics seemed to be this thing that was secluded for a minority of intellectuals these days you can't get away with that argument — you have to be attuned to what's happening, there's so much at stake. There's absolutely no excuse for people who aren't politically aware," argued Morrissey, because governments couldn't be trusted to be benevolent. "Ultimately people feel it's all beyond them — we want to change that. The Smiths will push people to think for themselves, to believe they can really do something."[58] They played gigs in support of Red Wedge, the GLC and Liverpool's reviled Labour council.

Morrissey went further than any other public figure in his criticism of Margaret Thatcher. He famously remarked to *Melody Maker* that the "sorrow of the Brighton bombing" of the Tory Party conference by the IRA in 1984 was that "Margaret Thatcher escaped unscathed"[59]. Morrissey's 1988 song 'Margaret on the Guillotine' led to his being called in for questioning by Special Branch officers. (Just a year later Elvis Costello got away completely with looking forward to Thatcher's death on 'Tramp the Dirt Down': "When England was the whore of the world/ Margaret was

[58] Pye, Ian, 'Magnificent Obsessions', *Melody Maker*, 26 November 1983.

[59] Fletcher, Tony, *A Light That Never Goes Out: The Enduring Sage of The Smiths*, Windmill Books, 2013, p371.

her madam/ And the future looked as bright and as clear as/ The black tarmacadam"). Smiths' songs weren't meant to be idle commentary on the fairytale, the deceit of the new bourgeois aristocracy of Britain, they were meant to be a spur for active protest and change. "I took pop music very seriously. I thought it was the heart of everything. I thought it affected everybody and moved everybody."[60] Moving hearts, minds and feet.

As so often, Morrissey's ideal of himself seemed to have coalesced around the black and white dreams of post-war British cinema. One hero was Mr Cringle in *I'm a Stranger* (1952) played by the father of Roger Lloyd-Pack (the classically-trained actor better known in the Eighties as the roadsweeper, Trigger). Mr Cringle was important to Morrissey in epitomising how an inspired rebel could dumbfound authority and expose the banality of the powerful who would never understand genius. "Others may have good looks and sexual success, but Mr Cringle's weapon of words carries enough punch to alter the texture of every life around him, partly because, as a fanatic himself, he has suffered enough to know better."[61] But how, in practice, are Smiths' songs political? There's none of Roddy's revolutionary gusto and no attempt to expose any particular social injustice, the crimes of regimes in Britain or anywhere else. It was one thing to deliver a withering one-liner, to occupy the higher ground, and quite another to get involved with the hand-to-hand combat of backing specific policies or parties. Morrissey, in effect, appeared superficially to have turned his back on the fight. And that's understandable: a sensitive mind faced with a barracking, daily assault of noise from every newspaper, every popular TV programme, every radio DJ, all sharing the same spirit of unscrupulous materialism. But still it looks as if Morrissey is just like the rest, preferring to keep his head down and look after his own affairs.

How important is music to society? asked i-D magazine. "It's probably the most major influence on life," Morrissey replied. "Every person has a favourite record or tune. It's the easiest way to effect and change people's lives. It's certainly more important than politics."[62] Politics in it-

---

[60] Ibid., p59.

[61] Morrissey, *Autobiography*, Penguin Classics, 2013, p135.

[62] 'The Smiths', *i-D*, February 1983.

self, as a machinery of practices, the game, was nothing. A personal resistance was what mattered to Morrissey: the invisible insurrection, the reworking of personality, attitudes and daily lives, and just trying to find a more human and kindly way of living. "To say everything is hopeless, which is what people have been saying up till now, is a pointless attitude and that's where our belief in beauty and charm comes in. It's not to do with having a perfect profile or alabaster teeth."[63] This partly explains Morrissey's aversion to petty forms of power, to the unkindness of parents, teachers, priests, employers. And his yen for old-fashioned community. "I think the main blemish on this country is the absolute segregation which seems to appear on every level, with everything and everybody. There is no unity, certainly not within popular music. But of course this is because of the present government, which thrives completely upon it. The country is governed by a government that doesn't really care that much about it."[64] Personality was what mattered, not issues like unemployment. "[J]obs reduce people to absolute stupidity, they forget to think about themselves. There's something so positive about unemployment. It's like, Now We Can Think About Ourselves. You won't get trapped into materialism, you won't buy things you don't really want…"[65] The only thing worth fighting for was beauty — a position that came to the attention of the *NME*'s Len Brown after a night at another Smiths' concert. "Those who have never seen The Smiths accuse Morrissey of being a miserable, egotistical, arrogant bastard. Yet live, in the flesh, these criticisms evaporate because it's all part of his tongue-in-cheek, self-deprecating humour. He's seriously obsessed with the elevation of beauty ('That which the bourgeois call ugly' – Wilde), with overturning conventions and establishing meanings."[66]

The impact of the changing political context on indie was a contradiction. It was only more business-minded thinking and record industry

[63] Black, Bill, 'The Smiths: Keep Young and Beautiful', *Sounds*, 19 November 1983.

[64] Hoskyns, Barney, 'These Disarming Men: The Smiths', *New Musical Express*, 4 February 1984.

[65] McCullough, Dave, 'Handsome Devils', *Sounds*, 4 June 1983.

[66] Brown, Len, 'The Smiths: Newcastle Mayfair' *New Musical Express*, 2 August 1986.

profits that gave musicians from outside of the mainstream the chance to be heard. It was also the relatively tolerant benefits system and new Enterprise Allowance scheme that helped so many indie bands come to life. But the system also meant, eventually, that indie bands had to conform. Sometimes only superficially and unconsciously, maybe only in small ways, but it still meant a constriction of attitudes and direction towards where the money and the success were going to come from. "It is no accident that punk purists cite 1979 as the year when many of the ideas and aspirations that inspired independent music got emasculated in the muscular beliefs of some key players who recognised that here was a market ripe for exploitation. Marginal became marginalised," wrote Rough Trade historian Neil Taylor[67]. "I think Rough Trade never became Thatcherite, but let's say it bowed down a bit; it was forced to. I think they adapted to survive," agreed former shop manager Steve Jameson[68].

The further along the road to success, the stronger the feeling of pressure. Aztec Camera's Campbell Owens remembers what it felt like to be subject suddenly to an unseen hand. "Once we started getting into charts we were into Thatcher's Britain. It all changed. We were making music for other reasons. It had been so bright and hopeful and it was over in a flash. We thought everything was going to be new, but it wasn't."[69] The genuinely political moment, when bands were willing to be an irritant, to shout about and believe in change, was short-lived. "Mixing pop with politics would become increasingly difficult," wrote Tracey Thorn, "and even seem irrelevant to a later generation, our level of commitment appearing to them to be somewhat quaint and hysterical."[70] There would be more charitable donations to popular causes, the phenomenon of Band Aid and Live Aid, but for the big names in music this began to seem more like a form of Corporate Social Responsibility. Good for reputation and stakeholder engagement, while at the same time knowing accountants would be

---

[67] Taylor, Neil, *Document and Eyewitness: An Intimate History of Rough Trade*, Orion Books, 2010, p20.

[68] Ibid., p189

[69] Owens, Campbell, telephone interview, 9th November 2018.

[70] Thorn, Tracey, ibid., p158.

looking carefully at what was tax deductible. Politics in music became corporatised and anodyne, a matter of selecting 'safe' causes that wouldn't alienate the customer base. In 1989, with the release of his first solo album, Edwyn looked back to the early days of his career. "So *Hope and Despair* is about how that was the last time that things seemed real, the first time you had youth threatening the establishment. It sounds corny and clichéd but I like the excitement you hear in music like 'Street Fighting Man' and 'Anarchy…', it had this threatening lyrical invective. Whether it was Rotten or Jamie Reid it was threatening the establishment, there was some intelligence at work there. Nowadays, post-punk, people sell this cosmetic angst, they sell despair as a commodity, cosmetic despair, completely selfish."[71]

The days when music made a serious contribution to debate over what matters — the possibility of new ideas, alternative ideologies — are long gone. In 1989, RAND corporation author Francis Fukuyama proposed the popular and convenient notion that with the collapse of Communism the world had reached the 'End of History'. The combination of democracy and capitalism had won the war and been proven to be the correct answers to the question of how we should all live. It was now simply a case of propagating the solution to every nation and refining the machinery of finance and technology to be as efficient as possible. While the End of History thesis has been discredited — when, in the modern era, has the potential for chaos been greater? — the energy, motivations and habits of independent thought in the early Eighties have eroded away. Our 'leisure society' demands too much from us. Exhausted and empty from the competition of careers and consumption and social media, the sheer effort involved in appearing even ordinarily successful, means we have to give up on the idea of individual will and instead plug into ready-made systems who have done all the thinking for us, the specialist service providers who stream our governance, work and entertainment.

*

---

[71] Brown, Len, 'Hope Springs Eternal: Edwyn Collins', *The Cut*, Fall 1989.

LIKE MAGIC IN THE STREETS

My life is glamorous and no-one else knows it. I'm waiting in line at the bus station after a Saturday of being a slave in Concept Man, feeling itchy and bleary from all the polyester and plastic.

A blue winter evening. The office blocks are emptying. It's raining and the air's a poisonous brown with bus fumes. Lads are chucking chips at each other down the other end of the station. Empty crisp packets roll along into a corner with the leaves and fag ends and cans. But nothing stops the show for me. Every drop of rain is part of the story, every shining piece of pavement is almost too much to bear.

Does anyone else see what I'm seeing? The line in front of me doesn't seem bothered. This is just a waiting place on the way somewhere else. The girl from Dorothy Perkins, buried in coat, scarves and bags, has plugged into her Walkman. I don't know what it is, why the feeling is so strong, but it makes me want to do stuff. Maybe I'll go over to the man on the corner. He's got a bucket for the miners and I've got a few coins. I can change anything because of how the bus station looks, and how it looks back at me. Everyone is talking about going to college or signing on. But all I want is more of this.

I'm keeping the glamour to myself. Dean would take the piss and say it was all about Pub Elaine. Lovesick teenager where nothing looks the same, all stars and roses. Maybe I am. Pub Elaine isn't worth any lost sleep according to Dean. He says she's pure toilet.

*

Back to the old house, a 1920s council semi in Stretford. The window of the box room at the front looks out over the privet hedge to the traffic of a never-ending arterial road, the non-stop traffic of every day and every night. Is this what days are for? The milkman running from door to door, a clatter, clink and sudden electric whirr. Bus after bus. A rusty Chevette, Escorts and Cavaliers in a dreary procession of going to work and coming back home. Tyres over rain-wet asphalt: slash, slash, sur-lash. Sometimes the dirt dries in summer and the traffic seems to send a high buzz and rumble above the houses, to the telephone wires and pylons, leaving a billow of dust left below. Open windows fill the bedroom with the smooth, strangely comforting smell of carbon monoxide, as addictive as cigarettes. Even when the roads empty at night, the convalescent city is kept going with its own life support machine. There's the radiance of traffic bollards, a streetlight glow on the ribbon road trees, the glare of shift-worker kitchens in the houses opposite.

Stretford is some four miles from Manchester city centre. The town was a by-product of the opening of the Manchester Ship Canal and its purpose-built industrial estate, Trafford Park, in the late nineteenth century. The planning of Stretford was originally infused with the Victorian spirit of optimism, a pride in what could be achieved by civilisation, how a local population could be elevated above its too-human tendencies. So young Stretford was designed around an Eden of parks, a botanical garden and other grand civic amenities built (like Glasgow) in red and yellow sandstone, where the bright ideals were made material in appropriately ornate, high-minded and rhetorical decoration. Then things fell apart. The most rousing and substantial of ideas and intentions can be mis-remembered, re-interpreted, misunderstood, forgotten. The 20th century was a different country with different demands and Stretford was allowed to atrophy, like so many other British places, in the name of utility and a new version of what was necessary. Factory workers needed housing. Traffic needed roads.

The middle-classes were able to buy property in suburbs away from Stretford in order to be separated from the mess in-between the old factory works and the bus depot, the railway lines and the Arndale. The Morrisseys were themselves part of an inner city slum clearance programme, moved from their settled local community to Stretford in 1970. Betty, a librarian, and Peter, who worked at the hospital as a porter, had arrived with Jackie and Stephen from inner city Hulme, a wasteland being cleared ready for the Crescent flats. A future of concrete brutalism for those who stayed behind.

11 year-old Morrissey slept in a room overlooking Kings Road, porous to Stretford and its Victorian Gothic of bad dreams, glowering in a landscape of feeble and ramshackle industry like Ozymandias sneering in the desert. A sinister Dickensian theatre of anonymous red-brick housing; derelict factories; lonely canal paths; the dark places under railway bridges where the tramps lived, roared on by trains passing angrily overhead. Manchester was already monstrous in his imagination. Morrissey had been seven years old when Ian Brady and his Mancunian lover Myra Hindley

went on trial, charged with torturing and murdering three local children who were nine, 11 and 17. Brady and Hindley had taken photographs and made tape recordings of the torture, including sexual abuse, before burying the bodies on Saddleworth moor. Other children were still known to be missing. "I happened to live on the streets where, close by, some of the victims had been picked up," said Morrissey. "Within that community, news of the crimes totally dominated all attempts at conversation for quite a few years. It was like the worst thing that had ever happened, and I was very, very aware of everything that occurred. Aware as a child who could have been a victim... it was all so evil; it was, if you can understand this, ungraspably evil."[72] The city streets had been fouled with old sufferings. "Local kids ransack empty houses, and small and wide-eyed, I join them," Morrissey remembered, "balancing across exposed beams and racing into wet black cellars; underground cavities where murder and sex and self-destruction seep from cracks of local stone and shifting brickwork where aborted babies found deathly peace instead of unforgiving life."[73] Across the iron bridge from Morrissey's Stretford home was St Mary's Roman Catholic Secondary Modern, an institution he would come to know as a place of other Dickensian grotesquerie. Teaching staff would uphold the routine of religious ceremonies with a dignified and supercilious air while at the same time being themselves part of a sub-culture of violence, Morrissey has suggested. Tough lads from families taken out of the slums enjoyed the rough-housing, the confusion of misrule.

The door shuts on Manchester and Morrissey is back inside a home that's hot and frowzy with emotions. The coal fire in the front room is a seething Halloween orange. Neighbours are round with their kids, gossiping, drinking tea and eating biscuits. The kids are in and out of the kitchen, they're arguing, greedy for treats, their mood boiling up and down. The blare of television can't compete. It's a typical family house in the higgledy Irish community where relations come and go with stories of who's sick and dying, who's lazy, who's finally found work, who's been seen out with who. "We were quite happy to ghettoise ourselves as the Irish

---

[72] Kent, Nick, 'The Smiths: Dreamer In The Real World', *The Face*, May 1985.

[73] Morrissey, ibid., p3.

community in Manchester," said Morrissey. "The Irish stuck rigidly together and there'd be a relation living two doors down, around the back or up the passage."[74] Love and hate ran through the streets like a fever. The soundtrack to King's Road came from the sound of Sixties' crooners singing songs of heaven and heartbreak. Peter and Betty themselves were known as a modern, good-looking couple. There were wolf-whistles when Betty was seen out, smartly-dressed and self-possessed. It was the kind of attention in the streets that upped the temperature of any argument or bad feelings, making marriage harder. And when Peter got into an argument he'd often finish things with his fists.

Johnny Marr (originally Maher) had the same Irish background, the same links to a home country where there were so many aunties, uncles and cousins, Brians, Kathleens, Marys and Brendans. "It was a loving but quite heavy, oppressive background," said Johnny. "There was a lot of wild talk, a lot of wild behaviour and a lot of drinking. But at the same time as being quite intimidated by a lot of wild, young Irish kick-ass guys, it wasn't half exciting for me and my sister."[75] Everything bounces off Johnny. He leaves home at 15 ("but that was fun. I think that was one of the best things I ever did"[76]). He goes on the dole ("I had a great time. OK, I could've done with more money, but I was living and I was playing...And honestly, all I really wanted to do was play guitar"[77]). By contrast, a few streets away, the bookish teenage Morrissey becomes caught on the thorns of everyday life. He challenges the authority of school, but it's a laborious form of suffering not an escape. "It was alright if you just curled up and underachieved your way into a stupor. That was pretty much what was expected really. Because if you're too smart, they hate and resent you and they *will* break you. When I found out that I wasn't being picked for the things I clearly excelled at, it became a slow but

---

[74] Morrissey interview, *Hot Press*, May 1984.

[75] Fletcher, Tony, ibid., p52.

[76] Garvin, Rex, 'Johnny Marr: The Man Who Caught The Common Cold', *ZigZag*, August 1984.

[77] Ibid.

sure way of destroying my resilience. They succeeded in almost killing off all the self-confidence I had."[78] His father leaves the family home in 1976. Jackie gets married and has children. Morrissey clings to what was left of the security of home, his mother, because he wasn't the adventurous Bohemian type. "I couldn't really face the gasfire that didn't work, the eight blankets on the bed, or the frost on the windows. I wasn't quite that resilient."[79]. Instead there's a long period, five, six years or more, of isolation. "I had lost the ability to communicate and had been claimed by emotional oblivion. I had no doubt that my life was ending."[80] There was constant creative expression — he worked furiously at his typewriter, his bedroom always "swimming in paper"[81] — but the only audience was himself. He wandered around the local parks. He flicked through the same-old rack of chart LPs and bargain leftovers available in Boots. Morrissey knew that something spectacular was coming or, even more likely, nothing at all. And that didn't matter because doing nothing always felt better than being inauthentic. "I can't even remember deciding that this was the way things should be," he told *Melody Maker* in 1984.

"It just seemed suddenly that the years were passing and I was peering out from behind the bedroom curtains. It was the kind of quite dangerous isolation that's totally unhealthy. I think, yes, there was in some ways a wilful isolation. It was like a volunteered redundancy, in a way. Most of the teenagers that surrounded me, and the things that pleased them and interested them, well, they bored me stiff. It was like saying 'Yes, I see that this is what all teenagers are supposed to do, but I don't want any part of this drudgery.'"[82]

---

[78] Kent, Nick, ibid.

[79] Kopf, Biba, 'The Smiths: Morrissey A Suitable Case For Treatment', *New Musical Express*, 22 December 1984.

[80] Morrissey, ibid., p201.

[81] Interview with Morrissey, *Earsay*, Channel 4, July 1984.

[82] Jones, Allan, 'The Blue Romantics', *Melody Maker*, 3 March 1984.

Those years turned out to be a time of gestation, the unconscious working through of ideas that gave his creations a stronger foundation of personality. An unavoidable him-ness. "The long period of isolation I had meant a very long period of self-development. If you're going to produce something of value, you have to think about what you're doing — you can't dive into it — and I gained a lot from being isolated. If I'd had the usual uncomplicated adolescence I wouldn't be here now, writing. It's odd how terrible things can be part of a learning process."[83] A lot of the lyrics, the material for his interviews, had already been written. This hardened Morrissey and gave him a stomach for action; for readying himself for a life in public that was connected, dramatically, if only in some small corner of his mind, to the glorious humiliation of the Catholic saints. "In a way, it's a type of revenge. You hate so many people... It sounds very juvenile now, I suppose, like smashing someone's window. But then what else can you do? It was like a weapon, something to make them gnash their teeth. Otherwise people will always have the finger on you. Always."[84]

*

Success came easily for Morrissey and Marr. For all those other indie guitar bands like the Go-Betweens who had given everything of themselves and seen nothing much in return, it looked depressingly easy. Morrissey and Johnny met in May 1982 and by December believed they had enough songs to conquer the world. The Smiths were a wildfire. "We planned a strategy and all of it worked," Morrissey told Radio 1's Kid Jensen. All their gigs and radio sessions were carefully handpicked in terms of credibility quotient, and that included turning down a tour supporting the Police. "We didn't want to waste our time or other people's time."[85] They wanted serious venues, especially in London, they wanted to be associated with the alternative vibe of Rough Trade, they wanted the validation of John Peel.

---

[83] Savage, Jon, 'The Smiths: Deliberately', *The Sunday Times*, 8 January 1984.

[84] Kent, Nick, ibid.

[85] Morrissey interview, *David Jensen Show*, ibid.

The early gigs, many of them at colleges and universities, started a buzz around informal networks of indie music fans. Marketing might get you sales but only word-of-mouth starts a cult. Simple stagecraft like the rainfall of flowers at the beginning of each show meant audiences could see and feel that they weren't in Kansas anymore. "Standing side-by-side are trendies in long leather coats, punks in exhausted combat gear and even the odd long-haired hippie or two. But all with something in common — they're all wearing flowers in their hair. You see, they've come to see The Smiths which, of necessity nowadays, means a trip to the florist beforehand," according to an early *Smash Hits* review of a gig at Westfield College in London. "The bobbing masses just below the stage laps up singer Morrissey's every gesture as he swings a huge bunch of flowers over his head, getting faster and faster until the stalks snap, sending yet another flurry of petals into the audience. Johnny Marr's melodic but forceful guitar lines perfectly frame Morrissey's finely-textured voice to produce pop with a delicate passion. The intention is pretty simple — vibrant, optimistic, uplifting songs; a celebration of youth, love and having fun."[86] "They're not just throwing flowers, they're wearing beads as well. Are these new underground raves going to prove yet another attempt at the psychedelic revival? Or perhaps another ride on the pastoral bandwagon? Whatever, they're sure to be extremely sensitive types..." (*Melody Maker* at Liverpool Polytechnic)[87]. Anthems of love, fun and the pastoral? These weren't impressions of the Smiths that would stick for long in the public imagination. Maybe new voices always start off by sounding optimistic.

NME readers voted the Smiths as 'Best New Act of 1983'; three Smiths' singles and an unreleased song made John Peel's Festive 50 for the same year (Factory's New Order, mind you, had five). Morrissey always suspected that Peel himself wasn't that much of a fan, he'd never be around when the band turned up to record sessions, and it was producer John Walters who'd pushed for so much Smiths' airplay. Meanwhile the Smiths were saying yes to everything. *Top of the Pops* and *The Old Grey Whistle Test*. *Pop Quiz*. *Pebble Mill at One*. Riding Charlie's Bus on *SPLAT* for

---

[86] Perretta, Don, 'Live Review - Westfield College, London', *Smash Hits*, 17 November 1983.

[87] Kiley, Penny, 'The Smiths: Liverpool Polytechnic', *Melody Maker*, 5 November 1983.

TV-AM. Because they were confident they were unstoppably subversive. Nothing could dilute them, so the more kitsch the medium the better. "We want to reach as many people as possible. We've hardly begun…We think we can do these things and walk away with enormous credibility because we are very strong-willed characters and our belief is very deep-rooted. We just have immense strength — the musicianship is quite special. There is a great deal of depth that just hasn't seen the light of day, yet. It's self-evident really," said Morrissey[88]. The music press could be just as giddy. "Even before they took the stage girls were being pulled aside for treatment after fainting and too much screaming. Talk about the Beatles! Clearly, The Smiths will go a long long way — but not just because they've come up with a unique image and loveable appeal. These flowerpower people have got a bagful of marvellously strong songs to back up their claims for a place in your hearts!…But the icing on the cake came when Morrissey clenched a bouquet and waved it proudly at the flushed relatives above him. It nearly brought tears to my eyes. Handsome one, Morrissey!" (*Melody Maker*)[89]

The backlash, as Morrissey predicted in his earliest interviews, was just as immediate. Reviewing a Sheffield University gig in October 1983, the *NME*'s Amrik Rai decided: "The Smiths write shallow, shrill and repetitive music, songs that circle slowly around still steady centres, bowling along, dipping into grey dripping metropolitan conurbations and swelling to gay drippy village greens. A spaced out and soft, spendthrift soundtrack, The Smiths are just bland and unsensational enough for Morrissey to shine."[90] By February 1984, just ahead of the debut LP release, *Melody Maker* had no doubt things were going to get messy. "Since the current speed of backlash is heading off the dial, it's a fair bet that The Smiths will be everyone's Aunt Sally in a week or two, but they will continue to attract rabid devotion and critical acclaim because they make the most perfect

---

[88] Wilde, John, Interview with Morrissey, *Jamming!*, 6 May 1984.

[89] Worrall, Frank, The Smiths live review, *Melody Maker*, 3 December 1983.

[90] Rai, Amrik, 'The Lackbash Starts Here: The Smiths/Sheffield University', *New Musical Express*, January 1984.

observations of the human condition and then wrap them up in the most memorable melodies since Lennon and McCartney put pen to paper."[91]

Rather than the 'strategy', the Smiths were mostly propelled by the hidden dynamics of a consumer society. When there's a hole in the market, some way it's going to be filled. The Smiths had to happen. The audience for new music — more alert and attentive than ever before — was altogether ready for pop thrills that weren't cheap or empty: unconventional, poignant, clever and sincere, and yet, somehow still pop. On the supply side, indie labels like Rough Trade had reached the stage as commercial enterprises when they needed chart-friendly bands to stay in existence.

In July 1983, the *NME* announced how "The Smiths, generally considered one of the brightest prospects to emerge this year, have signed a long-term deal with Rough Trade Records"[92]. The story suggested the band had turned down three major labels (one of them offering a six-figure advance), that it was their anti-corporate, ethical choice. Whether true or not, the Smiths were making sure they kept their indie image. It was a decision that was questioned by the 'professionals'. "The only problem the Smiths may encounter is financial," said DJ David Jensen in the *Daily Mirror* picking the band as one of his 'Red Hot Tips for 1984'. "They refuse to compromise their integrity by signing with a major record company. The limited budget available to independent company Rough Trade may prevent Morrissey and his group hitting the top."[93] The Smiths had avoided signing to Factory because they didn't want to be seen as 'another Manchester band'. But Morrissey was also holding his nose with Rough Trade. It was the Smiths and only the Smiths that made the label cool, he claimed in his *Autobiography*. "Rough Trade personnel in the early 1980s need never have feared sexual assault." The label had only built a reputation for being counter-cultural by releasing records "no one wanted to buy"; "it would take the Smiths to bring a level of success and glamour to Rough Trade

---

[91] Scott, Simon, 'Soul Shining: The Smiths/North Staffs Poly', *Melody Maker*, February 11, 1984.

[92] News in brief item, *New Musical Express*, 9 July 1983.

[93] 'DJ David Jensen presents his Red Hot Tips for 1984', *Daily Mirror*, 31 December 1983.

that the label had never dared hope for, and suddenly the smell of money replaced the smell of overcooked rice in the Rough Trade cloisters...In his wheelchair, Robert [Wyatt] was the very picture of the Rough Trade pop star, with a hit song that had cloistered nuns the world over tapping their habits."[94] The comments are ungracious, especially given the extent the Smiths were happy to exploit their rice-and-lentils indie credentials. As a CBS or Warner band the aura around the Smiths would have been very different. As would have been the reviews and attitudes of music papers like the *NME*. On their side, Rough Trade were forced into remodelling themselves, to get down to business and do everything they could to keep the Smiths — they couldn't afford them to be another Scritti Politti or Aztec Camera (or, let's not forget, another Orange Juice). That meant bending some principles, including making use of a major label's sales 'strike force', something that Rough Trade staff themselves considered to be "touching corruption"[95]. The Smith's subsequent success has deleted the immediate history of those early days at Rough Trade. Management hoped they might be another Aztec Camera but nothing was certain. The Smiths were a second prize, picked up because they were commercial and radio-friendly (more poppy than the Go-Betweens, more conventional than Orange Juice). Few people would have said there was anything unique about them. "The Smiths are Rough Trade's most commercial offering yet, deserving successors to Scritti and Camera," said the *NME* in early 1983[96]; and *Melody Maker* even a year later: "Too early to tell but right now The Smiths' nearest allies are Aztec Camera in that they're both Nick Heyward nicely out of tune."[97]

---

[94] Morrissey, ibid., p152/153.

[95] Taylor, Neil, *Document and Eyewitness: An Intimate History of Rough Trade*, Orion Books, 2010, p245.

[96] Hoskyns, Barney, 'Ridiculous and Wonderful: The Smiths/The Go-Betweens at the Venue, London', *New Musical Express*, 15 February 1983.

[97] Sutherland, Steve, Review of 'What Difference Does It Make?', *Melody Maker*, January 21, 1984.

At the centre of this whirl of discovery and elation among fans was a retro four-piece: vocals, lead guitar, bass and drums. The Morrisey/Marr partnership wanted to write classics that weren't just this week's thing (no single-use plastic here). They weren't interested in the contemporary music medium of video, it was "pantomime" said Morrissey, and "trivial"[98]. Electronica was fake and a cheapening of the material. "I think the songs have a certain quality because they are written on the guitar and that takes them through lots of levels of music: some of our songs could be [Phil] Spector songs and some could be Fairport Convention songs. Basically when I play I try to imagine a string part or a piano part as well as a guitar part," declared Johnny[99]. The musical model itself was closer to a tight jazz unit: the strong acoustic rhythm section, setting out a structure for elaborate blues guitar and emotional expression (with improvised, neurotic curlicues) laid on top. "The Smiths' sound rockets with meteoric progression," wrote Morrissey, "bomb-burst drumming, explosive chords, combative bass-lines, and over it all I am free as a hawk to paint the canvas as I wish."[100] It was Johnny who'd brought in the skills of two other members of the Irish community, Andy Rourke (bass) and Mike Joyce (drums). And at this stage Morrissey was keen to present their coming together as a miracle of felicity. He and Johnny were a natural partnership, a meeting of the melodic and the literary, and "Andy and Mike [were] the most capable musicians I've met," he told Radio 1. "We're a perfect little family."[101] Morrissey's role was words man ("I'm here principally because I write"[102]), and to front up to the press. He wanted to be a performance poet, to hear his words ringing out over an audience in his own voice and the quality of his singing lent an unexpectedly mellifluous weave to the blend. Soul without stylised contrivance. "He sounds capable of singing cabaret or pre-rock standards, backed by a jazz combo or string orchestra. But his

---

[98] Interview with Morrissey, *Earsay*, ibid.

[99] Deevoy, Adrian, 'The Smiths', *International Musician and Recording World,* October 1983.

[100] Morrissey, ibid., p148.

[101] Morrissey interview, *David Jensen Show*, ibid.

[102] Interview with Morrissey, *Earsay*, ibid.

voice will never sound better, or have more room to manoeuvre, outside the elegantly simple setting of the Smiths," said the *New York Times*[103]. It was a voice that perhaps would have been appreciated far more if it hadn't come from the mouth of Morrissey.

Another reason the Smiths entered the mainstream so quickly was their technical proficiency. They didn't throw themselves onto the gig scene, they booked rehearsal space and worked relentlessly in order to make sure that when they did finally enter the stage it would be with a professional flourish, delivering a set of songs that were ready-made classics. Months of rehearsals were also used as time to expose any lack of commitment from the rhythm section and to fudge over the lack of chemistry. There were inherent character differences to understand and get used to. Morrissey saw his bandmates as more "traditional", interested mostly in "beer, burgers and women"[104]. Mike and Andy preferred hanging around a PacMan machine to turning up for press interviews. "Morrissey and I are total extremes," said Johnny. "He's completely the opposite of me. Onstage Morrissey's completely different to the way he is offstage, he's extrovert and he's loud, whereas offstage I'm too loud and onstage I'm quite quiet. Everything — he's a non-smoker, he doesn't drink coffee, and I live off coffee and cigarettes. He's not a great believer in going out, cos he doesn't have fun when he goes out, whereas I go out every night, so we're two completely opposite cases."[105] From the beginning critics heard tensions rather than a workable counterpoint: Johnny's "slashing, chord-filled style suggests a dreamy, impressionistic landscape that at times seems directly at odds with Morrissey's grim lyrical musings."[106]

*

[103] Palmer, Robert, *New York Times*, 28 March 1984.

[104] Interview with Morrissey, *Earsay*, ibid.

[105] Hoskyns, Barney, ibid.

[106] DiMartino, Dave, 'The Smiths: We'll Meat Again', *Creem*, February 1986.

With so much hope and expectation on one side from the fans and so much reckless self-confidence on the other, fulfilling the potential of the Smiths in one LP was always going to require a heroic endeavour. Work began with producer Troy Tate, former guitarist with The Teardrop Explodes. "It's been a magical communion," Morrissey said of the work with Tate; it was just "a dilemma choosing from so many wonderful songs."[107] And in the run up to the LP's release he didn't waver from this promotional line, in spite of all he knew about what was really happening in the studio. Their first LP was "a complete signal post in the history of popular music", he told *Record Mirror*[108]. It was supposed to be, but after such a crafted beginning to their career there was suddenly a lack of ideas over what this monumental piece of vinyl should actually sound like. Smiths in the raw, with the crash and crackle of a live gig? or a smoother Smiths, where the beauty was protected from the rough surging energy of performance? It was a repetition of an unavoidable problem for indie: was it more important to be real or to get played on chart radio?

Troy Tate wanted to deliver on the first option, to try and bottle the skin-prickling enchantment felt by live audiences, the inspirational 'something' that wasn't in the written music. Tate was an inexperienced producer, meaning he was wiling to work hard and talk the band through choices, not try to control them. "When we did the first Peel session we were totally overpowered by the powers that be," said Johnny. "But Troy came in and relieved the situation…It was like we had the wheels and Troy set them in motion. The studio was really good as well, it had a good atmosphere – Elephant in Wapping. It's not Air but it doesn't have to be."[109] It was another Rough Trade production in a cheap studio, this time in a rundown dockland borough. The Wapping Wall sessions in the summer of 1983 were long and arduous. 14 tracks were recorded during a heatwave in a basement where the band struggled to keep their instruments in tune because of the warping humidity, no-one quite able to lose their clinging layer of sweat. While the rest of the band were only seeing the insides of

---

[107] Morrissey interview, *David Jensen Show*, ibid.

[108] Morrissey interview, *Record Mirror*, 11 February 1984.

[109] Deevoy, Adrian, ibid.

taxis and the clammy studio, Morrissey — so often a sheet of photo-sensitive paper — was absorbing what he saw in his wanderings around the nearby streets and along the mud-lumbering river Thames. "Apart from the Peabody Trust flats, empty warehouses, rats that talk, and the left-behind doggerel of deep regret, there is nothing at all in Wapping. The elderly poor still shuffle about, out of time and quietly insane."[110]

The Wapping tapes left everyone feeling nervous. Especially Geoff Travis. The financial future of Rough Trade was tied up in the success of the Smiths. He'd played the recordings to John Porter (one of the "overpowering" Peel session producers) who concluded they were out of tune and out of time and should be scrapped. "It meant so much to [Troy], he's thought about it all so much that I felt really bad about saying 'no' to some of his suggestions," said Johnny, "particularly as I'd got really friendly with him."[111] Johnny would have been happy with a new mix of what had already been recorded, but Travis didn't want to scuff the one shot they had at a Smiths' debut, and Morrissey also wanted to start again. There were rumours he'd been uncomfortable with how close Johnny and Troy had been in London.

The band re-grouped, working between studios in Manchester and the capital, where John Porter was given £100 and six days to lend some of his rock n' roll chic to proceedings. An English gentleman, Porter had played keyboards for Roxy Music (and Morrissey had loved the quirky glam album he'd appeared on, *For Your Pleasure*). That same year Porter had married Linda Keith, one of David Bailey's 'wild child' models and ex-girlfriend of Keith Richards and Jimi Hendrix. Again, Johnny was pleased to get musical input and support from a fellow musician. "All the elements of the Smiths are there. There's nothing lost, I'm sure of it. [Porter] was the perfect studio technician for us. He got some amazing subtleties but at the same time we were putting some things down in just a couple of takes."[112] He and Porter became a team in the studio, exploring possibilit-

---

[110] Morrissey, ibid., p158.

[111] Felder, Hugh, 'Scratch n' Smiths', *Sounds*, 25 February 1984.

[112] Ibid.

ies that didn't always work for anyone else. "[M]e and Morrissey would be sitting on one couch," said Mike Joyce, "and Johnny and John would be on the other, both grumbling away at the others."[113] Given the bravado of the Smiths, Porter was taken aback by the accompanying lack of nous. "Johnny and Morrissey were very close and had great faith in each other. They were really clueless at that stage — they were so clueless as to even ask me to manage them! The dreams and plans were wonderful, but there was a certain frisson."[114] Porter's friend and session musician Paul Carrack was brought in to add some piano lines (he'd been part of Squeeze, where he'd replaced Jools Holland, and was soon to join Mike + the Mechanics). Extra input came from Morrissey's friend (maybe even previously a girl-friend). It's Annalisa Jablonska's upset laughter on 'Suffer the Little Children', and voice saying "Oh really?" on 'Pretty Girls Make Graves'.

The process was rushed, and, according to Porter, Morrissey wasn't interested in any of the technicalities, he just wanted his vocal perform-ance left as it was. "I was totally into black music, and I think he saw that as a bit of a threat to their style," said Porter. "There was one famous oc-casion, where we were doing a vocal at Matrix in Bloomsbury. We'd got to the end of the first verse and Mozzer disappeared, so we chatted on for half and hour and it was like, 'Where's Mozzer gone?' Eventually we found out he'd walked out of the studio, got on a train and gone to Man-chester!"[115] Rough Trade had invested £6,000 (maybe £30,000 today) in the making of *The Smiths* and neither Geoff nor the band was convinced by the outcome. The grime and grunge was squared and prettied up, the tragedy given more of a comedic colouring. "The album ought to have been a dangerous blow from the buckle-end of a belt, but instead it is a peck on the cheek," concluded Morrissey in his *Autobiography*[116], maybe rueing the decision to ditch the Troy Tate sessions, the ones with exactly that rough intensity, whip and smack. The band shouldn't have allowed

---

[113] Perry, Andrew, 'The Smiths Smash Top 3', *MOJO*, March 2000.

[114] Ibid.

[115] Ibid.

[116] Morrissey, ibid., p160.

the final mixes to stand, he said, but the money had been spent. The level of disappointment with *The Smiths* was evident in the unusually rushed release of *Hatful of Hollow* just seven months after the debut LP, a batch of Radio 1 live sessions and two singles, an instant 'greatest hits'.

Unaware of the wan-faced wobble behind the scenes, the record-buying public saw *The Smiths* as the grand debut of the hottest British band around. Banks of lightbulbs flashed and an indie LP entered the mainstream charts at number two (behind the Thompson Twins). The band received an industry Gold gong for achieving more than 100,000 in sales (*Hatful of Hollow*, however, went Platinum) and even the pop magazines were on-board. "Current toast of the town, The Smiths are not to be denied. Morrissey relays ten tales of love missed or mangled, mixing gay abandon with his witty brand of melancholy. Johnny Marr's tunes are melodic joy...Best debut LP since U2. 5/5" (*No. 1* magazine)[117]. "Apart from a couple of dull tracks, this LP is genuinely wonderful (8 out of 10)" (*Smash Hits*)[118]. *Melody Maker* affirmed how the release was a world away from the razor-blade chill of bands like Joy Division, this was pop.

There really isn't much room for anything but perfection on this LP. There are moments here that float and shimmer with a spectacular inevitability, a timelessness, an opinion of their own enormous qualities that only the very best pop music can boast. And, like most of pop's most enduring moments, The Smiths' music is often bruisingly mordant in its preoccupation with states of melancholy, regret, an ironic nostalgia for the way things might have been, but obviously weren't and, perhaps, were never intended to be. Like most great pop, *The Smiths* is also consumed by an extravagant romanticism; a touching conviction that love can overcome the most critical of life's squalid realities.[119]

---

[117] Cooper, Mark, *The Smiths* review, *No. 1*, February 25, 1984.

[118] Ellen, Mark, *The Smiths* review, *Smash Hits*, 1-14 March, 1984.

[119] Jones, Allan, *The Smiths* review, *Melody Maker*, February 25, 1984.

The mood of excitability around the band meant there were question marks. The Smiths, and Morrissey in particular, were serious and substantial enough to be treated as an enigma that should be at least attempted to be understood. If the LP wanted to be art, then it was going to be subject to more assiduous scrutiny. Like this from the *NME*'s Don Watson:

> After contemplation of his flamboyant advances I've arrived at no conclusion as to what precisely he bears before him or what exactly he is after. What remains at the core of Morrissey's art is a mystique that has so far proved impenetrable — he affords the odd insight, but there is never enough glimpsed to dispel his fascination...Too frequently his philosophy of pop seems all too neatly prepared to appeal — the quaint campaign against the synthesiser for example. The mass appeal lies (unfortunately) in a form of traditionalism — so Morrissey offers the fictional tradition of 'great pop' — complete this sentence in six letters. The Buzzcocks, Orange Juice, The.......[120]

Morrissey quickly became the focus for criticism. He was the one with something to prove, the talented backing band were safe. "Advice: let the Smiths grow without the burden of unrealistic devotion. If Morrissey is one of rock'n'roll's great individuals let him prove it, don't be so damned accepting. The truth is that *The Smiths* is a disappointingly good album from a potentially exceptional band." (*Rip It Up*)[121]. Even *Smash Hits* felt how much the mystery of the LP might only rely on mutant karaoke, Morrissey vs Marr: "Morrissey's words are rather like his clothes — they're sombre, curiously old-fashioned and they don't quite fit. And, at times, the tunes seem barely attached to the guitars that chime like clockwork underneath them, making the strange little scenes they conjure up seem all the more mysterious."[122] What did Johnny really think when he first heard the lyrics being put to his amiable spangle of guitar patterns for 'The Hand that Rocks the Cradle'?

---

[120] Watson, Don, *The Smiths* review, *New Musical Express*, February 25, 1984.

[121] Kay, George, *The Smiths* review, *Rip It Up*, April 1984.

[122] Ellen, Mark, ibid.

Morrissey had taken the band into a situation where the words were taken seriously. He'd been made — and allowed himself to be made — by the music press. A media construct. Which is why the lyrics of songs on *The Smiths* made for easy news desk copy. It began in August 1983 with a *Sun* reporter ringing up a Tory MP. Did they know that a high-flying new rock band was singing songs about molesting children? ('Handsome Devil': "A boy in the bush/ is worth two in the hand/ I think I can help you get through your exams/ And when you're in your scholarly room/ who will swallow whom?") Moral outrage was duly supplied. The columnist then went through the motions of ringing Rough Trade. Morrissey explained the lyrics were nothing whatsoever to do with paedophilia. The story and its serious accusation was published anyway with a made-up (or at least, out of context) quote from Morrissey ("I don't feel immoral singing about molesting children"). "I've got a younger brother who is 11, who on the day it was in *The Sun* went to school and was hassled by kids, hassled by teachers," said Johnny[123]. *Sounds* followed up with their own attack in a gossip piece. Radio 1 quickly dropped its planned broadcast of a live 'Reel Around the Fountain' ("It's time the tale were told/ of how you took a child/ and you made him old."). The story was out there, living a life of its own and romping through the un-informed conversations of middle England. No matter how contrived, the implications of the accusation stuck. In September 1984, Boots and Woolworth's were withdrawing copies of *The Smiths*, this time because of 'Suffer Little Children'. Families of children murdered by Brady and Hindley had complained to the press — or had been encouraged by the press to complain — about "offensive" lyrics ("Lesley-Anne, with your pretty white beads/ oh John, you'll never be a man"). 'Pretty Girls Make Graves' and 'The Hand that Rocks the Cradle' ("I once had a child, it saved my life...I just looked into his wonderous eyes/ and said 'never never never again'") were also used by the tabloids as examples of Morrissey's perversity. For lyrics that were so personal, many of them the remnants of those years of solitude on Kings Road, the press scandals should have pierced Morrissey to his core. But instead he seems to have accepted the furore as confirmation of the stupid-

---

[123] Dorrell, David, *New Musical Express,* 24 September 1983.

ity of the modern mind and its hypocrisy, so it was a validation of his thinking in black-and-white ("And if the people stare/ then the people stare"). "I live a life that befits a priest virtually and to be splashed about as a child molester... it's just unutterable."[124]

The Smiths does look like a record obsessed by sex, both attracted and frightened. Tied up in regretful, unhealthy, morbid dressing-gown knots with it ("you tug my arms and say: 'Give in to lust/ give up to lust, oh heaven knows we'll/ soon be dust....'"). The cover is the naked torso of a 19 year-old Joe Dallesandro, a sex symbol from the New York underground film scene, star of Andy Warhol's Flesh (1968). A young hustler, the Artful Dodger of sex. Lou Reed references Dallesandro as 'Little Joe' on 'Walk on the Wild Side' (1972); his jean-covered crotch was used for the zipper cover of the Rolling Stones' *Sticky Fingers* LP (1971), and he made an appearance in Francis Ford Coppola's *The Cotton Club* (1984) as gangster Lucky Luciano. Like Edwyn at Postcard, Morrissey wanted to make his own covers and had found the photograph of Dallesandro among the mine of old papers and images stored up in his bedroom, a photo that he felt "had a tinge of sadness"[125]. Some critics wanted to make links between the cover, the lyrics, and Morrissey as a homosexual ('Still Ill' was interpreted as a reference to the de-criminalisation law and how some people would continue to describe him). *Rolling Stone* heard the sound of "homosexual isolation", "the daily ache of life in a gay-baiting world"[126]. "Morrissey writes intelligent, conversational lyrics about the things you worry about, but with predominant themes of frustration, sex and child molesting (our national sport)...Aren't these themes dodgy?...if Morrissey has only a minimal interest in sex, how come it appears so much in his songs?" asked one interviewer in October 1983. Morrissey sighed. Not again. But the question and answer are critical to understanding *The Smiths*. "[Sex is] this enormous blanket, and there are so many implications that can be put onto it. As far as the press see it what I do lyrically can almost be inter-

---

[124] Deevoy, Adrian, ibid.

[125] Interview with Morrissey, recorded as part of ICA's Rock Week, London, 5 October 1983.

[126] Loder, Kurt, *The Smiths* review, *Rolling Stone*, 21 June 1984.

preted as obscene, which of course it never can be. I think it's a sad reflection on modern journalism that this thing constantly comes up. To us it's just like asking about our verrucas or something. Simply to concentrate on one small distasteful aspect really belittles everything else we do."[127]

The working title for the LP was 'The Hand that Rocks the Cradle', and while this may well have been dropped in the wake of the *Sun*'s pursuit, it's fitting. In creating a dark little world from his Manchester days, rueful and anxious, the LP is casting a spell of protection. It's a set of songs about innocence, what is uncorrupted and irrepressible in spite of everything. Like one of the classic Disney films of the Forties and Fifties, the menace in the shadows is very real: childhood will be stolen, lies told. Sex is one of the potential traps waiting in the darkness, a culture and system looking to snatch innocence away, reduce relationships to the physical, to what can be possessed and degraded. The wraiths of Brady and Hindley are made to appear in a form where evil is palpable and ever-present ("a woman said 'I know my son is dead/ I'll never rest my hands on his sacred head'/ Hindley wakes and Hindley says:/ 'Wherever he has gone, I have gone.'"). As part of his protective spell Morrissey sings about the unexpected radiance of a "flower-like life", something still possible in the frightening Disney fairy-tale of corrupt authority, unreliable parents and bullying employers ("when the wardrobe towers like a beast of prey", "wavering shadows loom/ a piano plays in an empty room/ there'll be blood on the cleaver tonight/ when darkness lifts and the room is bright/ I'll still be by your side.") As a form of defence, poetry is a gentle and immanent force in everything, everywhere. Morrissey insisted his lyrics weren't crafted, they came in a flood with no effort, pulled from the aether: "I just sit down and kind of fall into a trance...I don't know where they come from."[128] In other words, from his instincts and experience, old memories mixed up with dreaming. They weren't a coherent script but dispatches from the war front. A rearguard rescue effort. And in this way the Smiths romanticised the streets of home as much as Orange Juice did with *You Can't Hide Your Love Forever* and Aztec Camera with *High Land, Hard Rain*.

---

[127] Deevoy, Adrian, ibid.

[128] Interview with Morrissey, ICA's Rock Week, ibid.

LIKE MAGIC IN THE STREETS

The Dallesandro body is so saturated with sex by its surrounding culture as to be non-sexual, the skin of a boy who's been used by a hypocritical society. Tellingly, the title 'Pretty Girls Make Graves' comes from Jack Kerouac. It was a line Kerouac would keep repeating to himself in order to remember the Buddhist cycle, how lusting after all the young women he sees on the streets in Mexico is part of a process that leads only to birth, suffering and death: pretty girls make graves. Morrissey's lyrics are glimpses of nothing more than a yearning for an ethereal Platonic affection: love as a longed for impossibility, only existing in the form of some scattered ruins of an ideal: ("she's too rough/ and I'm too delicate"; "I'm feeling very sick and ill today/ But I'm still fond of you"; "under the iron bridge we kissed/ and although I ended up with sore lips/ it just wasn't like the old days anymore"; "If they dare touch a hair on your head/ I'll fight to the last breath"; "it's not like any other love/ this one is different — because it's us"). Humour plays an essential part in making the chiaroscuro of threat and consolation work together as a living picture. It's charming, Sixties cinema-style wit, tempered by good-natured discretion and decency rather than smart insinuation ("people said that you were easily-led/ and they were half-right"; "I look at yours, you laugh at mine"; "take me to the haven of your bed/ was something that you never said/ two lumps, please/ you're the bees knees/ but so am I"; "I need advice/ because nobody ever looks at me twice").

The counter-cultural tradition is another nearly-organising strand, the rejection of work and ambition. 'What difference does it make?' is the standard response of Ray Smith, a Zen-hunting character in Kerouac's *The Dharma Bums*, whenever he's asked what he's going to do next. Morrissey doesn't mind playing the beatnik clown, the holy fool: "a beggar-man whom nobody owns", who admits "what a terrible mess I've made of my life", "I'm just a country-mile behind the world". 'You've Got Everything Now' is Morrissey's frustration at seeing the career success of the unthinking and thuggish while he was on the dole ("Back at the old school/ I would win and you would lose"). "It pays if you don't think," is how he explained the song to David Jensen[129].

129 Morrissey interview, *David Jensen Show*, ibid.

*

The singing, the words, the LP, were a politics of Morrissey himself, the need of the shy performer to get on stage and explain. In his autobiography *Words*, Jean-Paul Sartre reveals how he felt his youth had led to some misguided statements and ways of thinking. "Like all dreamers, I mistook disenchantment for truth."[130] Was Morrissey similarly mistaken? This suspicion was at the heart of his evolution into a hate figure. Cartoon Morrissey, the miserable, self-pitying vegetarian, the Anti-Normal so much enjoyed by popular media as a means to encourage a feeling of right-thinking among its readership. It was Morrissey's own fault. He enjoyed being misunderstood too much. Like Oscar Wilde who needed bourgeois disgust, Morrissey needed a narrow-minded pop culture. The myth and misunderstandings made him, and allowed the Smiths to become more than another guitar band. "I can understand that people can find me very irritating. And I accept that to an almost absurd degree, because I know that I'm not... I'm not... well, I'm not really a pop pushover. And that can irritate people, because they want their music to be quite simplistic, and they don't really want any fuss and bother and any seriousness. And I know I'll certainly never fit into that bill. But ultimately I feel that if people are saying no to the Smiths, they're saying yes to Madonna. And I find that the biggest sin of all."[131]

Morrissey came to realise there was another Morrissey going around town, looking and sounding just like him. The Bigmouth Morrissey was out of control and getting the real man into trouble. He got to the stage in his career when Bigmouth couldn't be caught anymore, he was running up far ahead — that knowing grin, running into photoshoots and striking Christ-like poses. The exit door on the other side of the room was always just closing behind him when Morrissey arrived, Bigmouth skittering with glee round the next corner and getting into the taxi first. Both the tabloids and the music press revelled in these games. "Sick" Morrissey says it's fine for boys to like boys as well as girls, they said. Morrissey turns up to

---

[130] Sartre, Jean-Paul, *Words*, Penguin, 1964, p101.

[131] DiMartino, Dave, ibid.

interviews in a tutu. Morrissey spent his youth hanging around public toilets[132]. "The Smiths are impossible to love unless you wish to mother Morrissey," wrote Tony Parsons in the *NME* in the summer of 1984. "There is a wistful optimism about the music they make that is very easy to like a whole lot but the main man-child's self-adoring ennui sticks in the craw once you realise that this is what he is going to be doing on his death bed. Ennui gets a little boring after a while."[133] The follow-up LP, *Meat Is Murder* (1985) was deemed to be weak, and the blame was directed towards Morrissey: "The suspicion is that there is no more real passion where those cries [on *The Smiths*] came from," wrote Barney Hoskyns[134]. The Smiths' record releases were becoming more like the soundtrack to a film of Morrissey's career as a cultural icon, the merchandising for the 'Pope of Mope' and tales of tabloid outrage.

To Morrissey, the Smiths might have been an ongoing project of expression, a place for him to work on potions and elixirs to help the ill-adjusted. But to Johnny it was a band. He was an exceptional musician who could be playing with anyone, and yet he was still being overshadowed. As they had to, the two different continents drifted apart. "I thought we'd boxed ourselves in musically and I didn't want to just carry on trotting out the old stuff, which was on the agenda. There was a lot of ego involved and a lot of paranoia...The relationship Morrissey and I had — ultimately, it was the making of the band and the breaking of the band."[135] There was no confrontation, no final argument, just the news that Johnny had gone in May 1987. A whimper. But to Morrissey it was another episode of high drama in the legend. "Johnny spits out my name, changing his story as he shifts from foot to foot; he says he had no idea, and then says he fully intended to 'move on'...Darting schizophrenically in the pursuit of self-interest, Johnny now looks pale on the scaffold — the

132 Morrissey, ibid., p188.

133 Parsons, Tony, *New Musical Express*, August 25, 1984.

134 Hoskyns, Barney, 'The Smiths: *Meat Is Murder*', *New Statesman*, Spring 1985.

135 Taylor, Neil, ibid., p305/6.

opportunism of wolves giving him a notably punished look."[136] Five years and the epic adventure was over. No-one bothered to stay in touch, no Christmas cards.

Morrissey has worked his way through 14 record labels since becoming a solo artist in 1988. The icon and his unruly Bigmouth Double have made a smouldering, demonic progress, trailing sulphur through the public imagination. In 1988 when a teenager threw himself in front of train, the *Daily Mirror* quizzed the mother about his record collection. Because there were Smiths records, the finger was pointed at Morrissey's miserabilism[137]. In 1993, Morrissey fell out with the *NME* after an article argued he was an errant Little Englander, a racist with sympathy for far-right parties: he'd appeared on stage wrapped up in a Union Jack flag, written songs like 'National Front Disco' and 'Bengali in Platforms' (followed later by 'England for the English' and 'This is Not Your Country'). Morrissey wouldn't speak to the *NME* again until 2005. In 2010 he called the Chinese a "subspecies" due to reports of their mistreatment of animals. He was a fan of Nigel Farage and Brexit[138]. In 2017, the release of *England Is Mine*, an unauthorised biopic of Morrissey's early life, was an opportunity for both re-assessment and fresh irritation. "Thirty years after the Smiths broke up, the 58 year-old's reputation is in dire shape, and not for musical reasons," argued *The Observer*'s review. "His albums are still well received and he remains a passionate live performer with enough diehard fans to fill stadiums. No, the problem is what he says. It is hard to think of another living artist who has squandered so much goodwill...Now a film that purports to show the birth of a star risks looking like the story of the apprenticeship of a resentful crank."[139] Morrissey has become the indefensible one. "'It stinks,' says Billy Bragg, who worked with, and loved,

---

[136] Morrissey, ibid., p265.

[137] Kent, Nick, 'The Smiths: *Rank*', *The Catalogue*, September 1988.

[138] Armitage, Simon, 'Morrissey interview: Big mouth strikes again', *The Guardian*, 3 September 2010.

[139] Lynskey, Dorian, 'When did charming become cranky? Why a middle-aged Morrissey is so hard to love', *The Observer*, 23 July 2017.

the Smiths during the 80s. 'They were the greatest band of my generation, with the greatest guitar player and the greatest lyricist. I think Johnny was a constraint on him… back then he had to fit into the idea of the Smiths. But now he's betraying those fans, betraying his legacy and empowering the very people Smiths fans were brought into being to oppose. He's become the Oswald Mosley of pop.'" (*The Guardian*, 2019)[140]

"Just how clinical and how innocent is this seducer of our imaginations? How genuine his successive (and often mutually exclusive) stances as corrupted and corruptor, reformed literary libertine and celibate gay bachelor?"[141] asked the *NME* in its review of *The Smiths*. Here's the rub. What was calculated to impress and inflame and what was real? In another apparently significant stunt, Morrissey appeared in close-up on the cover of *Record Mirror* in 1985 with 'FAKE' written on his neck. Around the same time, Morrissey met with ex-*NME* star Nick Kent for an article in *The Face*. "[S]tudy the words and deeds of this curious individual whose every spark of unfettered candour has kept the music press enthralled throughout the two mercurial years of The Smiths' existence," wrote Nick, "and one can only conclude that here is a man whose convictions tend to waver in certain key areas as mysteriously as they remain consistent in others."[142] He explained to readers how Morrissey's manager had tried to persuade him not to talk to any "former acquaintances". Everything needed to come direct from Morrissey. It was a desperate need for control that many interviewers would feel over the years. "What I am certain of," concluded poet Simon Armitage on meeting his hero in 2010, "is that nobody is more aware of being in the company of Morrissey than Morrissey himself. Call it self-consciousness, call it self-absorption, call it self-defence, but every gesture seems carefully designed, and every syllable weighed and measured for the ripples it will produce when lobbed into the pond. Sometimes it's in the form of a brilliant, Wildean retort, sometimes it's a self-deprecating comment of suicidal intensity, sometimes it's a shameless remark about the

---

[140] Jonze, Tim, 'Bigmouth strikes again and again: why Morrissey fans feel so betrayed', *The Guardian*, 30 May 2019.

[141] Watson, Don, ibid.

[142] Kent, Nick, 'The Smiths: Dreamer In The Real World', *The Face*, May 1985.

indisputable nature of his own brilliance, and sometimes it's a claim so mystifying that at first I think he's taking the piss."[143] The sexy celibate; the anti-business Rough Trade artist who just wanted to sell more records.

There's much about Morrissey's character that makes sense in the light of an archetype explained by Richard Hoggart in *The Uses of Literacy* (1957). It was a book published at the beginning of a parabola of interest in British working-class culture that led to all those Sixties kitchen-sink films and pop songs so important to Morrissey. Hoggart describes the newly-created anxiety of scholarship boys going to grammar schools. They'd taken to book-learning, found inspiration and consolation and poetry, and enjoyed the recognition that came with being the 'clever one' of the family. They were assumed to have a bright future ahead of them, because unlike their father and brothers they'd been fished out of a situation likely to condemn them to a life of manual labour. But in reality the scholarship meant alienation: "they are emotionally uprooted from their class, often under the stimulus of a stronger critical intelligence or imagination, qualities which can lead them into unusual self-consciousness before their own situation (and make it easy for a sympathiser to dramatise their *Angst*)."[144] Becoming a successful scholar meant spending more time alone. "He plays little on the streets; he does not run around delivering newspapers; his sexual growth is perhaps delayed. He loses something of the gamin's resilience and carelessness, of his readiness to take a chance, of his perkiness and boldness, and he does not acquire the unconscious self-confidence of many a public-school-trained child of the middle-classes."[145]; "He does not wish to accept the world's criterion — get on at any price (though he has an acute sense of the importance of money)."[146]; "He has left his class, at least in spirit, by being in certain ways unusual; and he is still unusual in another class, too tense and over-wound...He rarely laughs;

---

[143] Armitage, Simon, ibid.

[144] Hoggart, Richard, *The Uses of Literacy*, Penguin, 1957, p292.

[145] Ibid., p298.

[146] Ibid., p301.

he smiles constrainedly with the corner of his mouth."[147]; "He has great aspirations, but not quite the equipment nor the staying-power to realise them."[148] There's potential, Hoggart argued, for a creative outpouring that didn't fit within any recognisable tradition and lacked self-critical perspective. "From the Renaissance, from Robinson Crusoe, from Rousseau," concluded Hoggart, "various forms of romantic individualism proceed — and in part this is yet one more form of them, but one that has gone to seed in self-regard."[149] In other words, there can be such a thing as the wrong kind of sensitivity and intelligence.

In 2009, Morrissey appeared on the BBC's *One Show*. All the bluff and easy humour of an experienced presenter like Adrian Chiles was drained down to his toes. It was as if Chiles was interviewing an alien life form with a brain full of danger. He knew it wasn't going to be easy, but this? Why can't Morrissey just play the game? Make a few likeable anecdotes — the lovely celebrities he'd met and had a giggle with, the time he'd left his trousers behind on a train — and then get on with the product puff. The standard love-in turned into an uncomfortable exchange of opinions. Morrissey was being honest about what he thought about the unemployment figures, how he'd never wanted to be an employee anyway. It was thoughtful in a way that clashed with the *One Show* format like can-can dancing on *Newsnight*.

It's important to go back to interviews with Morrissey that are unmediated like this, not the result of editing and selection as they are in print. Especially the early interviews when he's shy, before his Double started to get around town. The tall, quiffed, pretty-eyed James Dean wannabe; a speaking voice with smooth, coffee-coloured tones. Northern but with a clip of propriety, a more mannered and effeminate Simon Armitage. Nervously he's listening to each question, hoping not to leave himself too exposed, often looking away from his interviewer to the corner of the room, a self-conscious tilt of his head; a fey smile when he's embarrassed or enjoyed his own erudition. Over the years Morrissey has become more

---

[147] Ibid., p302.

[148] Ibid., p304.

[149] Ibid., p315.

square-jawed, his eyes and head settled and fixed. But in those days he was still a flutter of tics, soft and silky as a moth. And it's difficult to reconcile this earnest young man — pleased to be a contrary voice, pleased to be asked serious questions and listened to — with the confrontation and arrogance portrayed in written media pieces published during the same period of 1983/84. We need to remember the times when Morrissey was at his simplest.

So why the disgust? The problem is mostly on our side. There are very few 'pop stars' who have been as honest and self-immolating as Morrissey, willing for their innermost thoughts to be analysed. "When one reads of this monster of arrogance, one doesn't want to feel that one is that person. Because in reality, I'm all of those very boring things: shy, and retiring. But, simply, when one is questioned about the group, one becomes terribly, terribly defensive and almost loud. But in daily life, I'm almost too retiring for comfort, really."[150] He could be intensely self-aware when it came to his states of mind. "We would be talking about the poetry of squalor and the ways in which even the most profound and heart-rending depressions might sometimes be illuminated by a kind of beauty, a sense of grace," wrote Allan Jones in an interview piece in 1984. "It was worth thinking about, [Morrissey] said, perhaps these moods were tests of our endeavour and the skill of living was simply learning how to cope with the depths and bitterness of our desperations; overcoming them, we might be capable of so much more."[151] The attempt to represent his character on film in *England Is Mine* isn't a success. The talented geek suggested has none of Morrissey's other-worldly flamboyance, the extremes of an artistic temperament, of someone who's given himself up to beauty and truth. Morrissey is infuriated by the ugliness of the modern world, the dishonesty and pretence for the sake of social convention, the lack of integrity. It's all so painfully obvious to him. Meanwhile we work and shop, and we believe in the perfection of our happiness, and we don't want someone ruining the party by looking unimpressed.

---

[150] Jones, Allan, ibid.

[151] Ibid.

Accusations of racism reveal how a society's ordinary sense of right and wrong can be stiffened and corrupted into a grotesque and self-serving political correctness. Morrissey hasn't changed. He's been consistent in his belief in the value of British working-class culture, in being anti-Establishment and pro animal rights. Morrissey has always been a relatively moderate thinker. It's our culture, instead, which has been radicalised: in the way language has been sensitised to the nth degree; the hunger for taking offence and the feeling of superiority that goes with it; the lack of maturity needed for having a conversation on any topic that may involve subtlety of understanding, grey areas, the undermining of absolutes. This is what the breaking up of traditional communities has done, replaced a rooted common sense built on lived experience with a homogenised and managed global culture of beaming stock-photo faces (each one of them secretly praying for the failure of the others). "If you call someone racist in modern Britain you are telling them that you have run out of words," explained Morrissey in an (unmediated) interview for his own website in 2019. "You are shutting the debate down and running off. The word is meaningless now. Everyone ultimately prefers their own race ... does this make everyone racist?"[152]

*

Eventually, when the fog of both militant fandom and outrage clears, it'll be clear how lucky we've been to have had a Morrissey at all. A small victory meaning the world isn't so bad after all. A shy, confused Romantic slipped through the crack of a door opened by that unexpected early Eighties moment in time. How many other lost souls made it through? And as a result, he's not a prophet of misery at all, but one of the most life-affirming artists of his time. From a background of psychological squalor he went on to transform all the limitations of the Manchester streets and their low canopy of clouds into high drama. Wagnerian rhapsody with chips. He was able to explain why the smallest, most petty-seeming emotions really were part of something more, a battle with convention, a reason to fight for a personal, emotional truth.

---

[152] Etsy Rayner, Sam, 'A Lark's Tongue in April', *Morrissey Central*, 24 June 2019.

His melancholy comes from its opposite, a belief in possible beauty. Like a Philip Larkin poem, drenched in the charm and tragedy of working-class lives, and that moment when somewhere becomes rain.

5.

Tinsel Town in the Rain
The Blue Nile, A Walk Across the
Rooftops (April 1984)

We've ended up in an odd place. We were following a route of influences from Orange Juice to the Smiths, finding along the way a model aesthetic of wilful, outsider guitar music. We'd seen some of the forces from those years that made for a broadly shared character and sensibility: the trials of love and making the world new; their bookishness, their politics. Okay — but the Blue Nile? Synths, drum machine, orchestral strings. The sound of men in Marks & Spencer raincoats.

This short history, though, has been following a twisting pathway. It's had a purpose other than tracing a musical genre. We've met the tricksters in the indie wood. The boy magician. The wimps and their witch. The handsome devil who comes along and upsets them all. Now, in the final act of the story, when we see the beginning of the end for indie Romance, come the knights of good heart and true. The Blue Nile weren't a tangent but an epitome of that Eighties moment, an unexpected apotheosis. They were indie at its most pure. Uniquely what indie was all about — or at least what it should have been about, because the Blue Nile weren't intended to be a commercial entity. *A Walk Across the Rooftops* was supposed to stand alone, to exist in itself and for itself, neither recorded for the benefit of product sales nor for visibility as a band. "At a time when every tyro in the field wants to force-feed their silage to a willing audience, when the artists of pop are looking more like pirates, the modesty here is a bit startling," said the *NME* at the time of the band's first feature-length interview in May 1984[1]. The Blue Nile didn't want their LP to sound like anyone else, or even like 'a record' at all. It was a labour of love motivated by a need to express something about the world and people's relationships with it, the feathery emotions that come and go between people and places, like a horizon filled with the movement of passing clouds. It was made with only a limited release in mind, giving Paul Buchanan, PJ Moore and Robert Bell the time and freedom to work with Calum Malcolm over months of painstaking sessions. The LP alone became a legend in those early years, the people behind it having disappeared back into the Glasgow streets. Paul even told the story of how an old school friend came up to him and recommended a breathtaking new album by some group called the Blue Nile; had he ever heard of it? Given the history of the band, nothing about the anecdote sounds apocryphal.

A Walk Across the Rooftops celebrates the alchemy of place: how we all respond to ordinary, the most ordinary and even ugly of landscapes; how places can appear somehow reciprocal, both prompting and absorbing feelings of heightened awareness, moments that lead to an unexpected curl of happiness; a more acute sense of memory and regret; a sweetly limpid experience of reality. "Is there a place in this city," sang Paul on 'Tinsel Town in the Rain', "a place to always feel this way?" Sounds like sentimental fluff. But it can also be tough-minded and revolutionary. Concentrating on the importance of individual felt experience in relation to places was a rallying behind the playful ideas of 'psychogeography' — whether intentionally or the result of a shared spirit — the movement originated by the French avant garde in the Fifties as an act of revolt against bourgeois culture. You don't follow the prescribed or even very sensible routes through the city streets, going to and from work the same way every day, making use of civic facilities or admiring the usual sights offered by guidebooks. You wander in free and eccentric ways. Take the back ways to the most unappealing and forgotten corners; make an effort to follow any route that makes you see and feel the city new, from alternative perspectives. Walking across rooftops among the clutter of TV aerials and ventila-

[1] Cook, Richard, 'The Blue Nile: I Can See For Niles', *New Musical Express*, 12 May 1984.

tion ducts? That would be ideal. In the practice of psychogeography there was a division between raw experience on the one hand, and on the other, the prescribed guide to what you're supposed to be seeing and thinking, the mediated version that acts as a constant confirmation of appropriate behaviour. Convention says the city is a machine for worldly success in which, one way or another, we must play our part: the cogs whirring, the race underway, we need to keep up, which means keeping to the accepted roads and highways to avoid losing time. In the newly rampant and domineering culture of the Eighties, the Blue Nile found a place that was out of the way of the traffic, all the nervous hurry of commuters and shoppers, and took a few moments to stop and look around.

*

Three graduates gave up their jobs and consigned themselves to years of shabby living, taking rented rooms, sleeping on floors and scratching around for meals. Middle-classness interrupted. They did it for the sake of making music, knowing they had no musical training or special ability, and no wish to be just another band trying to make it on the circuit. The band name they ended up choosing was the last consideration, picked up almost randomly from the title of a 1962 travel book by legendary war correspondent Alan Moorehead when they needed something to put onto the sleeve of their first single in 1981.

Paul and PJ had both grown up in Bishopbriggs, an undistinguished suburb of Glasgow compared with Bearsden, a scattering of mostly greyish council houses and bungalows covering a rise of land some four miles north of Glasgow's city centre. Paul's father had had a little success as a singer before settling into a career as a civil servant, but there were no other musical influences at home. Paul is still remembered by some older residents of Bishopbriggs as the boy who used to go door-to-door delivering bottles of cream.

All three went on to study at Glasgow University but occupied very different student circles while they were there. Paul was part of the English lit crowd, sometimes working on a magazine for a niche trade union, the Society of Scottish Playwrights. PJ was straddling his studies between both electronics and fine art. It was a seeming mismatch of a combination that in reality represented perfectly the cross-grain of some heartfelt interests. In recent years PJ has composed a set of songs on the work of nineteenth century scientist James Clerk Maxwell on electromagnetic waves, a phenomenon harnessed for use in radio, radar, microwaves and Wi-Fi[2]. Meanwhile, four years older than Paul and PJ, Robert was finishing his maths degree.

They stuck together after their studies, mixing part-time jobs with their obsessive cycle of rehearsals, moving deeper and deeper into a shared and binding sense of musical possibility. Sincere but not po-faced, these were still young men having fun. "We weren't sitting around stroking our chins…we're like the Marx Brothers, there's lots of falling down and knocking things over."[3] Slapstick with the compulsive quality of a quest. "It was good. We were happy," said Paul on his return to 99 Otago Street with a Dutch film crew in 2013. This was the address of the first-floor flat where they'd rehearsed, sometimes sixteen hours a day. "The room was a tiny rectangle. We had to stand in a line to practice."[4] Otago Street is a row of four-storey tenement buildings in blackened sandstone just around the corner from Kelvingrove Park. The rush of the River Kelvin runs underneath its back windows. Number 99 has steps leading up to the front door that make it more reminiscent of houses on a New York block. On the skyline opposite are flats and chimneys as well as the frowning Gothic features of what was the Hillhead Congregational Church (and now a Glasgow University building). Paul stood with the cameraman in an unlit hallway for the filming, hovering in front of what had once been a much scratched and flaky red front door, obviously affected by the spell of remembering the young man he had once been, careless with his happiness and loves. Before its recent gentrification, he said, Otago Street had an air of out-of-the-way neglect about it. "I preferred it how it used to be. Untidy." He takes the crew to a nearby street where there had been a grocery

---

[2] www.intimeoflight.com

[3] Sweeney, Ken, 'In Search of the Blue Nile', RTE Radio, December 2016.

[4] 'Tinseltown in the Rain (The Story Behind)', *ntr*, December 2013.

shop. "If we had enough money we'd buy a little packet of four cakes. Or yoghurt. That was our high living."[5]

The intensity of their commitment didn't mean a conscious plan to record music for a particular market or audience. To their minds, "no field of human endeavour offered the same scope for reckless vulgarity and preposterous pretension as the music industry," explained Allan Brown in the wonderful *Nileism: the Strange Course of the Blue Nile*[6]. Pop stars were the worst kind of kitsch according to the band. They were gaudy. Inauthentic. Egotistical. They didn't ever want to find themselves in some circle of hell where they stood in a bar and said "We're In a Band — As You Probably Know". "We've tried to make little bits of music that were compassionate and that were free of embroidery and self-advertisement. It's the equivalent of timing your walk across the road to coincide with some elderly person about to cross. You don't want to say, Do you want a hand? because that might be patronising. You just want to check they're okay. That would be a good enough parallel for what we opted to do."[7] Picture the expression on the face of a record label boss or Radio 1 DJ on hearing this manifesto of crazed and militant heresy.

Realising such a delicate vision in practice meant hard work and sacrifice, what *Melody Maker* summarised as the efforts of a "trio of gentle, stubborn, idealistic men". "We had very definite ideas about the music we wanted to create and we realised that it couldn't be done in half measures, so we quit our jobs and knuckled down to a whole year of concentrated rehearsing and demo-ing," Paul told *Melody Maker*. "We needed to work not only on developing our musicianship skills but we also wanted time to work on the songs. Up till then it had been frustrating — we had the ideas but not enough skill to work them through. That year of toil was gruelling, none of us had any money, and I mean *any* money, but it was worth the effort."[8]

---

[5] Ibid.

[6] Brown, Allan, *Nileism: The Strange Course of The Blue Nile*, Polygon, 2010, p5.

[7] Ibid., p2.

[8] Fitzgerald, Helen, 'The Blue Nile: Source of the Nile', *Melody Maker*, 28 April 1984.

Week after week, the Blue Nile persevered in their rectangle of space for creation, legs jammed up against PJ's single bed. PJ would like to say how they were gentlemen amateurs, "except [we] weren't gentlemen"[9]. They begged and borrowed equipment. An amp, a drum machine that only played Latin rhythms, and an ex-demonstration model of an Akai 12-track tape recorder. There was thrift, ingenuity and some electronics hobbyist know-how. PJ bought a zinc tray from a friend who worked as a waiter for £3 to sample as percussion; he rigged up a trigger balanced on a piece of wood between two stools to produce just the right kind of atmospheric low thud; the capability of his portable Wurlitzer organ and early generation Roland Jupiter synth were stretched to their limit. A cheap pair of headphones were bought from the Tandy shop to help keep the noise down for the neighbours on the ground floor while they rehearsed. "They were crackling and cutting out even on the day we bought them," said Paul. "And when we did get them working properly we couldn't move because they'd just cut out again. We had to stay frozen to the spot. Then one of the neighbours the next day said, Is everything okay, we heard this tremendous banging and thumping from the flat last night. We'd been doing everything with the headphones on, so we were stamping our feet very loud and talking very loud."[10]

These shoestring Monkees carried on their adventures with a clapped-out Volkswagen Beetle that had been bought for £15. The new wheels meant they could get all three members of the band and their equipment to play occasional casual gigs needed to keep them afloat and buy them studio time, playing restaurants with checked table cloths and candles dripping down old wine bottles. No new material, just the safest cover versions they could think of, all set to those unavoidable Latin American beats. "We tried indestructible songs like 'She Loves You'. You almost couldn't ruin them — although we tried…"[11]

---

[9] Sweeney, Ken, ibid.

[10] Brown, Allan, ibid., p48.

[11] Interview with Ken Sweeney, ibid.

It was the limitations that shaped the singular Blue Nile sound, its space and air, the aural interplay that forms a visual sense of lights shining in darkness. PJ's synth was monophonic, he could only play one note at a time, and this forced him into finding ways to use the 'sustain', the moments when sounds drift into silence. It encouraged songwriting and playing that emphasises the significance of each and every note. The same applied to Paul and his new Fender Telecaster guitar, bought for £50 with his share of the gig money. "Because I really couldn't play that well the chorus pedal meant the guitar would sustain while I tried manfully to get to the next chord."[12] The Blue Nile had other qualities that produced a metamorphosis of what might otherwise have been tentative and amateurish. They were using budget versions of tech being used by Madonna and Frankie Goes to Hollywood, said Stuart Maconie, but the output was from another world: "What's interesting about the Blue Nile is that a lot of their records rely on very 1980s instrumentation, which could be the most insincere, glib, dated sound imaginable, sort of treated drum sounds and processed keyboard sounds. But because of the sheer intensity of the performances, because there's so little going on, and because what does happen is so judiciously chosen and because of the obvious intense atmospheres these songs create, they kind of transcend that and it's starkly beautiful... it was eerie, it was empty, it was incredibly emotional, achingly sad."[13]

If music was such a technically difficult means of expression for them, why not make a film, write a play or poetry? Music worked best, said Paul, because it meant they had to work with their innocent, beginner's minds: "you could rely on your instincts because you'd not assimilated any techniques, you hadn't been educated — with music you could start afresh."[14] Being a self-conscious part of the industry or musical genre would be stultifying. "We were working in isolation so we didn't know what other people were doing, you know, we were just following our imagina-

[12] Brown, Allan, ibid., p45.

[13] Scott, David, *Classic Scottish Albums: A Walk Across the Rooftops*, BBC Radio Scotland, 2006.

[14] Sweeney, Ken, ibid.

tion."[15] This led to what Paul called a kind of "advanced speaking", communication augmented by melodies, sounds and atmospheres, where none of the musical methods involved were allowed to become too familiar. "That was the search for us. We didn't want to render the songs in recognisable chord patterns or in recognisable sounds, we were trying to make a picture or some kind of experience for people and therefore it was necessary to keep away identifiable sound and identifiable patterns and tones"[16] It was also agreed to be important that the players themselves were kept out of the musical picture. As lyricist, Paul insisted the songs wouldn't be about him, no confessionals or editorialising. The author would have no authority, no message. The search, instead, was to find a way to capture everyday epiphanies in music: special moments of feeling that had something true and important about them: a thread of yearning that was easily found and so easily lost again. "You work and work and work and have the life that you have, and once in a while, sometimes once in a decade, you see a few things you've got and think, yes, that's authentic," said Paul. "You try to stay true to that little moment whatever the costs."[17] There was no compromise in the quest. "The sound was always subservient to communicating the emotion…Very very low tech but what we do take care of is the emotional value of each of the sounds."[18] The working title for the project while they practiced their first original songs was the White Hats. No-one now seems to remember why, but it's exactly what might be expected from them — a reference to old American cowboy films, a salt-of-the-earth sense of honour and morality, a name that's typically Imagist, physical and specific: "We were very pure."[19]

---

[15] The Blue Nile interview with Rickie Lee Jones, 1989.

[16] Walker, Johnnie, *Johnnie Walker's Long Players*, BBC Radio 2, 24 May 2019.

[17] Thomson, Graeme, 'Paul Buchanan: "I felt lost after the Blue Nile"', *The Guardian*, 12 May 2012.

[18] Scott, David, ibid.

[19] Sweeney, Ken, ibid.

In practice the project demanded levels of sympathy and shared imagination unusual to a band, to any creative partnership. Humility rather than ego was the most important resource. "Robert, PJ and I, in our better moments, we were able to cast aside our vanities and insecurities and imagine — or see, or realise — the same picture, and did our best to record that."[20] It's a comment that alludes subtly to how membership of an artistic co-op wasn't always easy. There were different personalities and different interests. Robert was older, regarded as being the most grounded of the three, with a thing for heavy metal. PJ was the one with artistic talent married with technical know-how, who took charge of bringing the city soundscapes to life. PJ's work on championing the scientist Clerk Maxwell — an uncommonly earnest endeavour — has been an echo of his role in the Blue Nile, the shared belief with Maxwell in a work ethic, striving for the sake of knowledge rather than material rewards, and a belief in a beauty hidden within the mechanics of the physical world. Paul was perhaps the most complex personality of them all, always recognised as the modest and quietly-spoken frontman, but also skilfully persuasive. He was aware of the effect of his smiles, the slow gathering of laughter lines around his face and how they instilled confidence. It's been suggested his was a careful honesty, that Paul was always fully in charge of the impression he was making. To a small extent, maybe even consciously ingenuous. "Wily. Troubled. A seducer," concluded the boss of their future record label[21].

For the moment, the Blue Nile's sense of having a bigger purpose than the band was enough to keep them together. After all, it was only meant to be a one-off. They worked at identifying the moments and finding ways to make them resonate. "This isn't quotable because it sounds so pretentious," quoted the *NME* from speaking with Paul, "but one of the best things we saw in our first trip to London was a guy and a girl standing in Oxford Street, a couple of office workers, and they were obviously having a moment − breaking up or something, something that was wrong — and you just looked at it and you knew the feeling. It was a brilliant re-

---

[20] Rudden, Bernard, *Flags and Fences*, BBC Scotland, 1991.

[21] Brown, Allan, ibid., p68.

minder of what's worth all the hassle. You have to believe it's worth trying to encapsulate a feeling like that, summoning it through the music you're making. We're willing to keep trying and trying and trying — just to capture that feeling."[22] Somehow the elements of obscurity had to be pieced together. "The shape was in the stone before we did the sculpture, it was a question of just looking in there," said Paul, "We would speak to each other in terms that were probably odd to people outside. We started to think about making the components of the music reflective of the subject matter and the atmosphere of the song, rather than just about playing an instrument."[23] "It's the interior monologue of some character. I occasionally feel sort of slightly sheepish about the melodrama that's involved with it sometimes — and I'll say to Robert, you know, I'm having a Judy Garland moment or whatever."[24] The Blue Nile worked to their "own defiant internal logic" according to Allan Brown[25], with their own language and set of working processes. "Someone will say this needs more red or green in background, and we'll understand."[26]

The result was, and remains, a unique piece of work. "[*A Walk Across the Rooftops*] is so audacious in the way it's constructed, and I think it's constructed in a way that only a group of men isolated and determined and passionate and soulful and committed and mad enough could do it," said Irish DJ Donal Dineen. "They took it to the extreme, just went so far with it, and it sounds like them and it sounds like the place they made it, it sounds like Glasgow, it feels like I'm in Glasgow. And somehow they had that magic spirit in them…it requires magical thinking to turn something that you're inspired by into a work of art."[27]

---

[22] Cook, Richard, ibid.

[23] Thomson, Graeme, 'Paul Buchanan', *The Herald*, 2006.

[24] Scott, David, ibid.

[25] Brown, Allan, ibid., p21.

[26] Rudden, Bernard, ibid.

[27] Sweeney, Ken, ibid.

*

Bands are mostly remembered in shorthand (Orange Juice were the birth of jangle indie; Aztec Camera descended into mainstream pop; the Go-Betweens never had a hit record; the Smiths were miserable). In the case of the Blue Nile the cliché has been unshakeable: they were slow, fussy aesthetes who took five years or more to produce each of their four albums. One song per year of their career. As martyrs to a niggardly kind of art they severely limited the output needed for the recognition and commercial rewards they might have achieved, it has often been said, all leading to the band's demise after 2004. Paul himself admitted there could be "paralysis by analysis"[28]. Years later, Linn boss Ivor Teifenbrun claimed to have lost around £500,000 on the band. "At one point, I think when Virgin Records became involved, there was talk of a clause in a contract demanding, say, five albums in five years, something like that. The band weren't happy with that, it could have been a deal-breaker. I said to them, there's an easy way to deal with that clause and that's to record five fucking albums in five years. And if they'd done that they'd be massive today." And this all makes sense if the Blue Nile could ever have been part of the standard industry cycle, recording an LP, releasing singles and going on tour before beginning all over again. But as we've seen, they weren't even supposed to be making 'music' at all.

"There have been points in our career where — if we're being honest — you think, I wish we could shake that audiophile thing off," said Paul, ruefully, in 2012. "For us, it was always about the pictures and the emotion."[29] Tunes might have been easy, epiphanies weren't. Contrary to the Tiefenbrun solution, even if the Blue Nile had been capable of producing annual 'product', it would have ruined them long before 2004. Not even the biggest fan would want to listen to 35 re-makes of *Rooftops* and *Hats*, in the same way that no-one wants every moment of every day to be melancholic reverie. The poignancy only exists as transience, as fleeting as

---

28 Brown, Allan, ibid., p5.

29 Murray, Robin, 'Tinseltown in the Rain: The Blue Nile', *ClashMusic*, 20 November 2012.

the unexpected, uncertain and felicitous moments of awareness the Blue Nile were trying to describe. As Paul said (even though the answer is obvious enough to our modern minds) the real question should still be: "Why do people make so *many* records? What for?"[30]

*

The customers take a seat while Nigel walks away at a stately pace. These things can't be rushed. Once he's out the back he straightens his tie in front of the mirror, buttons his blazer and corrects his fringe.

"Big balls?" asks a colleague, smoking in the corner with his copy of the *Mirror*.

Nigel just nods. This one's his and only his. He picks an LP from the stacks on the side, makes sure it's not looking too dog-eared, and returns to the showroom, composing himself as he glides and smiles.

Of course sir, he would say. Quality speakers are one thing, but why bother amplifying music that's already been reduced to noise? The best possible listening experience for today's audiophile is the latest Linn turntable system, the Sondek LP12. Because of the precision engineering of the tone arm and cartridge you hear every last drop of the original recording as it was intended. Yes, that's right, you've heard of Linn sir? A Scottish luxury brand that has made use of the best of British scientific audio research. Manufactured locally. I can assure you that nothing from Linn has been within ten thousand miles of Hong Kong. You must hear for yourself sir. We don't trust mass produced LPs for demonstrating our products. They're often not even pressed correctly, the hole is off centre and the revolution is skewed, the surface of the vinyl is imperfect. This is one of our very own records pressed by our in-house engineers.

What was it again? Nigel asked himself. He could never remember what the LP was called, some experimental easy listening stuff that sounded a bit like Chris de Burgh so you had to crank the bass up. It definitely wasn't in the Dire Straits league.

---

[30] Brown, Allan, ibid., p13.

*

Linn were purveyors of the kind of hi-fi porn only read about in specialist magazines. A Linn system was known to cost as much as a high-performance sports car (and, fittingly, in 2002 Linn were given the deal to supply audio systems for Aston Martin). An LP12 record player was expected to be treated like a family heirloom and passed down through the generations. "If you want to install a state-of-the-art music system in your house, the guy from Linn comes out, and spends like, you know, two weeks measuring up your house and sort of testing the ambience of the rooms, and then the guy comes back with a truckload of gear and they install it all and you have the most incredible music system you've heard in your life," said Radio Clyde DJ Billy Sloan[31]. Set up by Tiefenbrun in 1973, Linn still exists as a niche business with an £18 million turnover, now under the charge of Ivor's son Gilad who has re-structured Linn for a digital marketplace. The LP12 is still being manufactured in Linn's own local factory, at a much higher cost than would be possible by outsourcing to operations in a country like China, sacrificing profit margin for reputation. Originally it had been an anomaly, a hi-tech factory situated in the midst of the social deprivation of Castlemilk. Since 2007 Linn has worked from a purpose-built building designed by Lord Richard Rogers in a greenfield location just outside the city.

The unlikely alliance between the lowly graduates in their garret and this realm of luxury business, the rags to (relative) riches tale, was made possible by sound engineer Calum Malcolm. It was because of his interest in heavy metal that Robert was asked by John Meyer, owner of Edinburgh's Phoenix Records store, to produce an album for his new indie label. The job took place at Castlesound Studios, Calum's recording suite he'd set up in 1979 in a derelict Victorian schoolhouse in Pencaitland, a rural village on the wrong side of Edinburgh from Glasgow. Inevitably, over the course of those days away from home, Robert talked about his friends the White Hats, how they hoped to some day record a song. At this stage, before Calum went on to produce acts like Simple Minds, REM, Wet Wet Wet, Mark Knopfler and Prefab Sprout (as well as having credits

---

[31] Scott, David, ibid.

for work with Orange Juice, Aztec Camera and the Go-Betweens), he was known mostly for his recordings of Scottish country dance music. This must have seemed like a suitably low-key, backdoor introduction to the recording world. The single recorded by Calum, 'I Love this Life', was a false start for the band in any case, only serving to confirm the band's opinion of the dubious character of the industry. Robert Stigwood Organisation (RSO) was the label that struck gold with the biggest-selling LPs of the Seventies, *Saturday Night Fever* and *Grease*. RSO released the Blue Nile's debut single in 1981 and then went bust a few weeks later, before there was chance to hear the demos of new material recorded for free by Calum that included 'Tinseltown in the Rain'. The track was instead played to a visiting delegation to Castlesound from Linn who were there to consult with Calum on the performance of their new speaker technology. Light bulbs of realisation sparked into life like strings of fairy lights all around the room. Because Linn wanted to record its own music to demonstrate the full capacity of its turntables, to have limited release LPs as part of the sales package, and here was an unknown band painting (Scottish) sonic landscapes.

It was the beginning of a strange relationship. The no-nonsense tycoon Tiefenbrun and his band of striving idealists. Linn would sometimes send straight-faced executives in their tidy suits over to Castlesound to check on the progress of their investment. The band was once summoned to a board meeting to explain how hair gel had ended up on the interior of a Linn company car (well, Robert was a tall feller). None of that mattered because the Blue Nile were given more than £10,000 and left alone for five months at Castlesound to complete *A Walk Across the Rooftops*. There would be Calum but no formal 'producer' as such to oversee the output. No A&R department on their shoulder. Compared with the two weeks funded by Rough Trade for the other four LPs this was a musical Shangri-La, allowing for the quiet and considered work of artist technicians. "In hindsight that seems to have been a real blessing, a real fairy-tale," said Paul. "I couldn't conceive of making the record we made if we'd been popped into a recording studio with a lot of industry wisdom — it just wouldn't have worked out for us."[32]

During the Castlesound sessions, Paul, Robert and PJ set up camp in a former Swiss Embassy building, an 'empty' just around the corner from Calum's flat in Edinburgh. By the end of the recording they were sometimes sleeping on Calum's floor. "Yvonne and I were not that long married, pre kids," remembers Calum, "we often had dinner at ours or got carry-outs. Lots of late night listening sessions."[33] Daytimes they gathered together in the neo-Gothic surrounds of Castlesound at the end of the main street of the village, in what might be taken for a miniature Scottish country manor. The bright studio space was based in the old wooden-floored assembly hall, illuminated by a high row of arched windows. As studio boss, Calum was much more than just sound engineer. "Crucial, absolutely integral," said Paul: Calum was the fourth White Hat, turbo-charged[34]. "He worked really, really quickly, he whizzed about the control room on a chair with wheels on it."[35] The Blue Nile kept careful accounts of time spent at Castlesound to make sure Calum was paid fairly for what turned into months of intense labour, including the invention of their own primitive sampling methods. "This was early days for sampling, and we had an AMS delay which could hold a sample of around one second," explained Calum. "That was enough for a single drum hit, and formed the basis of many of the drums and percussion sounds on the album. Some of the sounds were triggered manually, but Paul Moore built a little box which could convert a square wave into something a Roland TR606 drum machine could sync to. The tempo of the TR606 was proportional to the frequency of the square wave, so I would record the square wave onto tape, and then the TR606 could be synced to the tape machine. That way we could trigger the AMS to fire samples in time. Genius! Well, sort of

[32] Rudden, Bernard, ibid.

[33] Malcolm, Calum, Email exchange, 27 December 2018.

[34] Walker, Johnnie, ibid.

[35] Brown, Allan, ibid., p88.

genius, it was a bit haphazard to be honest."[36] Snippets of tape needed to be edited, cut, and physically taped together again for the master tapes.

> It never felt like a job [said Calum] but we started early enough and did fairly intense days. It was a mixture of fun and serious hard work. We had some uplifting moments when certain parts came together — a lot of surprises. It was a bit of an adventure, but it was obvious when we got something good going. I think a lot of the bands I worked with were keen to get away from rock and punk, and the new romantic thing was feeling a bit 'frilly' or showy. There was a move towards a more distilled type of song, simple and direct, sincere. Good sentiment but not sentimental. They weren't interested in musicianship as much as song quality — they talked more about colour and atmosphere. Most important to the LP's atmosphere was Paul Moore's synth sounds; the band's harmonic sense — which was unusual, all the clusters of notes, lots of seconds, fourths, sevenths. The choice of re-verbs was important — they helped with the drizzly sound.[37]

Back in the flat, Calum would make the band to listen to Bartok. Dark, bitter, glistening Bartok. It was a way of widening their perspective on what the LP could sound like: "horrific things, you know, but they had these great string sounds going on, especially because they were Eastern European orchestras."[38] String elements for the LP were performed by the Scottish National Orchestra. "They found they couldn't play it at first," Paul has claimed. "That took the wind out of their sails a bit. But I think they took it as a challenge. I mean, we found them practising in their break, which is very unusual."[39] Drums were mostly synthetic, but some drumming sounds were contributed by Nigel Thomas of the London Phil-

---

[36] Malcolm, Calum, ibid.

[37] Ibid.

[38] Brown, Allan, ibid., p87.

[39] Ibid., p84.

harmonic. For all the sophistication of the individual elements, Calum always argued these sessions were hit-and-miss. "You know I had no idea what I was doing during *A Walk Across The Rooftops*," he admitted to Paul after the completion of the fourth album together in 2004. That's all right, replied Paul, he hadn't any idea either. "That was what was good. We weren't part of any scene; we didn't have people who could play a lot of great chords on their instruments. We could play a little, but I was the worst by a long way."[40] The special quality of the LP came from having real strings and a good piano, said Calum. Robert's spacious bass lines. "Paul Moore's sounds are terrific. I enjoy depth in sound, I like getting that transparent 3D thing. And Paul's voice isn't bad either."[41] That voice. "Like velvet, a rock and roll Frank Sinatra crossed with Nat King Cole but with a modern, post punk sensibility," Billy Sloan has argued[42]. "[O]ne of those fine, timeless Celtic voices that finds rawness no stranger to poignancy, a dual quality you encounter more often in folk forms than pop contexts."[43]

Working on the LP turned into a concatenation of ideas and feelings and experience, a big city full of them. And for all of its diversity and confusion, a city that could be shared. "Everyone got very involved in the record," said Paul. "Like with Nigel it wasn't a conventional session situation where he would just play what he was told. He got involved in the songs and in the ideas — which was obviously better for us both."[44] "We thought it would be the only chance we got to make a record, so we tried our hardest," said Robert[45].

Given the heightened visual sensibility of the LP, choosing a cover image carried some of the same weight of responsibility as the recording

[40] Peschek, David, 'Some Sort of Surrender: An Interview with Paul Buchanan of the Blue Nile', *Quietus*, 19 July 2012.

[41] Malcolm, Calum, ibid.

[42] Scott, David, ibid.

[43] DuNoyer, Paul, Review of *A Walk Across the Rooftops*, *New Musical Express*, April 1984.

[44] Fitzgerald, Helen, ibid.

[45] The Blue Nile interview with Rickie Lee Jones, 1989.

itself. Reading the papers one Sunday morning in 1983, Paul came across a glossy supplement feature on the American photographer Ogle Winston Link (1914-2001) whose work was being exhibited for the first time in Britain at the Photographers' Gallery in London. Link was celebrated for his dramatic images of railway engines in the Fifties. He captured the glamour, the iron might and terror of steam locomotives grinding through the streets of small town America on the Norfolk & Western Line. They were scenes that Link made more theatrical by shooting at night, in black and white, with elaborate home-made rigs of flash bulbs that would explode all at once. A commercial photographer, Link was also a railway geek, travelling around the country loaded up with his equipment, heavy box cameras, thick cabling and reflector disks to the lines where old steam engines were still running, recording the sounds of far-off whistles and thundering arrivals as well as taking his photographs. There's something Expressionist about the Link images, in the mystery of harsh light and shadow and thick billows of steam; something Hopperesque in the mundane settings of railway branch lines; all of which appealed to the Blue Nile.

Link-inspired, they drove around the Glasgow streets at night with Linn's Malcolm Fielding, an industrial photographer more used to taking promo pics of turntables under studio lights, to try and find landscapes that could match the mood of the album. In Cathcart Road, part of the notorious Gorbals district, they wandered around a row of part-demolished tenements next to the lean-to shed of the Hermon Baptist Church, while Malcolm set up the equipment and portable generator needed to recreate the Link style. The trio mooched. They met and chatted with church-goers just leaving the evening service next-door. "You're an angel," Paul told one old lady as she emerged from the Hermon, always the charmer. "No," she replied sternly, "I'm a sinner saved by grace."[46] The band weren't originally meant to be in the picture at all, it just happened to work out that way. Malcolm caught them together: "looking through a window no longer there, [it] summed up the feeling of the album," according to Paul[47]. There's a sense of height in the resulting image, of an

[46] Brown, Allan, ibid., p71.

[47] Walker, Johnnie, ibid.

unseeable vantage point, as well as the look of a romanticised 'anywhere' city (the lettering on the side of the derelict building has a downtown Forties' America look).

Malcolm had to work fast on his photos. The longer they stayed on Cathcart Road the more they drew attention from a young Gorbals gang who were starting to move into an ominous-looking routine. The gang had started out with a few harmless jokes, some questions, a bit of aimless conversation to build up some trust, but all the time their eyes kept returning to Malcolm's equipment. The photoshoot ended with the band sprinting back to Malcolm's car.

*

Who are this magic band of men whose spells can capture and entice? How can The Blue Nile have come from literally nowhere and presume to wield such influence over the emotions? What game are they playing and just what are their intentions? An explanation is demanded. Three characters sit before me on the wicker couch of a bright and airy hotel bar near Virgin's Portobello headquarters. But the trendy bar with its wall to wall mirrors and pot plants is clearly not their native habitat. No rock 'n' roll warriors these, with their chunky hand-knits and tweeds. They look out of place in these surroundings, uncomfortable in this situation too — this is their first-ever interview and they're understandably nervous. They've been travelling up and down from their native Glasgow quite a lot recently and that's not a task that gives them much pleasure either. 'We're not cut out for all this wheeling and dealing, we'd much rather be at home working,' says Paul Buchanan, the man behind the amazing voice, a bit abashed at the sudden attention they've attracted.[48]

The Blue Nile were suddenly caught in the burning gaze of press attention. Big Country's Stuart Adamson had heard the album while he was recording at Castlesound and made introductions to his label, Virgin, for a distribution deal. Even so, sales weren't much of a blast because they were

---

[48] Fitzgerald, Helen, ibid.

being powered by word-of-mouth recommendation rather than the usual fuel of playlisting and *Top of the Pops*. The first TV play of the first single 'Stay' turned up on *Saturday Superstore* in April 1984, reviewed by a panel including strongman Geoff Capes, Esther Rantzen and Keith Harris with Orville the Duck. No-one liked it. The band turned down an invitation to appear on ITV's flagship programme for children *Magpie*. The Blue Nile were in no way anxious for more marketing spend or to join the Eighties publicity merry-go-round. It was all just as it was meant to be. In its first week the LP grazed the charts at number 99, reaching a peak a few weeks later at number 80. Over time though, *Walk Across the Rooftops* went on to sell more than 100,000 copies. "That first record sold exactly the same amount of records every month for two and a half years," said Paul[49].

Reviewers tried to find a category for the album and failed. Reflective moods, contrary melodies, spaces. It wasn't what music was supposed to be about, it wasn't even quite entertainment; it seemed to be saying a great deal without saying anything much at all, and that was unnerving. Still, they couldn't help falling for the story of suffering young poet-graduates. Looking back in 1989, *Q* magazine recalled how "the first album was a one-off, an album like nothing else we'd ever encountered. Nothing happened and everything happened. The music came out raw, tender, vulnerable, hard, achingly human, logical and, on the wrong days, almost unbearably emotional."[50] "The only problem is describing it," admitted the reviewer for *Sounds*, "all the claims for a record being 'different' and 'unique' have been so exhausted and devalued by overuse that I fear stretching my credibility until it resembles gullibility. Well. It's like ... Frank Sinatra's eerie work with Gordon Jenkins!"[51]. The *NME* concluded it might well be the "fruit of some reclusive, obsessive vision"[52]; "*A Walk Across The Rooftops* has something quietly (very quietly) magical about it.

---

[49] Harrington, Richard, 'Everyday Dreams of The Blue Nile', Washington Post, 8 July 1990.

[50] Black, Johnny, Review of *Hats*, *Q* magazine, October 1989.

[51] Robertson, Sandy, 'The Blue Nile: Acquamarines', *Sounds*, May 1984.

[52] DuNoyer, Paul, ibid.

This is a shaping of the rules to fit individual minds, instead of the customary reverse: charmed music that sticks to the memory like thistle burrs."[53] *Smash Hits* approved while categorising the Blue Nile, with its own kind of advisory warning sticker, as grown-up music.

The eventual influence of this one-off LP was out of proportion because of the people who bought it. Sound professionals, muso techies, artists like Tom Verlaine, Sting, Kate Bush, Rickie Lee Jones and Phil Collins. Peter Gabriel would bulk buy cases of 25 CDs of the album to pass round (and the influence on *So* (1986) is striking, especially in the tranquil, softened spaces of 'Don't Give Up', the gentle electronic pulse of 'Mercy Street' and 'We Do What We're Told', even the twittering birdcage intro to 'Sledgehammer'). In an industry working up storm after storm of novelty, making use of blunter, heavier, more screamingly obvious hooks, studios had been given an introduction to an alternative soundscape and a richer sensibility. What had been right under their noses all the time in the most ordinary and seemingly empty of things.

Outside of the music profession, the Edinburgh crime writer Iain Rankin was one of those deeply affected by what he'd heard. A contemporary of the band, he'd been working for a hi-fi magazine and struggling with anxiety attacks when he first bought the album on tape. He has described walking up and down Scarborough seafront listening to the songs on a loop and trying to find a calmer place, "getting my head back together again". "It's an extraordinary album, it's unafraid of dead air. It's one of the few albums I've ever heard where they'll allow silence, silence inbetween each note, between each chord. There are moments of incredible tranquility, it's such a laidback album...To think it's made by three guys, it sounds like complete orchestra at times, there's noises in there you still won't hear anyone else do, it stills sound revolutionary."[54]

*

---

[53] Cook, Richard, ibid.

[54] Scott, David, ibid.

On any normal plane of reality, releasing a critically admired LP was the beginning of something: getting round to shake as many hands as possible, making the most of being in the shop window for a few weeks, booking the world tour, talking about all the new material coming next. And most of all, manoeuvring to make sure the band could take the next step up the ladder to superstardom. As the property of labels and management and their tunnel vision of commerce it was hard not to. Paul, PJ and Robert saw things differently: the LP was an ending, maybe not *the* end, but an ending all the same. They returned to ordinary life, intent on evading any unnecessary posturing, not sure what all the phone calls and meetings were really for. Paul closed the case to his guitar when the *Rooftops* recording finished and didn't open it again for more than a year until the recording of the follow-up, *Hats*, began. They were too polite to say straight out that they didn't feel ready, that they couldn't just turn up and perform on command. So there were years of angst which turned eventually to panic and the burning of early new session tapes. There were stiff phone calls from Virgin, sometimes daily, but *Hats* didn't appear until 1989. "It's like shouting at a flower, it's not going to make it grow," said Paul[55]. PJ explained how the band hadn't even got together during that in-between year, there was no practising and no writing let alone public performances. "It was impossible…Paul obviously was driven crazy by the pressure that we were going to record in seven weeks…Suddenly we were back in the studio. For grown men it was very foolhardy, but again, other grown men were bullying us and telling us how much we owed them. Personally I would have kept releasing 'Tinseltown' until they realised what they had."[56]

Commentators haven't always been kind about the Blue Nile's low productivity rate, talking in terms of a lack of commitment, "excuses" to avoid playing live, perverse decision-making, "snatching defeat from the

---

[55] Sweeney, Ken, ibid.

[56] Ibid.

jaws of victory"[57]. And when they did make commercial deals they were the wrong ones, taking a chunky cash advance in 1992 to sign with Warner Brothers (after Linn and Virgin had let them go), which, in reality, was just a ball-breaking loan. They were incomprehensible, irritating, overly precious. Or, from another perspective, they had integrity. A simplicity that was always in line with the White Hats manifesto, the reason for being in the same room together.

Maybe it was the smallest of deviations by Paul, straying from the line of purity and the agreed *raison d'etre* (that it was fine to make music as long as it was done the right way) that caused the break in relationships in 2005. PJ made it clear he wouldn't be touring after the final *High* album. Paul hadn't thrown himself at celebrity-land in any promiscuous way, but there was a serious flirtation. Charlie Brennan, Tiefenbrun's deputy, had seen how "[Paul] liked the flame, he liked the warmth, but he didn't want to get too close to the fire in case he got burnt."[58] Paul loved his period in Los Angeles after *Hats* (seemingly in spite of himself, as the self-questioning Catholic). There were invitations to work with Julian Lennon, Annie Lennox, Robbie Robertson, Michael McDonald, and for a while Paul was often to be seen poolside, hanging around LA mansions. Peter Gabriel introduced him to actress Rosanna Arquette (star of *Desperately Seeking Susan* alongside Madonna in 1985), who became his celebrity girlfriend. "I really enjoyed it ... The great thing all the time was you were constantly wanting to phone friends and say, Guess who's in the shop? Guess who's in the supermarket? I'm not immune to all that. In the movies — celluloid's better than life isn't it? It makes everything glossy. I don't mean it's better, but it's so glamorous, I met lots of people — it was fascinating," said Paul[59]. A year earlier, in 2011, his attitude to the LA period had been more sober, or, at least, he'd been more on his guard. "We feel we're observers rather than pop musicians or artists, we're not one of them. The way pop musicians have been rewarded and treated over the years actually removes you from

---

[57] Carroll, Jim, 'A walk across the rooftops with The Blue Nile', *The Irish Times*, 10 February 2011.

[58] Brown, Allan, ibid., p113.

[59] Peschek, David, ibid.

the very thing that you're doing. You can't just go to a restaurant, any room there has to be a VIP room or table. I've experienced a tiny amount of it and I can tell you there is no magic realm, you don't get into a room where everything is better just because you get to hang out with Jennifer Lopez every day."[60]

It was a story as old as the Hollywood hills. The innocent from a workaday place is suddenly the centre of attention for an élite, our modern royalty. He is courted as a fresh and delightful talent. He's dressed up, fussed over and welcomed into an enchanted circle. He rides the glittery wave. But as it always must, the energy behind the wave becomes spent, builds and grows somewhere else instead. The innocent wakes up to find himself back in his old life wondering if it had just been a dream. Paul had kept his role as understated observer, but he'd broken from the White Hat ideal of anonymity, changed the proposition by establishing himself as a front man. Albums after *Hats* showed signs of a stunted relationship compared with *Rooftops*, a trio needing to work with past discoveries and ideas, even beginning to speak the same musical language as the pop mainstream. It wasn't meant to be like that. The White Hats were supposed to cause no more of a stir than a flight of birds over Sauchiehall Street, the sense of a change in the weather, enough to make you turn the collar of your coat up.

*

Teenagers in the Seventies and Eighties were the last generations to spend much of their waking hours outside in the streets. It was a time when they knew their kith — the little worlds that surrounded them — just as well as they knew their kin. Young people knew every house in their road intimately, the one with all the radio station and football stickers in the windows, the place with the Maxi on bricks and its curtains always shut; gardens where the posh families were showing off with crazy paving and rock gardens, their exotic puffs of pampas grass; they knew all the broken dusty cracks and trips in the pavements. The parks and bus shelters to go to, the

---

[60] Carroll, Jim, ibid.

back ways into town. All the NO BALL GAMES signs. TRESPASSERS WILL BE PROSECUTED. They knew the walls that could safely be used as football goals or somewhere to hit a tennis ball. Word would get round when there was an empty warehouse or building site to explore. There were always out-of-the-way places to ride bikes over jumps, places to just sit around, places to gob and somewhere for a wee.

There wasn't much to stay inside for. TV was made for either children or adults: a desolation during the day of programmes for schools, news and *Crown Court*, then *John Craven's Newsround*, *The Magic Roundabout*, more news, *Nationwide* and *Noel Edmund's Lucky Numbers*. Saturdays were kids' shows, wrestling and rugby league. Staying indoors meant having to find things to do and explaining what you were doing to mum and dad. A ticking clock. Old comics and magazines. Board games with half the pieces missing. A bookshelf like a museum, Enid Blyton and Agatha Christie.

Meanwhile, outside, there was real and vivid life going on in the streets. Open and free. A dirty, populated wild. Escape and surprises that had nothing to do with what parents knew anything about. Friends you wanted to meet as well as a whole load of threatening, unpredictable people you didn't. Freaky characters. Always the chance of seeing that particular someone you really wanted to see more than any other, that impossible and longed-for face, seeming to materialise magically out of the aether. Private places. Places to be seen and places to cause trouble. Places to take your troubles to. The streets were where you learnt about the boundaries of ownership, walls and fences, and how little of it all was open to someone like you (just 8% of British land is 'common' land accessible to the public; a third continues to be owned by aristocracy, dukes, barons and earls; in addition, the Queen's private possessions include more than 500,000 acres[61]). Having no money meant sticking to the in-between places, not planning to go anywhere or doing anything in particular. Maybe a few pence from taking back bottles to the local shop, enough for a can of Top Deck shandy to share. Relying on public clocks to know the time. Sent home by signs of twilight, seeing the menace of it in the streets

[61] Hayes, Nick, *The Book of Trespass*, Bloomsbury, 2021.

on a coal-smoke Saturday afternoon. Arriving back home in darkness to the sound of the football results and the itchy creep of the teleprinter.

And when teenagers left school and managed to find work, those jobs were more likely to have involved being in the streets, whether walking, riding bikes or taking buses to get there, or working outside in manual work and the non-service industries. It meant slow journeys into town, absorbing all those familiar sights, the church spire, office blocks, multistorey car park, high-rise flats, lampposts and treetops. Places tinted with morning and evening, where the landmarks were spread across the skyline, becoming too familiar to always be consciously present, but always there.

Living that way meant an immersion into the essential sensations of places: the mellow reek of exhaust fumes; sometimes a richer brew of cigarette smoke; the thick, fruity smell of a greengrocer's from an open doorway; café fry-ups. Dank places with their weedy corners collecting cans and old newspapers. Ordinary places with their own strangely affecting personality: the depot lined with a row of milk floats in a yard of patched up concrete; alleys cordoned off with wire fences, sun-spotted through trees; the gusty brows of hilltop estates. Always changing, with the seasons and their moods and character. Out on an autumn evening, the air thinning almost visibly, the blue lights of TVs turning on behind net curtains. The electricity of sun-bright spring mornings. Leaving home on a winter night, face down against the cold, whole empires of downtown lights waiting ahead.

There was a routine and ritual of walking, going places and being places, not travelling inside a car to centralised retail or leisure outlets. If you wanted to rent a video you went to the video shop in one road, you got a newspaper from the newsagents in another; alcohol and snacks from the off licence. Cars were expensive, not an assumed right. A boy racer might have their eye on a Ford Escort RS1600i but it would cost an entire year's salary for the average employee. Going out meant visiting the pub or social club down the road, the local places that were for people who lived in the surrounding streets just as much as the corner shop was. Local businesses at that time didn't need to invest in the kinds of standards of presentation, branding, fittings, features and levels of service that would later become an essential in a market dominated by glossy leisure chains. A night out drinking or to see a band could still be a cheap option, but you'd expect to smell the toilets before the catering.

The Eighties transition period divided the streets into separate zones of coagulated, market-oriented activity: home, work, shopping, leisure. Private car journeys were beginning to be needed to join the zones together. The first out-of-town supermarket in Britain was built in 1964, followed by the first shopping centre at Brent Cross in 1976. By 1987 there were 39 proposals for large-scale shopping and leisure developments across the country, all of them over 50,000 square feet[62]. The trend for disconnection has continued to be relentless. While strategic planning policy in local authorities and nationally has been against decentralisation because of the impact on town centres, between 2001 and 2012 there was a 34% increase in retail and leisure park schemes. 35% more out-of-town supermarkets were built between 2001 and 2011[63].

In 1970 there were 15 million registered vehicles on the roads, by 1989 there were ten million more. Walking the streets has continued to decline sharply according to official numbers. Between 1986 and 2005 the proportion of journeys by foot decreased by 32%[64]. The trend has had the most acute effects on the experiences of younger people. 86% of parents in 1971 said their children were allowed to walk home from primary school; by 2010 this figure had fallen to 25%[65]. It means that over the past 40 years, towns and cities have come to be seen and experienced very differently. No longer places that are wandered through from necessity, they've shrunk, become atomised, drowned out by TV, video, computer games and other media that come between us and the world outside; so places have been left to fade away into a background of semi-awareness. The in-between places of cities have evaporated. They're the nowhere-in-particular to be avoided or travelled through at speed. TV and magazine ideals of 'good living' have made us all the more anxious about those

---

[62] National Economic Development Office statistics, 1988.

[63] Trevor Wood Associates report, 2012.

[64] Ramblers figures, www.ramblers.org

[65] Fagan-Watson, Ben; Shaw, Ben, *Children's Independent Mobility: an international comparison and recommendations for action*, Policy Studies Institute, July 2015.

places. They're more likely to be occupied by the unemployed, misfits, the penniless elderly and other outsiders. Those who don't fit into the 21st century paradigm of the good life where we move from one site of power to the next, between the location of careers; cool, affluent forms of entertainment; and a home that serves as a location of possessions and lifestyle. Walking can be a leisure activity carried out in the right locations and situations — with family, with a dog — only when it has a socially appropriate purpose.

Digital access means the Eighties divisions of geography by activity have only been strengthened. We don't need places at all. We can be strictly selective about the places we want to inhabit. Even when we are in the streets it's rarely in an unmediated way, with an awareness that's free from a sense of responsibility or the presence of a digital device, looking to capture and share the moment in digital form, desiccating that moment into something much less than it is. People have lost their relationships with places, to the vistas and rooftops of home, and the feelings those places evoke. Responses have become diluted by managed, air-conditioned environments. So teenagers have interactions with more people than ever before and yet find themselves isolated. A study by the Office for National Statistics in 2018 found that 10% of 16-24 year-olds were "always or often" lonely, three times more than those aged over 65[66]. More material wealth, more leisure time, and still a confusing sense of somehow having much less — because their lives have become enclosed. The safe, controlled spaces of indoors have become the pre-eminent, swallowing reality. It's an enclosure of lives that appeared to have reached its sinister peak — but also somehow its natural and pre-destined peak — with the Covid-19 pandemic. Societies seem to get the catastrophes they are 'designed', in a twisted sense, to have. They trip over and fall into tragedies that relate to the psychology of their culture, the inmost desires of its populations. In the early 20th century the upswell of national pride in industry and technology and man's surging power over nature was followed by 'total' wars on a previously unimaginable scale and level of ferocity, where nothing and no-one was safe. In the 21st century, atomised communities of individuals,

---

[66] *Loneliness - What characteristics and circumstances are associated with feeling lonely?*, Office for National Statistics, April 2018.

fixated by security and personal space, get a global pandemic: staying indoors in biosafe bubbles becomes essential; the outside world should only be accessed and engaged with through digital devices.

Outside and walking in the streets, we're porous. We turn spaces into places by moving at a mooching walking pace, investing them with meaning. It's nothing consciously or rationally done, it's a kind of psychological heartbeat, not just reacting to but interacting with the streets. Because nothing reaches the intellect until it's been experienced through the senses. The streets happen first, they come freely and spontaneously, separate from any systems and conventions. And that's important, this space, a loose and limitless space, a relative 'wild' away from places where identity is imposed, inside at home, or work, where we more often take on a shell-like skin, confined and defined by our surroundings. What's discovered in the streets (the 'magic', if that's not too devalued a word) isn't either neat or obvious enough for explanatory prose. Music works better. Our five bands and their five LPs are examples of amateurs given the chance to express themselves and respond to the system, the 'thing', and to what there might be beneath the surface of conventions through evanescent moments of epiphany. Their magic often comes from the streets.

The importance of place to the LPs is not anything as intentional or formal as the practice of psychogeography. As Will Self has written, pyschogeography tends to be a distinctly male and nerdy phenomenon, for those people interested in the minutiae not poetry: "middle-aged men in Gore-Tex, armed with notebooks and camera, stamping our boots in suburban stations platforms, politely requesting the operators of tea kiosks in mossy parks to fill our thermoses, querying the destinations of rural buses. Our prostates swell as we crunch over broken glass, behind the defunct brewery on the outskirts of town…really only local historians with an attitude problem."[67] The notion of the flâneur doesn't fit them either. Those strolling characters of nineteenth century France, haunting the streets and arcades at their leisure, were connoisseurs of idling. They were always conscious of themselves and their reflections in shop windows, in the polished tiles and counters of brass, as being visible works of art of their own making.

---

[67] Self, Will, *Psychogeography*, Bloomsbury, 2007, p12.

Our artists had no purpose or hobby in the streets, they were young, everyday outsiders. That experience of the streets, as much as the need to talk about love, identity and politics, was the impetus for expression and the novel form it took. *A Walk Across the Rooftops*, wrote Allan Brown, is about "the search for independence, for a space where the demands of contingent everyday life are minimised, leading the singer to leave the red stone building and walk across the rooftops, where he starts to find the waiting country. It's an album located in the hinterland where experience becomes memory almost as soon as it's happened, where the quest is to find a 'place to always feel this way.'"[68] Each of the bands was outside the centre in provincial cities and suburbs. The brightest lights were always somewhere else. All of them were on the move, restless and unsettled — as young people starting out mostly are — and none in situations where the places they lived in had become too safe or steady or ignorable. They were always sparking with sensations, a mixture of Romance, yearning, anxiety and fear. Because along with the inspiration there was also the encounter with decay and desolation, something out of control.

*

Paul Buchanan was in his mid-twenties and living in a flat in Parkgrove Terrace, a few minutes walk around the corner from Otago Street, when he wrote the lyrics to the LP. "It's that blonde sandstone," he said, re-visiting the building in 2016. "Kind of my favourite really. It's lovely. Just across there's the park. You can always see, if you look up now, all the TV aerials. There's all the Sky dishes that weren't there then. You can see the roofs, the old slate roofs, and they're not that high, they're at an interesting angle so you can see. And the same's true of lots of flats in Glasgow, you can really see."[69] The *Rooftops* title, he said, came from "just me looking out of a tenement window and dreaming, as I still seem to be doing. It seems a bit creaky to say now, but I remember telling people the album

---

[68] Brown, Allan, ibid., p94.

[69] Sweeney, Ken, ibid.

was a kind of imagined documentary set in Glasgow — headlights reflected in a puddle, that kind of thing."[70] This was still the Glasgow of social deprivation and gang violence, kids hanging round the spare ground; families living in tenement flats with no indoor toilet or hot water; NO DOPE NO HOPE graffiti on the walls. The council had started to work on the pollution-stained facades of the city's Victorian sandstone, exposing the long-lost rose and honey colouring beneath (not always getting to the sides of buildings though, so they kept some of their look of having been scorched by history). "The window that I would sit at there in the kitchen...maybe just part of the idea was that you realised that whatever you were going through on the other side of the rooftops, on the other side of the world, people were probably going through very similar things, some far worse than you, some the same, some not so bad, that was really the idea of it — somehow if you would be able to get up from the kitchen table and step out and walk across the rooftops," said Paul[71]. There was still the romance of place, no matter how painful and unromantic the reality of heartbreak, crime and the struggle to pay the bills might be in those lives.

A journalist for *MOJO* magazine once asked Paul if there was any place he'd like to settle. He'd taken some time to think of an answer, because he'd been around the block a few times. Finally he told them: "I wanted to live in the first 16 bars of Marvin Gaye's 'Inner City Blues'."[72] It was PJ who led the work on creating this kind of inhabitable LP for the band, somewhere with scale and distance, post-industrial gloom as well as an innate and ineffable grandeur; somewhere that was populated with real people rather than pop characters. "We wanted height," said Paul. "We were very concerned about height on that record – and by extension, depth, obviously, and perspective."[73] Strings are plucked to sound like police sirens, synthesised effects used to evoke birdsong, the "vuv-vuv-vuv of

[70] McNair, James, 'Review: The Blue Nile – *A Walk Across the Rooftops* Collector's Edition', *MOJO*, January 2013.

[71] Sweeney, Ken, ibid.

[72] Irvin, Jim, 'Marvin Gaye: *What's Going On*', *MOJO*, May 2001.

[73] Peschek, David, ibid.

trains and buses and the chatter of people"[74]. Calum recorded a thunder-storm one evening from the back door at Castlesound "with cars swishing through puddles"[75]. The music was meant to be visual in other ways, even aiming to find "a sound that was like a rooftop, a sound that was like a fire escape"[76]. And that included trying to channel a spirit of quietness — not a void, nothingness — but a genuine and substantial peace in an occupied world. It was for this reason that the band would only work on recording the track 'Easter Parade' on Sundays, a song that's holding its breath, struck by the beauty of a vision of a "city perfect in every detail".

The LP's lyrics are a series of grainy photographs that capture the unnoticed moments of a city, what's happening when people are usually not looking: "I follow a broken thread/ Of white flags falling slowly down/ Flags caught on the fences"; "The traffic lights are changing/ the black and white horizon". The words also chronicle walks in the city, not driven by a purpose, not doing anything in particular but soaking up a simple existence: "Walk in the headlights, walk in the daylight"; "wandering into the daybreak"; "The rivers in the distance must be leading some-where"; "The wild is calling, this time I follow; "I am in love with a feel-ing/ A wild wild sky". Sometimes the city is a spectacle, a parade, that is overwhelming: "Here we are, caught up in this big rhythm". Paul is look-ing down on society's competitive angst, the race, and how irrelevant it all seems by contrast with the immanence of the streets. "I think like many people, I'm aware, possibly too much — and not just for me but for every-body — of the gap between… the advertisements and the traffic," he ex-plained. "There's a huge gap, an immense gap. However much we sell ourselves this winner culture, it's unsustainable. It has to be ok to lose, it has to be ok to be unhip. It brings me back to what I said before about the immense struggle in loving each other. That's the goal. Everything else is nonsense, people who don't really believe in it selling it to people who

---

[74] 'Tinseltown in the Rain (The Story Behind)', *ntr*, ibid.

[75] Malcolm, Calum, ibid.

[76] Walker, Johnnie, ibid.

don't really believe…"[77]. *Rooftops*, he recognised, was finally the moment when the gap between what he was feeling and the expression of it was gossamer thin. "It's a great time, when what you're experiencing and what you're making are right next to each other. Your life's so simple, it's just … simple. No cars, no phones, nothing."[78]

*

The Blue Nile were fine to wander the streets, the young fogeys in their sensible jackets and raincoats. Orange Juice meanwhile were a flashing neon sign of art school feyness. Spotted leaving a gig one night at Glasgow Technical College on Byres Road the band were chased and beaten up (Alan Horne had already run away). When Edwyn sang about the late bus "leaving from the lonely station" it wasn't necessarily with an idyllic scene in mind. Isolated night-time stations might be filled with memories, momentous meetings and goodbyes, but they also came with an edge of fear at being singled out, of outbreaks of confrontation and violence. There was a threat always there in the back streets, parks and shopping precincts like a plague. A look, a spit on the floor. It didn't ruin the possibility of romance, the aggro only intensified the contrast and made the romance feel more unlikely and unearthly, something to keep hidden and to yourself. So when Orange Juice go reeling around the West End's hipster stores and cafes, "Step we gaily, on we go/ Heel to heel and toe to toe", there's carelessness with a frisson of fatalism, a promenade going on inside a solipsistic universe: "Here I go around and around/ Sick inside and eyes to the ground"; "I step down to the arcade/ And I see my reflection in the window".

"I wanted to make beautiful records and always under strict conditions," said Roddy Frame, "like this one had to be made in Wales or this one in New York."[79] Places were major elements in his song-writing chemistry. Remember the cottage he bought in the countryside near Man-

[77] Peschek, David, ibid.

[78] Brown, Allan, ibid., p81.

[79] Braid, Mary, 'In the right Frame of mind', *Sunday Times*, 15 May 2005.

chester to work on *Knife*. And East Kilbride sings through *High Land, Hard Rain*. Roddy walks the streets, day and night ("We met in the summer and walked 'til the fall"), it's a scenic outdoors LP. Songs work their way down and around through the streets, "From the mountain tops down to the sunny street", alert to mystery and possibility, "I hear your footsteps in the street/ It won't be long before we meet/ It's obvious…". 'Oblivious' is in some ways the exception, written away from home while he was surrounded by the quintessential suburbia of Acton (and, appropriately enough, 'Highlands' Avenue) — "Bit of Reginald Perrin vibe. Sunny. Semi Tudor"[80]. But Roddy is soon back with the big skies, the rain, the murmur of distant trains in East Kilbride. He's out when evening falls, tuned into the faint essences of the unseen: "I got all the love and beauty/ In the spirit of the night." Even the cold, the empty and prosaic can't help but turn into poetry. "[A]ll that's left to warm your breast's the wine we stole tonight/ Bottle merchants both of us, overdosed on Keats, we smashed them all/ And watched them fall like magic in the streets." That Aztec Camera sound and rosy lyrical bloom evoked a powerful sense of place. So much so that fans didn't just want want to listen, they wanted to physically be there on the streets. Someone like the composer/musician Moby, commenting on a memory of himself from 1986, could say: "all I wanted was to live in Scotland and be friends with Roddy Frame…"[81].

The Go-Betweens found their muse in the most elemental of sources, the ur-city. Asked to describe the Go-Betweens' sound, Robert Forster called it: "like sunlight…a lost primitive civilisation"[82]. Grant McLennan's "prime, great love" was "fire, water, air, earth — men and women fitting into their landscape."[83] The wild, but the wild captured through a human gaze in its most simple, unaware and beautiful moments. "The Go-Betweens' imagery is wide screen, coloured in deep blue and

[80] Frame, Roddy, *Tim Burgess's Twitter Listening Party*, 3 May 2020.

[81] Moby, Facebook posting, 20 September 2018.

[82] Stenders, Kriv, *Right Here: the story of the Go-Betweens*, 2017.

[83] Nicholls, David, *The Go-Betweens*, Verse Chorus Press, 1997, p127.

bright yellow, peppered with isolated figures," said the *NME[84]*. When Robert read about his hero Bob Dylan and what was being described as his "wild mercury sound", he wanted the same kind of vivid phrasing for the Go-Betweens: "that striped sunlight sound": the essence of quiet moments of perception, the noise of convention shut out, when the light slants onto a landscape between clouds, trees, city tower blocks. On *Before Hollywood* this psychogeographical sensibility is translated into moments like these: "There's lightning on the hill tonight/ Over in the west/ The colour changes shape and slides"; "The thunder settles in and waits/ Trams on the rattle/ Windows banging shut like gates"; "I'm standing on a quay wrapped up in mist/ The steamer's left with someone that I miss". In the streets, spaces can be privileged, sealed off (like London's resident-only gardens) a mirror of all the power relationships that need to be subverted and transcended: "The main gate to the mansion is locked…I went in but I got chased off". Those barriers are immaterial when thoughts and perceptions are kept in the wild: "The garden is unkept and in bloom/ There is wilderness and flowers in my room".

"My childhood is streets upon streets upon streets upon streets," begins Morrissey's autobiography[85]. Streets were both the promise of adventure and limits of his universe, the subject of plaintive affections and miseries. Working-class streets keep an obscure magic in their palimpsest of ordinary lives. The unpretentious emotion and tragedy of the passing of days, all the cold Saturday evenings looking into illuminated shop fronts, fetching treats from the takeaway before returning to sit in front of the electric fire and the TV. When Morrissey played Battersea Power Station in 1997, he didn't think of it as just another live venue. "It is a beloved monument clinging to life and surrounded by bits of forgotten land that no-one seems to know what to do with. There are bent lamp-posts on cobbled streets where this happy breed surely lived out their lowly lives. It's all about to fall, yet doesn't quite. The Power Station is the pride of south London and fills the heart with love, yet nobody knows more about it than

---

84 Watson, Don, 'The Go-Betweens: Up From Down Under', *New Musical Express*, 26 November 1983.

85 Morrissey, *Autobiography*, Penguin Classics, 2013, p3.

that."[86] In recent years property developers have turned the proud monument into a place that has nothing to do with ordinary people anymore, selling two bed apartments for £3 million and up to £10 million for three bed penthouses.

"I could never live anywhere else — I absolutely adore England, I really do," Morrissey told the *Melody Maker* in 1987. "Not many people see what I see — so many romantic elements of English life buried beneath the corrosion. I'm the only person I know who can take a day-trip to Carlisle and get emotional about what he sees."[87] In 1985 he told *Spin* that Manchester was all the material he needed ("because I grew up there and everything that I feel now is because of certain incidents that happened there"[88]), but it was feelings associated with relationships with places rather than any single spot on the planet that moved him. In 2009 Morrissey was singing about that reciprocal feeling in another country: "I'm throwing my arms around Paris/ Because only stone and steel accept my love". Manchester was the source of a sour nostalgia. Where curtains were shut against more than just the coming of night-time. "The dark stone of the terraced houses is black with soot, and the house is a metaphor for the soul because beyond the house there is nothing, and there are scant communications to keep track of anyone should they leave it."[89]. The city centre streets weren't being managed and monetised in the Seventies. Johnny Marr remembers this from his constant walking in and out of town to the department store Lewis's on Market Street and to see who was hanging around Piccadilly Gardens. "You had to watch yourself walking through subways or cutting across parks in case you bumped into the wrong people, and you had to be especially streetwise if you were carrying a guitar."[90] Derelict sites around the city, the wasteland of rubble and burnt out cars,

---

[86] Ibid., p410.

[87] Quoted in Simpson, Mark, *Saint Morrissey*, SAF Publishing, 2004, p165.

[88] Savage, Jon, 'The Smiths', *Spin*, June 1985.

[89] Morrissey, ibid., p4.

[90] Marr, Johnny, *Set the Boy Free*, Century, 2016.

were places for travellers and skinheads with their own rules. Lads who'd been friendly and chatting one day would be waiting for him with bricks the next. Petty crime and violence were everyday rituals. "It could be a bit edgy around Ardwick," said Johnny, "and even as a little kid I had to watch myself. I was in the street one day when a much older kid grabbed me for no reason and started pounding my face into the pointed tail lights of a parked Ford Anglia car."[91] Morrissey's bête noire were the Collyhurst Perrys ("a vicious cult of midgets dedicated to Jumbo cords, wedge haircuts, Fred Perry tee-shirts and easy violence," recalled one Manchester-born journalist[92], or in Morrissey's own words, "non-human sewer rats with missing eyes; the loudly insane with indecipherable speech patterns; the mad poor of Manchester's armpit"[93]). Walking back home from the Central Library and the Arndale Centre, waiting for a bus at Piccadilly, meant holding his breath in case there was sight of a Perry. "They would smack you in the mouth and ask you what you were looking at after."[94]

The city streets had been read by the Smiths as epic history, chronicles in brick and concrete that were borrowed to give the music a ready-made grandeur: "rain lashed, smoky tales of young marriages failing in flats by the gasworks and illicit meetings under viaducts, a world populated by Albert Finney and Rita Tushingham, The Shangri-Las and Ena Sharples," wrote Stuart Maconie. "At this point The Smiths were more than just a group, they were a fully realised world."[95] Smithsville is populated by people left-behind by the Eighties' surge of wealth, people stuck in streets blighted by ugly scars of demolition, in lives bogged down in boring jobs, selling their time for the lowest possible pay, only managing to find ordinary comforts in the streets and each other.

*

---

[91] Ibid.

[92] Owen, Frank, 'Home thoughts from abroad', *Melody Maker*, September 1986.

[93] Morrissey, ibid., p138.

[94] Owen, Frank, ibid.

[95] Maconie, Stuart, *Cider with Roadies*, Ebury Press, 2004, p165.

The Eighties' imagination was pervaded by dreams of escape from the British landscape and its palette of greys, greyish greens and browns. The freedom of going abroad and experiencing the 'foreign' became a mass consumer product made up of ritual technicolour displays of gaudy beach towels, cocktails and sunburn. Travel, in the form of package holidays in particular (making sure there was no need to speak to 'foreigners' or eat their food), had become a cheap luxury. There was an end to regulation on travel pricing and the increase in competition meant discounting. More travel agents were turning up in the High Streets, where young pretender Lunn Poly was overtaking Thomas Cook. Most popular for British escapees were the Costa Brava, Madeira and Malta, and even the USA was looking a good deal compared with a British holiday.

High Land, Hard Rain betrays a yearning for the dusky south, somewhere Roddy could walk the streets at night without two jumpers and an overcoat. The band name name may have been a careless choice, novelty words, but there's also a streak of affinity there for that lost Aztec civilisation, a sun-worshipping, socialist simplicity, that chimes with Roddy's Caledonian flamenco. "Yeah, I can't help playing like that. Campbell says I'm just like a Gyppo!! But I've never had any training, it's just the way I taught myself to play, and it's still there. I'm sorry, I can't help it!"[96] When it came to choosing a cover image for early Postcard release 'Mattress of Wire', Roddy cut out a picture from an encyclopaedia of a young Roman girl, classically dark-eyed, her head wreathed in Mediterranean laurel leaves. In the photoshoot for the LP, Roddy clings longingly to that glowing Greek island[97].

The exoticism of the name chosen by the Blue Nile hints at the band's mental geography: rooted in the real life of Scottish cities but with an instinct for fantasy — adventure and reverie at the edge of crystal waters, a simpler land. There are few of Glasgow's actual landmarks in *A Walk Across the Rooftops* except for the bells of St Steven's and the "red car

---

[96] Dessau, Bruce, 'Roddy Frame', *Jamming!*, October 1984.

[97] The sound of summertime Roddy exists on record. *Dreamland* (1993) is a rhapsodic London-Barcelona travelogue, of walking in a summer where "the streets just sparkle silently".

in the fountain" which had been displayed as a quirky curio in a local club. The image of Golden Age New York is more powerful — because of the influences already mentioned, from Edward Hopper, Charles Bukowski, Raymond Chandler — but there are others. Glasgow, more than any other British city, felt an affinity with the USA. Its classless, blue-collar culture, the Country and Western music, Frank Sinatra, the easy sentiment and hard-boiled humour. "The city almost considered itself an American consulate, or a misplaced state," wrote Allan Brown[98]. Attracting more tourists from the US to Glasgow had been seen as an important tactic in addressing economic decline. There are also echoes on *Rooftops* of the peculiarly New York-shaped musical form of minimalism. Popularised from its avant grade beginnings in the late Seventies by Philip Glass and Steve Reich, minimalism was the sound of New York, not the people or their culture but the modern mechanics and visual patterns of the city itself: simple repetitions of architecture, traffic, factory machinery, automation, the new mainframe computers, the beauty of tessellated forms. Sampling sounds from the streets was all part of the minimalist composers' method, along with overlaying simple rhythms and synthesised phrases. In the history of music, following on from the disturbing post-war noise of serialism, minimalism was intended to be a re-emphasis onto the harmony between people and the streets. When Glasgow celebrated its role as the first European Capital of Culture in Britain, both Frank Sinatra and Philip Glass performed live. When Orange Juice was starting up, the advert for new members talked in terms of a "New York band forming in the Bearsden area", because New York was the home of disco as well as the Ramones. Morrissey was famously the New York Dolls biggest fan, setting up and running the British appreciation society, and made plans to visit the city in 1979 (that came to nothing). It would have been too late for Morrissey anyway according to Grant. "Robert and I have talked about this — we went to fucking England first. We should have gone to New York. But by the time I went to New York, at the end of 1979, the scene had gone anyway, had come and gone."[99] New York remained the dream metropolis:

---

[98] Brown, Allan, ibid., p25.

[99] Nicholls, David, ibid., p132.

"uttering 'New York' and 'Paris' not as honeymoon destinations, but as cities to one day walk through and work in."[100]

*

Would Dad ever remember not to start cooking the peas before turning on his fish fingers? wondered Sarah. She'd go over on Sunday afternoon to see him and as usual he'd be doing the hoovering. He'll have got Mr Kipling's French Fancies in. Dad was different though, looking different. Older in his face, in the lines and shadows, but younger in his eyes and the way he talked sometimes. He was making plans and talking about a holiday in Spain that was all bought with pet food. Even Adrian was making conversation about college and girlfriends like a real person.

No looking back though. Her flat was home now. Gas fire burbling, the sheets hung out over the clothes horse were steaming. Fray Bentos in the oven. Coming home from work at the Council offices every evening was still a dream. The dim little entrance hall and the flaky paint were there to welcome her. The threadbare carpets had been covered up with rugs and she'd painted the walls. Dad had given her the living room lamp and the record player.

In the summer she was going to open up all the windows. The sun would flood in. She'd sit in the sunlight and turn the music up loud.

---

[100] Forster, Robert, *Grant & I: Inside and Outside The Go-Betweens*, Omnibus Press, 2017, p31.

Outro

*W*hy does 1985 look and feel so much closer in character to the 21st century than even just two or three years earlier? Maybe because, by then, a neoliberal mindset had been popularised and settled in. Union power had buckled, socialism had been turned into an alien concept. The cycle of big business and consumerism was seen to be winning and become the accepted reason for living. It was a cycle given revolutionary impetus by IT: 1984 had seen the launch of the first Apple computer, as well as the introduction of the Windows operating system. The FTSE 100 Index was set up. There was the first major sell-off of public assets, British Telecom and the Trustee Savings Bank. The increase in share ownership was trumpeted as a demonstration of the benevolence of capitalism, where anyone could benefit from the power of global financial systems (it was a myth — there were more small investors in the Sixties than there are now). Sir Richard Stone was awarded the Nobel Prize for Economics for his work on developing accounting systems that allowed the life of nations to be assessed in terms of their economic activity, consumer demand and the Holy Grail of 'growth'. In 1985 there were the first mobile phones, the first internet domain names were registered. Europe's largest indoor shopping centre opened up in the West Midlands. Most significantly of all for the music business — and the culture of British music-making as a whole — there was Live Aid.

July 13th 1985 was a hot day across the country, brilliantly blue-skied. But families stuck to their sofas for an afternoon and evening of TV that had turned into something bigger than was ever anticipated. More than a follow-up to the Band Aid Christmas single, more than just raising funds for NGO work in response to the famine in Ethiopia. Live Aid was the global feel-good event of a generation, a superconcert at Wembley

Stadium and JFK in Philadelphia that was televised to a billion people in 110 countries. It served as an epitome of the victory of the Eighties' zeitgeist, the combination of commerce, technology and pop culture led by an Anglo-American neoliberal axis. However valid the cause and the impact of the $127 million raised for initiatives by NGOs for saving lives in Ethiopia, the element of philanthropy was always muddled by scenes of fist-punching and flag-waving. Glamorous celebrity activism. The celebration of 'us'. Live Aid was opened, inevitably, by the Prince and Princess of the fairy tale, Charles and Diana. They were followed by a jukebox of household names. In other words, the biggest global brands, a musical Unilever: Queen, David Bowie, Elton John, Phil Collins, Sting, Status Quo, Dire Straits, Paul McCartney, Spandau Ballet. Even bands with a huge transatlantic following like Depeche Mode, renowned for stunning live performances, weren't invited.

The music business learnt a great deal from that single day. Why put so much money into a pipeline of risky, unknown bands? Talent, rebellion, a new sound and a new message — none of those things paid the bills; it wasn't a reliable product in itself. Bands assumed to be out of fashion and sliding into obscurity were given another chance by the fierce global publicity of Live Aid. The event demonstrated the potency of a new sugar-coated formula: how familiarity, affection and mass marketing made for a valuable heritage pop product. Even Adam Ant, who'd been allowed one song at Live Aid, went on to say the concert marked "the end of rock n roll"[1].

That didn't mean no more interest in new product potential among the major labels, just more risk management. "They save huge amounts of work, time, and money because they can just wait until a band emerges fully fledged from the independent network and then offer them the capital investment which the independents don't have," explained Geoff Travis in 1987[2]. There was no Smiths at Rough Trade anymore and any new

---

[1] *Louder than War* interview, 'Adam Ant brands Live Aid a "mistake" and a "waste of time" and the end of rock n roll', 26 August 2011.

[2] Cooper, Mark, 'Rough Trade Records: Rough At The Top', *The Guardian*, 30 February 1987.

Smiths who came along would be expected to take their shot with a major label as soon as possible. Very few of the indie bands emerging from ramshackle indie stables were believed to be worth the investment. Of the 22 bands featured on the *NME*'s *C86* mail order cassette showcasing the 'new' indie scene, only two had any lasting success (The Wedding Present, and a re-invented Primal Scream).

C86 is controversial. For some it was a renaissance: "It was the beginning of indie music. It's hard to remember how underground guitar music and fanzines were in the mid-80s. DIY ethics and any residual punk attitudes were in isolated pockets around the country, and the *C86* comp and gigs brought them together," wrote Bob Stanley of Saint Etienne in the sleeve notes to a *C86* re-issue. Other commentators only heard second-rate imitation, a manufactured branding. Indie in general seemed to have settled for a low bar just in order to keep on existing, with no more talk of changing the world. "The heroic phase of the independent movement was long past. By 1985, it had settled into steady but unspectacular growth. Independent culture no longer imagined it could supersede or even challenge the mainstream," wrote Simon Reynolds in his history of post-punk[3]. It was the indie music of 1985 that led John Peel to say: "I don't even like the records I like."[4] Indie kept going because its archetypal jangly, shambling self had become a market. A small one with its own formula and set of expectations and limitations. And as a market, it was one the major labels wanted for themselves, in order to knock over the competition, eke out credibility and be in position to bag the bands who might crossover into the mainstream. They set up mock-indie labels that were subsidiaries linked to independent distribution networks. The music press stopped caring whether there was anything genuinely independent behind a band's output. It didn't really matter as long as the sound was suitably lank. It was a trend that culminated in the marketing strategy for Britpop in the Nineties; palatable, singalong pop given a mock-indie hallmark of credibility. Edwyn was appalled by the suggestion he was somehow the 'Godfather of Britpop'. "Britpop was little more than a commercial foot-

---

[3] Reynolds, Simon, *Rip it up and start again: postpunk 1978-1984*, Faber & Faber, 2005, p518.

[4] Ibid.

note to The Smiths," according to Mark Simpson, "a belated and massively overhyped attempt by the record industry to cash in on the legacy of the original 'Indie' four-boys-and-guitars band whose commercial potential was never fully realised in their lifetime."[5] An exaggeration, but along the right lines.

It would be easy to assume that our five fell out with major labels in the Eighties because they were choking on their precious indie credentials. That was rarely the case. Edwyn, admittedly, was often pricked by the attitudes of A&R departments and managerial suits into a state of cussedness. But the machinery behind getting music out into the world wasn't what mattered. At worst it was a necessary evil, at best a useful machine that could be manipulated. Back in 1981, Edwyn was quick to mock the newly-announced indie records charts because it only took sales in the low thousands to reach the top: "If you're in the alternative charts it means you're on the dole."[6] "I don't see what you gain on a small label. You only make life more difficult for yourself," agreed Roddy, just after signing for Warner. "The independent idea is very strange. What exactly are you independent of? You are competing with the big labels and often using their distribution networks, but miss out on not having the money to back it up. We are really happy with our deal, we have plenty of freedom and total artistic control, and being on a big label means there are people to organise things for you so that you can concentrate on more important things like writing."[7] Morrissey always believed the Smiths made the mainstream in spite of Rough Trade: "Nothing surrounding the Smiths was ever positively *exploited* – it seems such an ugly word but sometimes it can be handy."[8] "In the music business it's a cliché to claim that every word of *This Is Spinal Tap* is true. But it is — every word," said Paul[9]. But even the

---

[5] Simpson, Mark, *Saint Morrissey*, SAF Publishing, 2004, p169-170.

[6] Pye, Ian, 'Juicy, fruity, cheap 'n cheerful', *Melody Maker*, 17 January 1981.

[7] Dessau, Bruce, 'Roddy Frame', *Jamming!*, October 1984.

[8] Kent, Nick, 'Morrissey: The Deep End', *The Face*, March 1990.

[9] Brown, Allan, *Nileism: The Strange Course of The Blue Nile*, Polygon, 2010, p9.

Blue Nile eventually hired a Spinal Tap-style manager in the form of Ed Bicknell in 2004, a larger-than-life character who had manoeuvred Dire Straits to MTV stardom.

By 1985, the conversation about the mainstream had changed. It might have sounded the same, but the mental sums being worked out were different and the logic of what constituted 'success' even more so. "For some reason we now felt under pressure to have hit singles, to compete in the pop marketplace, rather than exist somewhere else entirely," wrote Everything But the Girl's Tracey Thorn in her biography. "In the early 1980s this kind of ambition had seemed new and positive, and was born of a genuine belief that those of us from the post-punk generation were poised to take over the charts and reinvent the rules of pop music. But instead that takeover hadn't happened, and we were all left somewhat adrift, without a clear alternative home to inhabit and still battering at the doors of the charts, doors which, much of the time, remained resolutely shut."[10] The walls of the music world were closing in, its financial channels hardening against anything amateur or that didn't fit a product formula. Post-punk had nowhere to go. The flowering of Romance represented by those five LPs by Orange Juice, Aztec Camera, the Go-Betweens, the Smiths and the Blue Nile was at an end. The battle for the soul of pop had been lost, and the original spirit of the bands began to separate and become diffuse, drained of any coherent outsider position and the reason for the Romance.

*

There's more music being recorded than ever before. Digitisation has allowed for democratisation and no limit to experiment, the number of individual voices or access to what's produced. Major labels still lump themselves behind market strategies and what's known to sell. And meanwhile, without the need to fund expensive recording, distribution or marketing costs, the 21st century version of the independent label has proliferated. It sounds like a utopia. But it's a situation that shares the same problem as

---

[10] Thorn, Tracey, *Bedsit Disco Queen: How I Grew Up and Tried to Be a Pop Star*, Virago Press, 2013, p180/81.

the equally fine principle of political democracy: if everyone has the vote then no-one has any power. If anyone can make music the more likely whatever's crafted is ignored by everyone except a tiny circle of followers. We're divided, atomised and powerless. And that only makes it easier for an Establishment to maintain its comfortable position. For post-punk, taking over the mainstream had at least been a possibility, there was a platform to aim for, and the occasional excursions to the cynosure of the charts and *Top of the Pops* meant it was impossible to be ignored.

These five LPs aren't the only examples of outsider indie Romance[11], or necessarily the 'best' music of that period (how could there be such a thing?). In both their idealism and scepticism, the LPs were made by the dynamics of a curious Eighties fairy-tale. When a cultural and commercial window opened for an unusual sincerity to show itself. A glorious futility. They didn't change the world or the history of music in any obvious, substantial ways. But people keep returning to these five LPs as one-off wonders, having meant something more than just music at the time, and having since become a part of an identity. A mental mosaic of independence. In this book I've tried to explain why that might have happened.

The LPs are minor artefacts from a long gone world that could be black-hearted, trivial and shoddy. But they are artefacts that are still providing clues to another Eighties adventure, where there was a spirit of devotion to what was transcendent about ordinary lives. What could sometimes be found in the magic in the streets.

*

At our party there's none of the youthful intensity left from the old days. No touchy sensitivity either. Cups of tea are being passed round with polite smiles. This time we're in a rented hotel suite overlooking the glassy, leaf-strewn surface of a lake, conveniently close to the M1 motorway and with plenty of parking. Soft lighting shimmers over an expanse of wooden floor and sympathetic ivory-coloured furnishings. A few remains from the

---

[11] See: Further Listening.

bagels, satay and sushi platters are left lying around. A circle of what are now only half-familiar faces has gathered, laughing at the fuss over their youthful outpourings after all this time. How can it be forty — yes, forty — years ago?

They're still making music, Paul, Morrissey, Robert, Roddy, Edwyn. So there's plenty of talk about making streaming and touring models work somehow, until they eventually fall into twos and threes to sit in the padded chairs normally reserved for wedding parties, and go deeper into conversation about their lives.

Everyone wants to catch-up with Edwyn and how he's getting on in the old family home of Helmsdale, his remote sea-rich haven. The 62 year-old keeps a cane by his side to walk with. After the two brain haemorrhages he suffered in 2005 it's a miracle and a blessing he's still alive[12]. The Eighties and the early Nineties had been a thin time (being on *Top of the Pops* had been as much a guarantee of future stardom as being on *Love Island*). Edwyn was living in a one-bed flat without a major record deal in 1995 when 'A Girl Like You' became a global hit and funded the further development of his West Heath Yard Studios in London, giving him the chance to at least persist with his solo recording career. He was just 45 when he began to have severe headaches and sickness, what he at first put down to a case of food poisoning. Grace and his son saw Edwyn through the years of rehabilitation, as he patiently (and impatiently) learnt how to walk and use words again. Roddy was in and out to see him, plotting new schemes and playing the guitar parts when Edwyn wanted to gig again. It was just two years after his period in intensive care that they appeared on stage together, followed by another appearance at Glastonbury in 2008. Both Roddy and Johnny Marr played on Edwyn's first album of new material after his illness.

At 57, Roddy is a spry Notting Hill bohemian, not often back in Scotland, but he'll try and catch up with Campbell Owens when he's there. Campbell is senior lecturer in music at Glasgow College and sometimes plays bass for James Kirk. They're working on a new album of songs together. Does Roddy know his old partner in crime Bernie Clarke has

---

[12] Documented movingly by Grace Maxwell in *Falling and Laughing* (2009), and the film *The Possibilities are Endless* (2014).

been playing jazz piano at a London restaurant? Roddy exchanges notes on London venues with 64 year-old Robert, who's working on a follow-up to 2019's *Inferno*. How about *Quick Changes* as a title? Looking like a Professor of English Lit, a statesman of indie pop, Robert is very used to doing this kind of thing on his own now. But every now and then something he's just said will niggle at him, especially when it's about a book or a film. A picture of Grant — that steady questioning look, that tilt of the head — will come freshly to his mind once more. A toll crossing in Brisbane was renamed the Go Between Bridge in 2010. But why should he pay the $3.72 to cross his own bridge? asks Robert, keeping a serious face. Just a small cut from the tolls would have made him and the rest of the band more money than all of their recordings put together. Lindy, he knows, continued to do campaigning work for charities until her retirement in 2021, still falling out with journalists who ask stupid questions. He guesses she won't ever read his autobiography.

Morrissey's presence in the room, the quiff, the suit, the big shirt collar, is like that of a celebrity lighthouse. He's an imposing, solitary landmark even when part of a group. At 62 he's been living for years in the anti-Manchester, the city of Los Angeles and its exclusive district of Lincoln Heights. Sun-drenched and plastic, but closer to a warmer and simpler source of fan-love. Paul approaches him with a gentle smile, ready with reminiscences about his own days in LA. Unlike Morrissey, Paul (now 65) would much rather have come in company, with Robert and PJ. Maybe they could talk about getting together to play again, write some songs. Even just say hello and talk over old times. Paul's still looking out over the Glasgow rooftops around Byres Road, but without the Blue Nile it's lost its sharper purpose. He's been walking around in circles, feeling disconnected. The solo album in 2012, *Midair*, wasn't the Blue Nile, however heartbroken and beautiful. More like something to do.

Morrissey's explaining why his biggest fans are in LA's Hispanic community, while Paul is keeping an eye on the door to the hotel suite. Because you never know.

Further listening

Josef K, *The Only Fun in Town* (1981)
Scritti Politti, *Songs to Remember* (1982)
The Pale Fountains, *Longshot for Your Love* (material from 1982-84, not released until 1998)
Tracey Thorn, *A Distant Shore* (1982)
Ben Watt, *North Marine Drive* (1983)
REM, *Murmur* (1983)
Aztec Camera, *Knife* (1984)
The Pale Fountains, *Pacific Street* (1984)
Everything But The Girl, *Eden* (1984)
The Go-Betweens, *Spring Hill Fair* (1984)
Lloyd Cole & the Commotions, *Rattlesnakes* (1984)
Orange Juice, *The Orange Juice* (1984)
Prefab Sprout, *Swoon* (1984)
The Smiths, *Hatful of Hollow* (1984)
The Pale Fountains, *From Across the Kitchen Table* (1985)
Prefab Sprout, *Steve McQueen* (1985)
The Go-Betweens, *Liberty Belle and the Black Diamond Express* (1986)
The Smiths, *The Queen is Dead* (1986)
Aztec Camera, *Love* (1987)
The Go-Betweens, *Tallulah* (1987)
Lloyd Cole & the Commotions, *Mainstream* (1987)
The Smiths, *Strangeways Here We Come* (1987)
Shack, *Zilch* (1988)
The Go-Betweens, *16 Lovers Lane* (1988)
Morrissey, *Viva Hate* (1988)
Prefab Sprout, *From Langley Park to Memphis* (1988)
The Blue Nile, *Hats* (1989)
Edwyn Collins, *Hope & Despair* (1989)
The Sundays, *Reading, Writing and Arithmetic* (1990)
Prefab Sprout, *Jordan: the Comeback* (1990)
Trashcan Sinatras, *Cake* (1990)
Trashcan Sinatras, *I've Seen Everything* (1993)

Acknowledgments

Thanks to the band members and producers who so kindly contributed their reminiscences and insights: John Brand, Craig Gannon, Adam Kidron, Calum Malcolm, Lindy Morrison and Campbell Owens. I really appreciated having your input.

This book is steeped in the (brilliant, inspiring, daft) work of music journalists since the early 80s. A world that's been bulldozed by the Internet. So it's a belated kind of thank you.

Rob Wringham for a quick lend of his razor-sharp wit and good taste.

Harpreet! Superstar. Whisky god. The man behind the shades of Rodrigo Flores. Your version of 'Spanish Horses' will always haunt me x

Adrian! (Nothing to do with *that* Adrian). 30 years as a perfect drinking companion x

Always for Ruth, Noah and Theo x